Settler Colonialism

FireWorks

Series editors:

Gargi Bhattacharyya, Professor of Sociology,
University of East London

Anitra Nelson, Associate Professor, Honorary Principal Fellow,
Melbourne Sustainable Society Institute, University of
Melbourne

Wilf Sullivan, Race Equality Office, Trade Union Congress

Also available

Empire's Endgame:
Racism and the British State
Gargi Bhattacharyya, Adam Elliott-Cooper, Sita Balani,
Kerem Nisancioglu, Kojo Koram, Dalia Gebrial,
Nadine El-Enany and Luke de Noronha

Reinventing the Welfare State:
Digital Platforms and Public Policies
Ursula Huws

The Politics of Permaculture
Terry Leahy

Exploring Degrowth:
A Critical Guide
Vincent Liegey and Anitra Nelson

Pandemic Solidarity:
Mutual Aid during the Covid-19 Crisis
Edited by Marina Sitrin and Colectiva Sembrar

Settler Colonialism
An Introduction

Sai Englert

First published 2022 by Pluto Press
New Wing, Somerset House, Strand, London WC2R 1LA

www.plutobooks.com

Copyright © Sai Englert 2022

British Library Cataloguing in Publication Data
A catalogue record for this book is available from the British Library

ISBN   978 0 7453 4497 3   Hardback
ISBN   978 0 7453 4490 4   Paperback
ISBN   978 0 7453 4500 0   PDF
ISBN   978 0 7453 4498 0   EPUB

Typeset by Stanford DTP Services, Northampton, England

Simultaneously printed in the United Kingdom and United States of America

To Noëmi and all those who loved her.
May her memory be a blessing.

Contents

Series Preface

Addressing urgent questions about how to make a just and sustainable world, the Fireworks series throws a new light on contemporary movements, crises and challenges. Each book is written to extend the popular imagination and unmake dominant framings of key issues.

Launched in 2020, the series offers guides to matters of social equity, justice and environmental sustainability. FireWorks books provide short, accessible and authoritative commentaries that illuminate underground political currents or marginalised voices, and highlight political thought and writing that exists substantially in languages other than English. Their authors seek to ignite key debates for twenty-first-century politics, economics and society.

FireWorks books do not assume specialist knowledge, but offer up-to-date and well-researched overviews for a wide range of politically-aware readers. They provide an opportunity to go deeper into a subject than is possible in current news and online media, but are still short enough to be read in a few hours.

In these fast-changing times, these books provide snappy and thought-provoking interventions on complex political issues. As times get dark, FireWorks offer a flash of light to reveal the broader social landscape and economic structures that form our political moment.

FireWorks

Acknowledgements

A book can only be the outcome of numerous collective processes – whether in terms of its production, or of the ideas it contains. It is not possible to name (or even identify) every one of the participants in these shared efforts, but I am nonetheless indebted to them all. There are also many specific people who have generously given me their time, help, insights and support. I want to take this opportunity to thank them from the bottom of my heart. Without them, this book would not have seen the light of day, and the quality of its content would have suffered considerably. It goes without saying that all remaining shortcomings are mine and mine alone.

First and foremost, I want to thank the *Firework* editors, Gargi Bhattacharyya and Anitra Nelson for trusting me to write this book and contribute to their series, as well as for their comments on earlier drafts. Gargi in particular deserves all my gratitude for her encouragement, detailed feedback, and the several hour-long phone conversations without which the manuscript would never have made it across the finish line. I am also grateful to David Castle and the whole Pluto team for all their work in putting the book together.

In addition, several colleagues and friends have taken the time to read the draft, in whole or in part, and shared their insights with me. They have not only considerably improved the present book in doing so, they have also given me the confidence to keep going when the writing got tough. My deepest thanks go to Ashok Kumar, Heba Taha, Jamie Woodcock and Tanzil Chowdhury for their generosity and comradeship.

In addition, Chiraz Hassoumi has been a wonderful student assistant. I am very grateful to her for her careful reading of several drafts of the book and her insightful feedback. Angus McNelly, Cristiana Strava, Jeff Webber and Maïa Pal generously shared books and articles with me, and expanded my knowledge significantly in doing so. Thank you to all of them. I only wish the lack of time and my limited reading speed had not prevented me from engaging with the material they suggested in greater detail.

A special word of thanks also to those who patiently listened to me complain, hesitate, doubt and work through the challenges I faced during the writing process, before kindly encouraging me and getting me back to work. Hannah Dee deserves a very special mention here. Being able to count on her calming advice and hilarious insights into my crisis management models is one of the great blessings in this life. I am also indebted to every member of KMN(PF) for their support and for filling my academic life with more moments of joy and hilarity than one is allowed to expect. Thank you all.

The ideas in this book are not only of academic concern, nor developed solely within the confines of university buildings. They are the outcome of endless discussions, debates and collective processes of political education. While it is not possible for me to name them all, I am profoundly thankful to all the activists I have had the honour to organise alongside over the years. In particular,

I want to express my deepest gratitude to all the socialists, Palestine solidarity and anti-casualisation activists, that I've worked with in Brighton, London and Leiden, and who have made the world feel like a better place and the struggle feel worthwhile. I hope you will find some of yourselves in these pages.

Finally, I have not gone through this process alone. I have been blessed with the love, comradeship and support of Malia Bouattia throughout – both in our shared life, as well as in our political pursuits. Words do not suffice to express the depth of my gratitude, but I also dedicate these pages to her. She knows, much more than most, the cost of fighting back.

Introduction

On 2 May 2021, a crew of five members of the Zapatista Army of National Liberation (EZLN) set sail for Spain. To mark 500 years since the beginning of the Spanish colonisation of Mexico, the majority Indigenous Maya movement was launching what it called an invasion in reverse. However, an EZLN spokesperson noted that this invasion would represent the exact opposite of what happened five centuries before: 'We're following the route that they came from 500 years ago.' However, unlike back then, '[i]n this case, we're following the route to sow life.'[1]

As they disembarked on Spanish soil, Marijose, a transgender member of the group, announced, in a sarcastic mirroring of the Spanish invaders' naming and claiming of the Americas:

> In the name of women, of children, of men, of elders and, of course, of other Zapatistas, I declare that the name of this land, which its natives today call 'Europe' will henceforth be known as: SLUMIL K'AJXEMK'OP, which means 'Rebel Land', or, 'Land that doesn't yield, that doesn't fail'. And thus it will be known by its inhabitants as well as by strangers as long as there is someone who will not abandon, who will not sell out, and who will not capitulate.[2]

In a further inversion of the process of European settlement in the Western Hemisphere, the Zapatista envoys quarantined before leaving Chiapas in order to comply with COVID-19 regulations and avoid spreading disease as they arrived in Spain. While the trip and its declarations were primarily symbolic, the struggle that they represented is not. The voyagers were using the opportunity to raise awareness of their ongoing struggle for liberation from the Mexican state, and the connection between that fight and those waged by the oppressed and the exploited across the globe. In fact, the internationalist element of the EZLN's struggle is long-standing. The movement gained renown in 1994 when it launched an insurrection in Chiapas, Southern Mexico, that coincided with the signing of the North American Free Trade Agreement (NAFTA). In doing so, as the insurgency made clear, they resisted not only the Mexican state but also global processes of neoliberal reform, as well as US imperialism in Central America.

In the first communique about the 'invasion', in October 2020, which announced the group's intention to voyage to Europe, Subcomandante Insurgente Moisés noted the many ills that the contemporary 'socially sick world' faces: ecological crisis, the systematic privileging of profit over people, femicides, the growth of nationalism, chauvinism and fascism, as well as war.[3] Yet, he also noted the ongoing 'resistances and rebellions that, even when silenced or forgotten, do not cease to be vital indicators of a humanity that refuses to follow the system's hurried pace toward collapse'.[4] He placed the Zapatista struggle for liberation within that global context and announced that the movement would eventually travel to every continent, to meet with the world's people in resistance. The statement further noted: 'You didn't conquer us. We continue to resist and rebel.'[5]

The Zapatistas are not alone. Indigenous movements continue to define much of the current global moment. Whether it is the struggle against Israeli colonial expansion and Apartheid, mass mobilisations against pipeline construction and natural resource extraction in North America, the campaigns in New Zealand/Aotearoa to reclaim, protect and recognise the rights of the natural world, or the movements across South America resisting US-backed coups, right-wing reaction, and the extractive policies of local states and transnational companies – Indigenous peoples, through their struggles for liberation, are at the forefront of the fight against the many crises of our age. While the structures of control, dispossession and coercion that Indigenous peoples face are local and specific, their struggles are neither parochial, discrete, nor containable within the nation states and dominant economic models that define our world, as a particular liberal narrative – of Indigenous recognition without liberation – would have it.[6] Instead, they are a crucial aspect of the struggles against capitalism, ecological catastrophe, racism, sexism and other forms of oppression and exploitation.

This is the point that the EZLN's inverted invasion was making in practice, a point also made by Manu Vimalassery, Juliana Hu Pegues and Alyosha Goldstein, when they argue that, 'Settler colonial histories, conditions, practices, and logics of dispossession and power must necessarily be understood as relationally constituted to other modes of imperialism, racial capitalism, and historical formations of social difference.'[7] This is how this book approaches the issue of settler colonialism. Not as a discrete, self-contained structure of domination, but one that interacts with – and is co-constituent of – key processes of domination that continue to define the present moment, both in and beyond settler colonial regimes. Capitalism, racism and dispossession, as well as different forms of state violence and gender oppression, emerged within, through and/or in relation to settler colonial expansion and domination. To make sense of them, an understanding of settler colonialism is crucial. Conversely, to understand the latter, the former must be included. This also implies that – as chapter 5 will draw out more fully – Indigenous struggles for liberation from settler colonial regimes should not be seen in isolation from other struggles across the globe, nor consigned to the specific locales where they unfold. These struggles concern us all and are part and parcel of everyone's liberation.

WHAT IS SETTLER COLONIALISM?

Settler colonialism has received growing attention in both academic and activist circles over the last two decades. Unfortunately, many of the debates surrounding it have largely remained confined to those circles, and have not managed to transform broader popular understandings of settler regimes and the struggles against them. Palestine, for example, continues to be widely understood either as a fragmented territory under occupation, or as contested by two peoples with equal and conflicting claims over it. Indigenous people in Oceania and the Americas are often discussed as defending specific ways of life, without an acknowledgement of the ongoing dispossession they face at the hands of the different settler states that they confront. Moreover, these populations tend to be described as 'disappearing', representatives of a people and a world that is already no longer there, gone forever and irretrievable, if not all together backward and refusing to adapt to modernity.[8] Understanding settler colonialism is then a crucial aspect of making sense of the world in which we live as well as the ongoing struggles to change it.

When colonialism is discussed, it is usually franchise, rather than settler, colonialism that comes to mind. While closely connected, through flows of labour and goods, to say nothing of the colonial powers that rule them, the two formations also have distinct characteristics. Most importantly, if franchise colonial regimes rule the colonised through a mixture of military power, colonial administrators and collaborating local ruling classes, they do not try to permanently transfer citizens from the metropole to the colony, in order to establish a new colonial society on conquered lands. Settler colonial formations, on the other hand, do aim to do so, by transferring settlers – hence the name – onto Indigenous land. In terms of the former, think, for example, of British colonial rule in India or French colonial rule in Syria. On the other hand, the establishment of European societies in Argentina, Algeria, or Australia, are all relevant examples of the latter. Settlers settle. They (aim to) make colonised lands their permanent home and in the process enter into continuous and sustained conflict with the Indigenous populations, whom they (attempt to) dispossess, exploit and/or eliminate. This aspect of settler colonialism is often summarised in the words of Patrick Wolfe: 'The colonisers come to stay – invasion is a structure not an event.'[9]

In the process, settlers become a vanguard of colonial rule and expansion, as well as a continuous presence on Indigenous land. As such, they enter ongoing conflicts with Indigenous people, as long as the colonial structures (states, property regimes, etc.) that give settlers access to Indigenous land, labour and resources, persist. If franchise colonial regimes focus primarily on extracting wealth from the colonies to the metropole, settler colonial formations also siphon resources, labour and – crucially – land towards the development of settlement. This is not to say that the process of colonial plunder to the benefit of the colonial power is irrelevant to settler colonialism. Quite the contrary is true, as this book will show in greater detail. It is however to point out that, as a 'third factor'[10] in the words of Arrighi Emmanuel, between the colonial metropole and the colonised, settlers develop their own, autonomous, accumulation of Indigenous land, resources and labour.

So rapacious is settler hunger in this process, that it can in turn lead to conflict with, and at times also secession from, the colonial metropole – as was the case, for example, with South African, South Rhodesian, or US independence. Settler colonialism remains, in these cases, after the colonial empire leaves – and can even intensify in the aftermath of settler independence, as chapters 2 and 3 will touch upon. It is therefore inaccurate to describe such processes as decolonisation or, as is often the case with the United States, for example, post-colonial – despite its continued settler colonial rule over, and conflict with, millions of Indigenous people.[11] That said, the primary, structuring, conflict of any settler colonial formation is not with the colonial power, but with the Indigenous people who settlers (aim to) dispossess, exploit and/or eliminate. In his 1970 comparative study of settler colonialism in Palestine, South Rhodesia (Zimbabwe) and South Africa, published by the Palestine Liberation Organisation (PLO), George Jabbour remarked:

> Once established in their new settlements, the settlers, as befits all colonialists, used to deal with the natives inhumanly ... Declared espousal of discrimination, on the basis of race, colour, or creed, without the need to feel apologetic about it, is the distinguishing feature of settler colonialism. Because the settlers are well entrenched in the lands they acquire, settler colonialism is not as easy to dismantle as traditional colonialism. The colonialists here were not overseas agents who came to the colonies on duty; they were permanently stationed in the colony, permanently in control of the natives and permanently fortifying their positions of strength.[12]

In his study, Jabbour developed themes that have remained central to understanding settler colonialism, and to which we will return throughout the book: the relatively enduring presence of settlers and their states, the ongoing conflict between them and the Indigenous population, the importance of land and control over it, as well as the centrality of racism in structuring social relations in the settler colonial world. However, Jabbour was also writing from the perspective of an ongoing liberation struggle against settler colonial rule. The fact that settler colonial regimes are more entrenched does not mean they cannot be defeated – as indeed they were, for example, throughout the African continent.

LIBERATION

In their critique of many existing analyses of settler colonialism, Corey Snelgrove, Rita Kaur Dhamoon and Jeff Corntassel point to the danger of overstating the stability of settler regimes and, in doing so, presenting colonisation as a done deal. Indigenous resistance, let alone liberation, is then sidelined, and settler colonial power is, indirectly, assumed and reinforced. They therefore ask their readers: 'What good is it to analyse settler colonialism if that analysis does not shed light on sites of contradiction and weakness, the conditions for its reproduction, or the spaces and practices of resistance to it?'[13] Understanding the workings of settler colonial regimes cannot simply be an intellectual exercise. It must be connected to the ongoing struggles for liberation and decolonisation waged against such regimes across the globe.

Making sense of how they emerged and developed, and how settler colonial processes connect to others – such as capitalism, imperialism, racism, sexism, nationalism – must also mean setting out to think through how these structures of domination can be dismantled. In fact, this goes to the core of the intellectual traditions that have written about and theorised settler colonialism. Jabbour was writing from the perspective of liberation and decolonisation. As Rana Barakat has noted, in the 1960s and 1970s, an analysis of Zionism and Israeli settler colonialism was put forward by a variety of Palestinian authors, writing from the perspective of, and with a commitment to, the liberation of Palestine.[14] She points out, for example, that Fayez Sayegh did so in *Zionist Colonialism in Palestine*,[15] and that the concept of 'elimination', so central to contemporary analyses (see below), was put forward by Rosemary Sayigh in her book *The Palestinians: From Peasants to Revolutionaries*.[16] These analyses took as their starting point the ongoing struggle for liberation from settler colonial rule, and aimed to make sense of it within this framework.[17]

Palestinians were not alone. In the same period, the Red Power movement, through organisations such as the American Indian Movement (AIM), re-energised the Indigenous liberation struggle and launched a new wave of militant actions against the US state.[18] Much like their counterparts in Palestine, Indigenous activists and scholars in North America developed political and historical analyses of settler colonialism, which were part and parcel of their engagement with Indigenous struggles, history and intellectual traditions. They also centred the subject of land as key to both their political and scholarly concerns, and prioritised Indigenous epistemologies as the framework for their writings, an issue reviewed in chapters 2 and 5. Nor were these concerns developed in isolation or particularistic. These movements were also influenced by, and connected to, the wider liberation movements that were taking place, both in North America and around the world. The civil rights and Black Power movements, the campaigns against the war in Vietnam, and the anti-colonial revolutions across Africa and Asia, influenced Indigenous activists as well as scholars, and shaped the politics of their own re-emerging liberation struggle.[19] Engagement with, and study of settler colonialism in the second half of the twentieth century took place within a context of both local and international waves of resistance and revolution. It was to understand the specific circumstances faced by Indigenous peoples, and thereby participate in the liberation process itself, that these analyses emerged and were developed.

Moreover, as Omar Jabary Salamanca, Mezna Qato, Kareem Rabie and Sobhi Samour point out, just as analyses of settler colonialism were connected to the struggles against it, so there was a connection between the retreat of these analyses and the defeat of the movements that had developed them. Writing in the context of Palestine, the authors point out that as the Palestinian leadership increasingly turned towards (quasi-)state building, and in so doing abandoned anti-colonial liberation, the analytical framework of settler colonialism receded also:

[T]he Palestinian liberation movement has seen a series of ruptures and changes in emphasis, and in many ways scholarly production accurately mirrors the dynamics of incoherent contemporary Palestinian politics. Recent Palestinian political history has been a long march away from a liberation agenda and towards a piecemeal approach to the establishment of some kind of sovereignty under the structure of the Israeli settler colonial regime. In this environment, it is not surprising that even scholarship written in solidarity with Palestinians tends to shy away from structural questions.[20]

The authors therefore also identify the importance of the settler colonial framework within a political project that seeks to recapture crucial elements of the struggle for liberation: international alliances and unity across different sections of the Palestinian people. The contemporary remobilisation of settler colonial analytics in Palestine, including the work of the authors mentioned above, is therefore part and parcel of a wider political reorganisation (see chapter 5).

My hope is that this book, and the references throughout, will serve as a first step for readers to engage with the issues it raises – and make a different understanding of our contemporary world possible. Indeed, to understand settler colonialism is also to start engaging in a different way with a number of local and international social movements, political struggles and solidarity campaigns. It means connecting the specific to the universal, the contemporary challenges to settler power to ongoing Indigenous liberation struggles, as well as the latter to the freeing of us all. If this book can contribute, in however modest a way, to clarifying readers' understanding of the world and encourage them to participate in the fight to change it, it will have achieved its purpose.

NOTES ON THIS BOOK

Settler Colonialism: An Introduction is not an original piece of research, nor does it claim to break new ground. Its aim is to contribute to making settler colonialism a more widely accessible and better understood concept. It offers readers an introduction to the history of settler colonial expansion, and identifies some of the ways in which settler colonialism intersects with, and is co-constitutive of, other forms of domination, exploitation and oppression, as well as the struggles against them. The task is gargantuan. This book provides a broad overview of an ongoing global process, stretching over five centuries, and involving millions of people. To do justice to each and every one of the topics and issues touched upon in these pages would require considerably more time and space.

While the book does not contribute new material to the existing literature, it does cast the net wider than many when it comes to selecting examples of settler colonial regimes. This decision emerges primarily out of a rejection of what Patrick Wolfe and others have identified as *the* defining characteristic of settler colonialism: the 'elimination of the native'. To avoid any misunderstanding, and because of the very wide use of Wolfe's approach in much of the literature on the subject, it is worth explaining this divergence in more detail.[21]

A central aspect of Wolfe's contribution has been to bring both the ongoing as well as the genocidal character of settler colonialism to the fore. His approach can be – and usually is – summarised through two statements. On the one hand, in his first major contribution, *Settler Colonial-*

ism and the Transformation of Anthropology: The Politics and Poetics of an Ethnographic Event, Wolfe explains that settler colonies 'were (are) premised on the elimination of the native societies. The split tensing reflects a determinate feature of settler colonisation. The colonizers come to stay—invasion is a structure not an event.'[22] On the other hand, in his most quoted text, 'Settler Colonialism and the Elimination of the Native', he restates this approach in the following terms: 'settler colonialism is an inclusive, land-centred project that coordinates a comprehensive range of agencies, from the metropolitan centre to the frontier encampment, with a view to eliminating Indigenous societies.'[23]

Here the key elements of Wolfe's approach emerge. First, settler colonialism is not limited to the past. It is an ongoing reality, which continues to define settler societies in many places, such as North America, Oceania, or Palestine. Second, it is a structural form of domination in which conflict with, and the murder of, Indigenous people should not be understood as isolated or random events, but instead constitute the very nature of settler colonial regimes. Indeed, the third and central claim made by Wolfe is that because settlers challenge Indigenous people's right to the land, the basis of all collective life, settler colonialism's defining logic is the elimination of the native. Whether physically, culturally and/or through assimilation into the settler population, settler colonialism is differentiated from its franchise counterpart by settler power's eliminatory drive, necessary to lay claim on Indigenous land. The strength of this approach is that it facilitates comparison between different settler regimes, identified by their similar logics of Indigenous elimination, while simultaneously accounting for the specific ways in which settlers, in different places, at different times, dispossess Indigenous populations.

However, Wolfe and those that follow his approach also run the risk of making reality fit into their definition, rather than the other way around. There is absolutely no doubt that, as this book will repeatedly show, settler colonialism has been and continues to be eliminatory in the ways that Wolfe theorises. Nonetheless, this alone does not cover the entirety of the settler colonial arsenal of domination. As will become clear in what follows, some settler colonies are based primarily on the exploitation of the Indigenous population, for example, Algeria and South Africa. In addition, exploitation can also coexist with eliminatory practices, as in the Spanish settler colonies in the Americas. Yet, Wolfe, and others after him, precluded this possibility.

For instance, in explaining the difference between settler and franchise colonies, Wolfe wrote: 'In contrast to the kind of colonial formation that Cabral or Fanon confronted, settler colonies were not primarily established to extract surplus value from indigenous labour. Rather, they are premised on displacing indigenes from (or replacing them on) the land.'[24] A striking issue with this formulation is that Algeria – the colonial formation confronted by Fanon – was a French settler colony. Similarly, Veracini, in his *Settler Colonialism: A Theoretical Overview*, writes, 'while the suppression of indigenous and exogenous alterities characterises both colonial and settler colonial formations, the former can be summarised as domination for the purpose of exploitation, the latter as domination for the purpose of transfer.'[25]

This sharp distinction between settler and franchise colonialism on the basis of elimination and exploitation, is difficult to square with reality. On the one hand, elimination and genocide are a reality across the colonial world, by means of war, famine, forced or enslaved labour, and mass murder.[26] On the other hand, many settler colonial regimes were based primarily on the exploitation of the Indigenous populations. By precluding the possibility of settler colonial regimes being structurally dependent on the Indigenous population's exploitation, Wolfe's model closes off large sections of the settler world from analysis. This can lead to an overwhelming focus on the Anglo-settler world – especially Canada, the United States, Australia and New Zealand – with the partial exception of Palestine. Shannon Speed has made this point, for example, in relation to the lack of engagement in the literature on settler colonialism with Spanish settlements in the Americas.

Speed identifies the causes for this absence in the way exploitation is, by definition, located outside of the analytical framework of many studies of settler colonialism. She writes, '[i]n places like Mexico and Central America, such labour regimes ... were often the very mechanisms that dispossessed indigenous peoples of their lands, forcing them to labour in extractive undertakings on the very land that had been taken from them.'[27] Similarly, in his discussion of settler colonialism in South Africa, Robin D.G. Kelley points out that elimination and exploitation went hand in hand: 'the expropriation of the native from

the land was a fundamental objective, but so was prole-
tarianization. They wanted the land and the labour, but
not the people—that is to say, they sought to eliminate
stable communities and their cultures of resistance.'[28] We
will return to both examples, and others, where exploitation is a structuring aspect of settler domination and
dispossession.

In attempting to resolve the tensions between Wolfe's
theoretical framework and the diversity within the
settler colonial world, rather awkward formulations can
emerge. For example, in his *Land, Labour, and Difference:
Elementary Structures of Race*, Wolfe states that '"pure"
settler colonialism of the Australian or North American
variety should be distinguished from so-called "colonial
settler societies" that depended on indigenous labour (for
example, European farm economies in Southern Africa
or plantation economies in South Asia)'.[29] Why Southern
African 'colonial settler societies' are disqualified from
being fully settler colonial, remains unclear. Colonisers
came to stay – to settle – while also exploiting Indigenous African populations as the driving force of their
economies.

Lorenzo Veracini, in his discussion of settler colonialism in Palestine, similarly makes a distinction between
those Palestinian lands colonised in 1948 and in 1967,
characterising the former as settler colonial and the latter
as colonial, because the elimination of the native was not
achieved in the latter occupied territories.[30] Rana Barakat
has convincingly challenged this formulation, not by ques-
tioning the centrality of elimination to the settler colonial
process, in fact, but by pointing out the importance of

accounting for specific material circumstances rather than relying on theoretical assumptions.[31] It is not that Israel stopped trying to eliminate Palestinians in the territories conquered in 1967 – it has not been able to achieve this goal because of the 'sheer numbers of Palestinians still present'.[32] Settlers are not able to simply impose their goals in a vacuum, they must engage with the material realities they encounter, not least the Indigenous population and their resistance to colonisation.

Here another danger emerges, which is to collapse settler colonial *aims* with material *realities*. For example, if a settler colony aims to eliminate the native, it does not automatically follow that it will achieve this outcome. Indeed, in the process of attempted elimination, it must continuously engage with Indigenous resistance, which can frustrate, delay, or defeat its plans. Jean O'Brien has made this point, noting that it is not because settlers desire to eliminate Indigenous populations through miscegenation, for example, that they can necessarily achieve this goal.[33] She therefore stresses the difference between 'the *logic* of elimination as an *aspiration* of the coloniser', and its actual success, continuously challenged by the ongoing resistance of the Indigenous population.[34] This further underscores the importance of integrating Indigenous liberation struggles into the analysis of settler colonialism.

We will return to the question of Indigenous resistance in chapter 5. For now, it will suffice to note that the question of Indigenous agency also relates to the issue of settler exploitation of the Indigenous population. It is striking, for example, that in those settler colonies where the economy was most dependent on Indigenous labour

– such as Algeria, South Africa, Kenya, or Rhodesia – Indigenous liberation movements have been able to mobilise their structural power to overthrow settler rule all together. It therefore matters considerably to how one thinks about settler colonialism's stability and longevity, and whether one excludes those settler regimes that relied on the exploitation of the Indigenous population, or not.

Even if one accepts that the *logic* of settlement is one of elimination *in opposition to* exploitation – and as argued here it is not clear that one should – the historical record remains that many settler regimes never did overwhelm Indigenous populations through large-scale immigration or importing enslaved populations, and that they therefore remained dependent on Indigenous labour. Those regimes that did – primarily the Anglo settlements in North America and Oceania – were able to do so because of the industrial transformations of the economies in the metropole and the huge population transfers this enabled, which we examine in chapters 1 and 2.

This book aims to avoid the pitfalls identified here, and thus departs from the approach that starkly counter-poses elimination and exploitation, that sees the former as *the* defining characteristic of settler colonialism. As the title suggests, this book hopes to introduce the reader to a variety of settler colonial regimes, distinguishing different relations between settlers, their states, and the Indigenous and enslaved populations over which they attempt to establish their rule. These techniques certainly include logics of *elimination*, as pointed out by Wolfe and others. However, we will see that settler domination also expressed itself through the *exploitation* of the Indigenous population.

OUTLINE

In order to make the points described above, the book proceeds as follows. Chapter 1 provides an overview of European settlement from the end of the fifteenth century onwards. While necessarily broad, the aim of this bird's-eye view of settler expansion is to familiarise the reader with the subject matter, give a sense of the scale of this global process, and identify its centrality in the emergence of the contemporary global order. In particular, it discusses the role the wealth accumulation by means of settlement, plunder, genocide, enslavement and exploitation played in the emergence of the global capitalist economy. In addition, it identifies the connection between enslavement and conquest in the (settler) colonial world, the dispossession of the peasantry in Europe, and the subsequent transformation of production and consumption these changes engendered. In doing so, chapter 1 provides the necessary background for the rest of the book. In addition, by clarifying the connections between settler colonialism and the emergence of capitalism, the chapter also underscores the contemporary importance of engaging with settler colonialism and the struggles against it, in order to extract ourselves from the twin and related threat of ecological catastrophe and capitalist exploitation.

In chapter 2, we move on to think about how settlers dispossess and what the consequences of this process are for Indigenous populations. It starts with an overview of the debates on dispossession and looks at how Indigenous studies' scholars have critically engaged with the work of Karl Marx, to make sense of these processes in the settler colonial world. In particular, we examine the way settler colonialism dissociated dispossession and proletarianisation in the Anglo-settlements. In England, peasants were cleared off the land and forced into the new manufacturing urban centres, while in the settler colonial world, it was possible for settlers to dispossess Indigenous populations *without* integrating them into the workforce. Here the logic of elimination, so central to the model developed by Wolfe, described above, is directly visible.

The genocide of Indigenous populations was made possible, in part, by the dispossession of peasants in Europe, turning the latter into new settlers available for the colonies. This was especially true in the Anglo-settler world. Moreover, importing enslaved populations, overwhelmingly from Africa, was another way in which dispossession and elimination were linked. In this case, Indigenous labour was bypassed through chattel slavery. However, the chapter also illustrates how in other settler locales, such as Mexico, Algeria, or South Africa, there was a more direct connection between Indigenous dispossession and exploitation. Finally, we look at the ways in which dispossession was organised and accelerated throughout the nineteenth century, especially by forcefully driving Indigenous peoples off the land and into reservations. The chapter details the way the reservation, as a technique of dispossession, travelled across the settler world.

The twin processes of accumulation and dispossession, covered in the first two chapters, require both extraordinary levels of violence as well as different methods to stabilise settler rule over Indigenous and enslaved populations. It is to this latter process that the book turns in the following two chapters.

Chapter 3 discusses the emergence of racism as a central aspect of social control across the settler colonial world, beginning with a discussion of racism's prehistory, located in both the conquest of the Iberian Peninsula as well as the English invasion of Ireland. In both cases, new forms of difference, constructed as fundamental, inalterable and innate, were imposed on the defeated. First, the chapter details how Jews and Muslims were expelled from the Iberian Peninsula, while those who managed to remain were targeted through the concept of *Limpieza de Sangre* (cleanliness/purity of blood), even after conversion to Christianity, and across multiple generations. Similarly in Ireland, the English justified their domination by constructing the Irish as savages in need of civilising, to be achieved through conquest and miscegenation. Once again, Christianity was of no help to the Irish. Both concepts of fundamental difference – impure blood and savagery – would travel with settlers across the Atlantic.

The chapter then traces the emergence, in colonial Virginia, of racism as a central organiser of social relations between African, European and Indigenous populations. We see how racism emerged as a response to joint revolt against plantation owners by both European and African bonded labourers, who demanded greater access to Indigenous land. The chapter ends with a discussion of the turn to what is termed 'scientific' racism and identifies how different 'biological' characteristics were imposed on enslaved and Indigenous people in different settler locales. Throughout, the chapter highlights how these forms of racialisation played a key role in naturalising the theft of land and the exploitation of labour.

The narrative turns to the social conflicts amongst settlers in chapter 4, discussing the apparent contradiction between militant and well-organised settler labour movements, which made claims to solidarity and internationalism, and the extremely rare examples of unity between settlers and Indigenous people in anti-colonial struggles. Although some exceptions exist, for example amongst committed anti-colonial communist and syndicalist movements of the early twentieth century, the overwhelming tendency was – and is – one of settler labour movements fighting for greater Indigenous exclusion and dispossession. Through the examples of the White South African and the Zionist labour movements, chapter 4 shows how settler class struggle, even when highly combative, is primarily fought over the internal redistribution of colonial loot. Rather than fighting for decolonisation or the dismantling of the settler state, settler workers tend to fight to increase their benefits, in terms of access to land and work, to the detriment of the Indigenous population. This process illustrates a key stabilising tendency within settler colonial regimes: the ability to redistribute colonial loot among settlers in order to diffuse internal social strife. It explains why in both Palestine and South Africa it was the settler labour movements who fought for greater exclusion of the Indigenous population from the settler economy – and even did so at times against the settler ruling class.

The book concludes with a turn towards the key destabilising factor faced by settler colonial regimes: Indigenous resistance and liberation struggles. Chapter 5 returns to Indigenous critiques of different approaches to the study of settler colonialism, and restates Indigenous agency's centrality in undoing the processes of domination and dispossession imposed by settlers and their states. We then turn to contemporary Indigenous struggles, in Palestine and North America, to illustrate these claims. In the case of the former, the chapter focuses on the recent mobilisations across historic Palestine in the face of Israeli dispossession in Jerusalem and military assault on the Gaza Strip. In doing so, the chapter follows the ways in which Palestinian organisers and scholars have repeatedly located their current efforts within longer-term processes of resistance, and have understood them as the latest iteration in an ongoing struggle for liberation. The chapter then turns to Indigenous struggles against pipeline construction and resource extraction in North America, highlighting how organisers and scholars have underlined the historic continuities between present-day mobilisation and the longer-term struggle for decolonisation and liberation. They also point to the connection between alternatives to settler colonialism, ecological catastrophe and capitalism that are developed through these processes of resistance.

SCOPE

A few last points should be made about the scope of this book. First, it engages almost exclusively with European settler colonies and their inheritors, a decision made primarily for reasons of space. However, this decision is also justified by the fact that, while other nation states have and continue to settle other people's lands in ways that resonate deeply with the processes described here, the overwhelming majority of settler colonial processes originated from, were implemented through, and continue to be supported by, European states and their settler descendants. Nonetheless, settler colonialism has been used to describe Japan's expansion into Korea and Manchukuo, India's policies in Kashmir, or the Chinese state's actions in Tibet and Xinjiang.[35]

Second, the book is limited in time, starting with the European invasion of the Americas. While arguments could be made that other powers and empires have moved and settled their populations in other peoples' lands, European settlement is not only quantitatively but also qualitatively different. This book locates this difference in the interconnection between European settler expansion and the emergence of capitalism (see chapter 1).

Third, we are currently living through a period in which it is becoming increasingly normalised to hear politicians, commentators and academics attempt to minimise or even question the severity of the crimes committed by European colonial empires, settlers and slave traders. Even more extraordinarily, the supposed benefits of this process are being extolled once again – apparently in order to present a 'balanced view' of the historical record. While not this book's principal objective, the material found here will hopefully participate in challenging these narratives by re-stating some basic historical facts. To put it simply:

genocide, colonial domination, and the dispossession of millions, on a global scale, are undisputable. They were made possible by the continuous exercise of prodigious amounts of violence against colonised and enslaved populations. Nothing positive can or did come from such acts, except for the setters and the ruling classes who were able to accumulate extraordinary amounts of wealth in the process. In two recent books, Gerald Horne has described these processes as an 'Apocalypse'. No better word comes to mind to describe either the scale or the depth of the horrors that unfolded.[36]

Finally, following most of the literature mentioned here, this book takes as its starting point that understanding settler colonialism and its role in the development of the global capitalist economy is necessary in order to bring about their end. By identifying the specific ways in which our contemporary world developed, how power relations were and are imposed, reproduced and challenged, and why this is so, we can start to change it. Structuring logics of dispossession, racialisation, elimination and exploitation need to be denaturalised, before they can be overthrown. It is the aim of this book to show that no aspect of settler rule was, or is, inevitable, and therefore that its continued existence is not inevitable either. The ongoing Indigenous struggles for liberation, despite five centuries of global processes of genocide and dispossession, continue to demonstrate this fact in practice.

CHAPTER ONE

Accumulate, Accumulate!

In 1492, the Spanish Catholic Monarchs (Isabella I of Castile and Ferdinand II of Aragon) established their supremacy over the Iberian Peninsula, leading to the expulsion from their kingdom of hundreds of thousands of Jews and Muslims. In the same year, serving the royal house of Castile, Christopher Columbus undertook the voyage that would initiate an era of European global dominance, and unleash unprecedented violence and destruction on the people of the Americas, Africa and Asia. This event has often been imagined as signs of a pre-existing European supremacy, which led it, almost as a matter of course, to rule the world. However, the so-called 'discovery' of the 'New World' was far from a feat of European superiority.[1] It was instead an outcome of its historical backwardness.

Faced with the inability to break the Muslim empire's control over the trade routes to the East, European powers were pushed into the development of new, more costly and insecure maritime trading routes. It was during this process that the Portuguese first sailed around Africa, settling trading ports on the West African coast and at the Cape of Good Hope. They would also conquer and establish a crucial trading centre of the new slave trade in São Tomé. This same desire to gain access to trade routes to India encouraged Columbus to look for a short cut and land, entirely by chance and unbeknownst to himself, in the Americas. European domination of world trade and of important swathes of the globe was not indicative of any existing, or innate, civilisational superiority. It was a stroke of luck, drenched in blood and forged in fire, which fundamentally changed the position of its kingdoms and empires in the global balance of power. Europe was made through its colonial expansion, and in the process, it remade the world.[2]

It was also during this process that many characteristics that continue to shape the contemporary world emerged, such as borders and nation states, inequalities between what is euphemistically called the Global North and the Global South, global racist regimes, and the structuring logic of capitalism.[3] This chapter will discuss the interrelation between settler colonialism and the emergence of the latter, and give the reader an overview of the expansion of European settler colonial regimes across the globe. The invasion of the Americas by the Spanish crown, Portugal's establishment of the early Atlantic African slave trade, and the extraction of silver and gold through the forced labour of Indigenous peoples in the Americas, facilitated new forms of accumulation on a global scale, which in turn participated in transforming social relations in Europe.

The huge amounts of gold and silver that these new conquests yielded led to the transformation of the colonisers' economies, while simultaneously facilitating the further expansion of European colonial empires. Strikingly, these flows of wealth led to the rise of new global hegemons – first the newly independent Dutch Republic, and then England – rather than strengthening the power of the colonial period's first hegemonic powers: Spain and Portugal. While the wealth plundered in the Americas led to a solidifying of existing social relations – and military overreach – in the Iberian Peninsula, it facilitated the growth of new productive and mercantile activities in North-western Europe.

These changes, in turn, increased demands for goods – sugar, tobacco, cotton, all produced in the American plantations – and facilitated the expulsion of peasants from the English countryside. As dispossessed peasants flowed into urban centres in search for work, they also were made available to participate in the settler colonial enterprise, thereby accelerating again the process of Indigenous dispossession. Settlement was a key element in the transition to capitalism, while also being an important pressure valve to resolve (or at least lessen) social strife at home. It allowed European states to expel growing numbers of the poor in urban centres, as well as religious or political rebels (who were often one and the same), and other 'undesirables'. This simultaneously undermined rebellion at home and mobilised the same population for the expansion of empire in the settler colonial world.

CAPITAL, VIOLENCE AND EXPANSION

'Accumulate, accumulate! That is Moses and the Prophets.'[4] With these words, Karl Marx summarised the structuring logic of capitalist social relations. The always expanding need to generate and capture surplus value, created by the labour power of workers, pushes capitalists to continuously look for new, more effective forms of exploitation and dispossession, as well as new markets to control. This insatiable thirst for more is not only self-generating. It is continuously renewed by the competition between capitalists. To fail to capture as big a slice of the pie as possible, is to allow the competition to do so. A double process then runs through capitalism's systemic logic: to deepen and to expand its power.[5] The former refers to the need of capitalists – individually and as a class – to extract always more value from those over whom they already exert control. The latter refers to the continuous need to capture, conquer and subjugate new resources, people and lands.

Marx does not limit his analysis to a general or theoretical level. He proceeds, instead, from the general to the specific, and points to the ways in which these structuring logics play themselves out in practice. He pays close attention to how capitalism concretely expands and imposes its power, both within Europe and across the globe. Ridiculing classical political economy and its romanticised vision of capitalism's emergence, which speculated about the responsible pecuniary practices of the early capitalists, he famously described the connection between the rise of capitalism and colonial expansion:

> The discovery of gold and silver in America, the extirpation, enslavement and entombment in mines of the aboriginal population, the beginning of the conquest and looting of the East Indies, the turning of Africa into a warren for the commercial hunting of black-skins, signalled the rosy dawn of the era of capitalist production. These idyllic proceedings are the chief moments of

primitive accumulation. On their heels treads the commercial war of the European nations, with the globe for a theatre.[6]

In these lines, he powerfully summarised the connection between the emergence of a global capitalist economy and the expansion of European colonisation. He also emphasised that this relationship rested, first and foremost on extreme levels of violence, which made the accumulation of wealth – through exploitation, enslavement and murder – possible, both at home and across the world.

While European peasants were forcibly dispossessed of their land and moved into the developing urban manufacturing centres to sell their labour power in order to survive, the peoples of the Americas, Africa and Asia were subjected to plunder, murder and enslavement. This twin process made possible the emergence of capitalism. This history of expropriation, Marx wrote, 'is written in the annals of mankind in letters of blood and fire.'[7] Capitalism can then not be reduced to its economic logic alone. Instead, that logic needs to be placed within a wider network of social relations that are shaped by the violent imposition of its power and the resistance to it. In the words of Alex Anievas and Kerem Nişancıoğlu:

... capitalism is best understood as a set of configurations, assemblages, or bundles of social relations and processes oriented around the systematic reproduction of the capital relation, but not reducible – either historically or logically – to that relation alone ... [T]he reproduction and competitive accumulation of capital through the exploitation of wage-labour presupposes a wide assortment of differentiated social relations that make this reproduction and accumulation possible. These relations may take numerous forms, such as coercive state apparatuses, ideologies and cultures of consent, or forms of power and exploitation that are not immediately given in or derivative of the simple capital–wage-labour relation, such as racism and patriarchy.[8]

This attention to the 'numerous forms' that these social relations take will continuously return throughout this book, as it engages with different forms of settler domination such as dispossession, exploitation, racism, or sexism. For now, we turn to an overview of the interconnected and co-constitutive processes of European settler colonial expansion and capitalist emergence.

SPANISH SETTLEMENT IN THE AMERICAS

The first three centuries of settler colonial expansion, from the late fifteenth to the end of the eighteenth century, are best understood as European global supremacy's emergence through the mass transfer of wealth accumulated in the 'New World' to the metropoles of the Old. Throughout this period, this process intensified as European rule was organised through the development of new colonial societies – primarily in the Americas – where a number of interrelated processes took place: the dispossession of Indigenous communities through conquest and genocide, the accumulation of land and natural resources that these developments made possible, the violent imposition of unfree labour regimes on Indigenous and African populations, and the creation of European settlements which ruled over both.

The process started with a monumental blunder. When Columbus presented his plans to find a short cut westwards to India, he was met with vigorous opposition. Not, as popular mythmaking would have it, because of a dominant belief in a flat earth and the possibility that he would fall off, but because his calculations of the earth's circumference were wrong. Both religious and secular elites, to whom the spherical nature of the earth was well known – and had been for centuries – pointed out that the distance between Europe and Japan (the closest known land mass) was so large, that any expedition that tried to cross the sea between the two would run out of water and food well before arriving at its destination.[9]

Columbus and his crew would indeed have died at sea if they had followed their projected route. However, they encountered – entirely by chance – a continent of whose existence they had been unaware. Docking first in the Taino island of Guanahani in 1492, which Columbus renamed San Salvador, Columbus then established the first Spanish settlement in the Americas in present-day Haiti – renamed Hispaniola – which he still believed to be an island east of India.[10] The development of economic and political relations on the island in the next decades serves as a useful illustration of what was to come across the Spanish and Portuguese empires in the Americas.

The settlers, discovering that the island was rich in gold, set out to accumulate as much of it as possible.[11] This insatiable hunger for the mineral would lead to conflict with the island's Indigenous populations. The following year Columbus returned to the island with over a thousand settlers and re-established his settlement, the Indigenous population having risen up against the Spaniards and destroyed the settlement he had left behind. The settlers set out to impose forced labour on the island's Indigenous population, in both gold mines and in food production for the expanding settlement. Food resources were diverted away from the Indigenous peoples towards the settlers, while increasing amounts of gold were extracted from the mines through forced Indigenous labour, and sent back to Spain. Simultaneously, growing numbers of Indigenous people were captured and sold into slavery in the 'Old World' – an number estimated to be 650,000 by 1580.[12]

On his second voyage to the Caribbean, Columbus also brought sugar cane from the Canary Islands into the island, setting in motion the production of a cash crop which would shape much of the region's economy – up to the present day.[13] The crop would also travel between different settlements, first to Brazil and then to the English colonies in what would become the United States. Replicating plantation organisations as developed in Mediterranean and Atlantic islands, the Spanish imposed mass sugar production for export to Europe throughout the sixteenth century. Sugar rapidly became a monocrop, impoverishing the soil and making it necessary to import food to keep the plantation economy functioning. From 1503 onwards, Spanish settlers started importing enslaved Africans, and also militarily defeated Muslims, to work in the plantations.

In just over a decade, the trajectory of the next five centuries of settler colonialism had been set in motion: an economy built on stolen land and resources, exploitation, mass murder and enslavement, on the back of which the settlers and the metropole grew rich. By the end of the sixteenth century, these patterns had been reproduced by the Spanish and Portuguese across much of the Western Hemisphere. They would in time be joined by France, Britain and the Netherlands. Other European powers, such as Sweden or Belgium, established a short-lived presence in the Americas, but remained peripheral to the process, with the important exception of the Russian colonisation of Alaska. If previous empires had built their wealth and power on the extraction of taxes from newly conquered peoples, often dependent on existing ruling classes, European colonialism demarcated itself in this period by the large-scale plunder of Indigenous wealth and resources, the mass enslavement of both Indigenous and African labour, and the genocide they unleashed on the Indigenous population of the Americas – all for the enrichment of the metropole and the settler societies.

GENOCIDE AND RESISTANCE

Settler violence and forced labour – topped off by the new diseases brought by the *conquistadores* (a title the Spanish soldiers had brought over from the wars in the Iberian Peninsula) to which the Indigenous peoples' immune systems were unaccustomed, unleashed a genocide of apocalyptic proportions. By the end of the sixteenth century, in the words of Eduardo Galeano:

The Caribbean Island populations finally stopped paying tribute because they had disappeared: they were totally exterminated in the gold mines, in the deadly task of sifting auriferous sands with their bodies half submerged in water, or breaking up the ground beyond the point of exhaustion, doubled up over the heavy cultivating tools brought from Spain. Many Natives of Haiti anticipated the fate imposed by their white oppressors: they killed their children and committed mass suicide.[14]

Similar horrors would be repeated across the hemisphere. Less than a century after Columbus' arrival, even the official Spanish estimates were that a third of Latin America's Indigenous population had been killed, while another 50 years later no more than 3.5 million Indigenous people survived – compared to the 70 million present when Columbus landed.[15] Today, the consensus is that the Indigenous population of the Americas was reduced by 90 per cent, from 100 million to 10 million people: a genocide of unmatched proportions, carried out across the hemisphere.[16] It is worth noting that while disease was an important part of this process, its role is often overstated – or at least extracted from a more general picture of settler violence and murder. As Roxanne Dunbar-Ortiz pointedly argues:

> If disease could have done the job, it is not clear why the European colonisers in America found it necessary to carry out unrelenting wars against Indigenous communities in order to gain every inch of land they took from them – nearly three hundred years of colonial warfare,

followed by continued wars waged by the independent republics of the hemisphere.[17]

Wars and confrontations, which as this book will return to, continue to this day – as does the resistance of Indigenous peoples in both North and South America.

The scale of the genocide unleashed on the Caribbean's Indigenous populations was such, and the number of available settlers so lacking, that growing numbers of enslaved Africans would be sent to replace them. As Gerald Horne has argued, the inability of the Spanish to mobilise enough settlers – largely due to their heightened religious sectarianism towards Protestants, Jews and other 'heretics' – increased their dependence on African and Indigenous labour.[18] The former were even recruited into the Spanish military's ranks, when considered to be religiously compatible. So-called 'Black Conquistadors' participated in conquest and settlement throughout the Americas;[19] this served as a powerful destabiliser for the empire, which found itself stuck between geographical overstretch and growing revolts amongst both the Indigenous and African populations upon whose labour it depended. These revolts, which (as pointed out above) started immediately upon Columbus' initial arrival, would continue to challenge the Spanish throughout their history – and remain a central aspect of settler colonialism up to the present. Horne writes:

> Madrid was dimly aware of the dilemma it had created for itself. Enslaved Africans were being imported to the Americas by 1503 ... But as early as 1505 ... there was

a suspension, albeit temporary, of the importation of slaves into Hispaniola, as quite ominously, this would-be chattel had been fleeing and setting up outlaw settlements of their own in the mountains and forests and from there executing violent raids on Spanish towns and haciendas. Thus, by 1522, the first large-scale uprising of the enslaved occurred during the Christmas holiday … That same year an enslaved man named Miguel led an army of 800 former chattel that forced the closing of profitable mines and delivered horror to the homes of settlers due south. By 1529, four years after being built, Santa Marta on the northern coast of South America was razed by rebellious Africans. In Mexico, there were slave insurrections in 1523, 1537, and 1546. Puerto Rico experienced severe trouble of this type in 1527, and by the 1540s it was again Hispaniola's turn … Slave revolts hit Cuba in 1530, not to mention the capital along the coast of today's Colombia that same year, which was destroyed. Africans fled to today's Ecuador and formed an independent polity that Madrid was compelled to recognize in 1598.[20]

As enslaved Africans revolted and escaped from servitude, they set up free communities, often alongside or in contact with Indigenous peoples, from where they would continue to challenge settler power, attack their cities, and free more of the enslaved. While these communities were fought vigorously by settlers and their states – whether Spanish, Portuguese, Dutch, French, or English – they remained a permanent fixture of these regimes.

THE EMERGENCE OF THE NATION STATE

In 1494, under the tutelage of the Papacy in Rome, the colonial world was divided between the two 'Catholic crowns' of Spain and Portugal in the infamous Treaty of Tordesillas. Portugal was granted the Eastern empire, including its trading outposts in Africa and Asia as well as the interior of contemporary Brazil, while Spain was awarded all the lands to the West. While the exact line of separation was never respected, the current division of Latin America between Portuguese-speaking Brazil and the rest of the continent is a remnant of this early distribution of the colonial world.

The treaty, it is worth emphasising, inaugurated a long colonial tradition in which the lives of millions of peoples around the world were decided on in the colonial metropoles, amongst the colonial powers. Indeed, similar agreements were implemented throughout the history of European empire building. For example, and perhaps most famously, the Berlin conference of 1884 divided the African continent between European colonial powers. In 1916, during the First World War, the secret Sykes-Picot Agreement divided the Ottoman empire between France, Britain, Russia and Italy, in anticipation of post-war colonial expansion. Even in decolonisation, European colonial powers would continue to behave in similar ways, as illustrated by the partitions of both India and Palestine in the 1940s.

Not only did the Treaty of Tordesillas impose colonial rule over the peoples of the Americas, it was also a key process in the emergence of the nation state as the new global order's central organising mechanism – both in the colonial world and the metropoles. While the process would take some time to develop fully, it inaugurated a new era of territorial control, through the imposition of borders and states, dividing populations and establishing clearly demarcated zones of sovereignty. These 'novel conceptions of *linear geographical space* and [their] concomitant modern form of territorialised state sovereignty' represented a fundamental break with previous forms of domination in Europe.[21] Anievas and Nişancıoğlu explain that:

> ... the originality of colonial conceptions of linear territoriality can be found most clearly in the treaties of the period. In the Old World, treaties concluding wars typically emphasised nonlinear or noncontiguous territoriality, and the spoils of conquests were divided according to places rather than territories. This was evident as late as the Treaty of Westphalia of 1648, which despite its purportedly modern credentials, still listed every noncontiguous 'place, jurisdiction, and right to be granted to one party by the other'. In contrast, treaties pertaining to the New World used cartographic or geographic language in order to delineate territorial claims based on linear demarcations and supposedly 'natural' frontiers. Territories could be claimed in this way precisely because the known political authorities – that is, the Amerindians – were not recognised, were denied their right to sovereignty and were therefore excluded from any such treaties.

We will return to the juridical place, or more precisely the lack thereof, accorded to Indigenous peoples in colonial legal doctrine. For now, it is sufficient to point out that these novel forms of territorial sovereignty would travel back to Europe and give rise to the modern nation state. In addition, the imposition of states, the breaking-up of territorial continuity, as well as the control and separation of peoples that they facilitated, would remain a key feature of the (settler) colonial world.

While these treaties – alongside Spanish military victories in the 1530s and the establishment of the Kingdoms of Peru and New Spain (Mexico) in the 1570s – marked the establishment of new settler states, the totality of their victory should also not be overstated. It took a whole two centuries, from the early sixteenth to the late seventeenth century, for the settlers to fully militarily defeat the surviving factions of the different empires, city states and kingdoms they conquered. Others, like the Mapuche in the South (today's Chile) would not be militarily conquered until the mid-nineteenth century.[22] By then, the Spanish empire had crumbled under the pressure of mass uprisings in which both Indigenous and enslaved populations played a central role. In addition, continuous revolts by both African and Indigenous workers, separately or together, continued to challenge the empire throughout its history.

Although the Spanish settlers managed to hold on to power in the newly formed independent states and their economies, Indigenous struggle did not (and has not) faded from the scene. In Mexico, Indigenous resistance would establish effective control over the Yucatan for much of the nineteenth century, while revolting miners would transform the global economy by effectively ending silver production in the north of the country (see below). In Peru, an Indigenous uprising led by Túpac Katari challenged Spanish rule, even laying siege for over three months to La Paz in 1781. In Bolivia, largely Indigenous miners would form the backbone of numerous insurrections, up until the present. They played, for example, an important role in the uprisings that made the rise to power of Evo Morales possible in the early twenty-first century.[23]

PORTUGAL AND THE SLAVE ECONOMY IN BRAZIL

Having claimed the land that would become Brazil at Tordesillas, it would take the Portuguese several decades before the successful establishment of their first lasting settlements. Indigenous peoples' continuous resistance against the invaders, the concomitant inability of the latter to impose their rule, as well as the high death rates among those Indigenous people that were forced to labour in the sugar plantations, led the Portuguese to turn much of the northern area into sugar plantations worked on by large numbers of enslaved Africans: 'Close to five million enslaved Africans were taken to Portuguese America (Brazil) alone between 1501 and 1866 ... whose labour became the driving force for the sugar economy in the early 1600s, and gold and diamond mining from about 1690 onwards.'[24] The Portuguese at first used their colony in Angola as the primary source for the slave trade, before easing the import of enslaved Africans by other European states such as England and the Netherlands.

The geographical proximity between Brazil and Angola also made travel faster and less costly, which in turn led to the Brazilian economy depending increasingly on importing new enslaved populations. As Patrick Wolfe has argued, this meant that the slave economy in Brazil was both dependent on high levels of mortality – enslaved people were worked to death because they could easily be replaced – as well as high levels of manumission – that is, it was cheaper to free those who did survive but were no longer able to produce as effectively because of declining health or age. This grisly arithmetic of exploitation and death also facilitated the boom of the transatlantic slave trade under Portuguese domination, until their effective monopoly over the trade was first weakened by the Dutch and then broken by the English in the second half of the seventeenth century. So central was the slave trade to the Portuguese economy, that Wolfe notes: 'Instead of talking, in the manner conventional to comparative slavery studies, of slaves in the sugar industry as distinct from, say, slaves in the rice industry or slaves in the cotton industry, we might do better – at least, where Portugal is concerned – to talk of sugar, rice, or cotton in the slave industry.'[25]

Indeed, Brazil would be the last country to officially outlaw slavery (in 1888) and enslaved Africans would be put to work in different areas and different sectors throughout its history. For example, at the turn of the eighteenth century, due to a combination of factors including growing sugar exports from Cuba, environ-mental degradation – such as soil exhaustion – caused by overproduction, and large-scale slave revolts, the Brazilian sugar economy entered a period of sustained decline. At the same time, however, gold was discovered in Brazil's south-east. The gold rush that ensued moved a million people to the area, making Ouro Preto (Black Gold) the largest city in Latin America by the 1730s. While new settlers came from Portugal and across the empire, large internal population transfers took place also, including the forced movement of enslaved African populations from the North. The mines of the South, much like the plantations in the North, remained dependent on their cheap labour.[26]

INDIGENOUS LABOUR IN THE SPANISH EMPIRE

The Spanish, on the other hand, moved from the early settlements in the Caribbean to the colonisation of much of the hemisphere. There they waged war on – and defeated – the three most powerful civilisations in Latin America: the Aztec and Maya empires in contemporary Mexico and Central America, and the Inca empire that stretched from contemporary southern Colombia to the middle of today's Chile. Military victory was made possible by Spanish exploitation of existing social tensions and rebellions within these empires. Allying themselves with warring factions against the central power, the Spanish were able to lay hold of those states' existing institutions, in establishing their early colonial rule. The civilisations they conquered were largely agricultural, and their lands were densely populated, which facilitated the imposition of an extractive economy to the settlers' benefit.

Indigenous agricultural produce was diverted to the Spanish settlements, as they were in the Caribbean, while millions were forced to work the land, and in mines and manufacturing. Three different forms of labour regimes were imposed on Indigenous peoples throughout the Spanish empire, that were not so different from chattel slavery. The first of those was the *encomienda*. This system, introduced in the early years of the sixteenth century, meant that 'the Crown conferred on individual settlers or officials the responsibility for protecting and civilizing native communities, together with the right to demand their labour in place of tribute due to the Crown.'[27] In practice, this meant that those who were given such a grant could impose forced labour on Indigenous populations through the extraction of tribute, in the name – of course – of civilisation. The *encomienda* was superimposed on existing Indigenous forms of tribute extraction, which it intensified considerably.

The system also remained dependent on an intermediary class of Indigenous elites (*kurakas* or *caciques*) that served as a conduit between the conquistadores and the Indigenous population: 'From the early seventeenth century, the Spanish regime in the Americas ruled native majorities with scarce military force. Everyday power relied on mediation by native leaders and colonial courts – more the former in the Andes, the latter in Mesoamerica.'[28] In certain areas, such as the Rio de la Plata, these relations were also solidified through marriages between settler men and Indigenous women[29] – pointing to the ways in which settler power relied also on the (re)production of male domination over women.

The second form of labour regime, imposed from the middle of the same century, was called by different names: 'the *mita* in Peru and the *repartimiento* in New Spain'. It relied on 'Indian villages, through their headmen ... to provide a proportion of their labour force to work in rotation throughout the year. This labour was allocated by local officials either to public works or to privately owned mines, factories or farms ... it lasted until the end of the Spanish American empire.'[30] Finally, the third method through which Indigenous labour was forcefully extracted was through debt peonage. Once the Indigenous people were indebted, 'factory owners and farmers reduced them to virtual slavery, and some of the worst labour conditions existed in textile mills and silver mines where Indians were held in this way.'[31]

These forced labour regimes were often accompanied by forced displacement also, in order to destroy pre-existing forms of communal life – and therefore undermine potential communal resistance. In the process, sexist gender norms were imposed and solidified. On the one hand, collaborating Indigenous elite men were reinforced in the process, as they were positioned at the head of these resettled villages. On the other, Indigenous women experienced the brunt of the process of dispossession: '... they were denied access to land and water rights that had previously been communal. New regulations banned them from freedom of movement independent of men, and demanded that women either become wives or be classified as maids, thus redefining them as the property of men.'[32] Women therefore often played a central role in resistance and uprisings against the Spanish across the

Andes, emphasising a return to Indigenous culture and pre-colonial social relations. In turn, the Spanish focused much of their ire and repression against women specifically, using, for example, 'charges of witchcraft ... to subjugate women and redefine their position in society, establishing a new system of patriarchy that undergirded colonial rule and exploitation'.[33]

Indigenous people were sent to work to their deaths in the mines, first in the area surrounding Potosí and then north of Mexico City, in a desperate attempt to pay back debts, labelled as 'tribute', to the settlers: '... between 1760 and 1809 ... silver and gold exports [from Mexico alone] has been estimated at some 5 billion ... dollars [at 1971 prices]'.[34] The very fabric of Indigenous society was fundamentally altered in the process and the devastation was of unthinkable proportions. An estimated 8 million died over three centuries in Potosí's mines alone.[35] In these societies, settlement, resistance and pre-existing agricultural production led to a different outcome than in the Caribbean and Brazilian contexts. Cheap, hyper-exploited labour was provided by the militarily defeated Indigenous populations, often made available to the Spanish by collaborating Indigenous elites. At the same time, White settlements emerged around the mining centres, where luxury goods, services and trade provided the settlers with employment.

AMERICAN SILVER AND THE RISE OF A NEW GLOBAL ORDER

The previously unheard-of quantities of minerals extracted from the new colonies, as well as the availability of land, trade and rapid social ascension, in conjunction with oppression and poverty at home, attracted growing amounts of European settlers seeking wealth and a new life. Myths of such places as El Dorado, a city hidden in the tropical forests of the 'New World', might have been popular inventions, but they represented the reality that making the crossing was a way to acquire land, status and otherwise unattainable riches. The city of Potosí, for example, made famous by its mines, had grown to become one of the largest cities in the world by the mid-seventeenth century. In the period '[b]etween 1503 and 1660, 185,000 kilograms of gold and 16,000,000 of silver arrived at the Spanish port of Sanlucar de Barrameda',[36] which, as Galeano reminds us, is likely to be an underestimation.

These imports tripled existing European reserves: 'By 1650, the estimated flow of precious metals from the Americas reaching Europe amounted to at least 180 tons of gold and 17,000 tons of silver. Between 1561 and 1580, about 85 per cent of the entire world's production of silver came from the Americas'.[37] The silver extracted by Indigenous workers in the Americas became a central driver of the world economy – as well as a key conduit for the transformation of Europe's place in it. Silver continued to serve this role up until the early nineteenth century – well after Iberian power had been eclipsed by its competitors on the European continent. John Tutino, for example, writing about the Bajío – a mining area north-west of Mexico City, points out:

Under Spanish rule an expansive mix of silver mines, commercial estates, and textile workshops generated rising flows of silver that stimulated world trade from the late sixteenth century. After 1700 the Bajío was the American engine of global commercial capitalism, ruling the world's money supply (still under a Spanish monarchy struggling in Euro-Atlantic power politics). With few landed republics, the Bajío was built to serve capitalist dynamism. Native people drawn by rising incomes and a minority of Africans forced by slavery mixed in lives of labouring dependence.[38]

These Indigenous and African workers, he argues, were not only central to the new global economy, centred on Europe and American bullion. It was also the miners of the Bajío, a century later, who brought an end to what Tutino calls 'silver capitalism', through a sustained revolutionary uprising in 1810.

While increasing the available wealth for the Spanish Crown in the short term – in the sixteenth century, 'as much as 25 per cent of the Habsburgs' revenue'[39] came from the precious metals extracted from the Americas – in the long term, these flows of silver led to the rise of new European empires and accelerated the global transition to capitalism. However, instead of further propping up Iberian power, this new development was centred on North Western Europe. Indeed, a contradictory process took place. As the Habsburgs' coffers filled with loot from the Americas, the wealth so accumulated reinforced the dominant social relations in the empire, by enriching the Crown and the nobility. In addition, increased wealth encouraged Philip II – famous for having been at war every year of his reign[40] – in his military campaigns, waged against the Ottomans in the Mediterranean as well as Central Europe, the English Crown, and the Dutch revolt. This overstretch was encouraged by the unprecedented wealth coming from the Americas, which appeared to be endless. However, spending surpassed even those massive flows of gold and silver. The Spanish Crown indebted itself, always further, largely to financiers in Amsterdam, London and Antwerp, as well as Paris and Genoa.[41]

In this sense, the wealth violently accumulated in the Americas was transferred into the hands of financiers and merchants in North Western Europe, especially in the Low Lands: '[A]lmost half of the gold and silver acquired by Spain ended up in Holland',[42] still a part of the Habsburg empire until the 1580s. In turn, the bullion so transferred laid the foundation for the growth of Dutch and English trade in Asia. Until then, merchants in China and India had little interest in the goods that their European counterparts had to offer, given the latter's comparative economic backwardness in the global economy. Silver, on the other hand, was in high demand, especially in China. American silver, extracted through the genocidal violence meted out against Indigenous populations, passing through the Habsburg military into Dutch and English merchants' coffers, powered the growth of the Asian trades in spices and textiles.[43] 'Even down to the end of the seventeenth century, "treasure" accounted for 70 to 90 per cent of the English East India Company's total exports.'[44]

The growth in European commercial capitalism, financed by American silver and centred first on the Dutch Republic and then on England, would have massive consequences for the processes of production, both in Europe and across the world. First, merchants organised in trading companies increasingly established their control over production – at home and abroad – imposing new forms of organisation that could boost productivity, diminish cost and increase their competitiveness on the world market.[45] Second, the expansion of global trade networks necessitated the construction of new infrastructure and the development of new industries. These, in turn, transformed labour relations in Europe, further accelerating the spread of wage labour and population movements from the countryside to the expanding urban centres that colonial empire both required and made possible

> … a large mass of proletarians were integrated into forms of work that presupposed colonies – shipbuilding, harbour building, and later sugar refineries and textile production. For example, huge quantities of labour were required to clear forests and transport timber, which would subsequently be used to build the ships that formed the backbone of English colonial expansion. Similarly, colonial enterprises were the precondition for the extensive construction of ports for long-distance trade. Pre-existing towns and cities such as Bristol and London expanded significantly in the 17th century, while entirely new conurbations – Liverpool most notably, but also Glasgow and Derry – later sprang up as nodes in the growing network of international shipping spurred on by the Atlantic trading system. The construction of ports and harbours was based on the labour-intensive activities of reclaiming marshy coastal

lands, felling and transporting timber and rubble, and constructing seawalls, breakwaters, piers, quays and jetties.[46]

The process of enclosures, through which these workers were made available, picked up speed in the late fifteenth century in England and reached fever pitch by the late eighteenth. The development of new technology, as well as the growing daily intake of calories, made possible through the mass production of sugar in the American slave plantations, increased productivity.[47]

It goes without saying that this circuit transformation operated in both directions. The intensification of trade and production, in turn, boosted European demand for natural resources and cash crops, such as sugar, which intensified pressure on production in the colonies. Slave plantations equally became disciplined by, and integrated into, the emerging global capitalist economy. They 'mobilised modern techniques in crop specialisation, cultivation, book-keeping, packaging and shipping',[48] while 'intensification of cultivation – its increasing commercialisation, mechanisation and industrialisation – brought with it an intensification of exploitation for the slaves who worked the plantations.'[49]

In short, the accumulation of wealth in the Americas, based on the murder, enslavement and dispossession of Indigenous and African peoples, kick-started the rise of European empires on the world stage. Moreover, this accumulation of wealth also led to the transformation of power relations between European powers. Precious metals extracted in the Americas led to growing Dutch and English power in global trade – via Spain – which in turn laid the ground for an accelerated emergence of capitalist relations of production and the intensification of exploitation at home.

THE RISE OF ANGLO SETTLEMENT

The processes described so far also made new forms of settler colonialism possible, which would become central to the emerging English empire. Indeed, as peasants were increasingly cleared off the land and moved into growing urban centres, a new phenomenon emerged, so central to capitalist labour relations: so-called 'surplus populations'. This was also accentuated by the growth in overall population that the dual process of colonial enrichment and capitalist transition made possible. Between the beginning of the sixteenth and the end of the eighteenth century, 'the population of ... England and the Low Countries almost doubled.'[50] The unemployed or underemployed – often euphemistically labelled 'the urban poor' in contemporary developmental speak – who accumulated in the cities, primarily in England, played an important economic role (keeping the wages of the employed low), but also posed potential political dangers. Poverty and jobless-ness risked leading to revolt. Much ink was spilled at the time on the need to resolve this issue, as well as on the perfect opportunity that the settlements in the Americas represented in that regard. Deporting the poor (and the rebellious) to the colonies would serve a double purpose: lessen social tensions at home and strengthen settlement abroad. From the end of the sixteenth century onwards, laws were passed in England that allowed the deportation of 'beggars', 'vagrants', or 'criminals' to the English settlements in North America. In the space of a century, 'some 200,0000 people were moved' in this manner.[51] A hundred years later, in the late eighteenth century, this process would be repeated by the (now) British in order to settle the newly colonised lands of Oceania.

It is worth noting that a very different and, until then unique, form of settler colonialism emerged in this process. Settler societies emerged, most strikingly in the colonies that would become the United States, which attempted to develop polities free from a reliance on the Indigenous populations. Their economies would be primarily dependent on settler smallholders and European bonded labourers on the one hand, and imported enslaved African populations on the other. In the first century of English settlement in North America, the enslavement of Indigenous people would also take place, albeit in very different proportions to the process described above, in the Spanish empire. In the second half of the seventeenth century, as the English became increasingly involved in (and dependent on) the slave trade, enslaved Indigenous labour would often be deported and sold in the Caribbean, in order to avoid their escape or rebellion, and replaced by Africans.[52] Chapters 2 and 3 will return to these issues in detail. For now, it suffices to say that these North American settlements were unique in the early seventeenth century in being built on Indigenous land but also, increasingly, at the exclusion of Indigenous labour.

The process by which the peasantry's dispossession in England led to an intensification of settlement in the

Americas, further reinforced the loop between colonial expansion abroad and social, political and economic transformation at home. The extraction of wealth, labour and resources in the (settler) colonies facilitated accumulation in Europe, which in turn supplied the settlements with the goods and (military) technology from its developing manufacturing centres – as well as, crucially, more settlers. This apparently never-ending flow of settlers would play a crucial role in overwhelming Indigenous societies in North America, and later in Australia and New Zealand. Wolfe notes that Indigenous

> … resources were not tailored to the unequal confrontation that settlers' endless renewability set in train. Natives' finite local stock was no match for imperialism's global elasticity. Rather, they were reduced to relying on a shrinking pool of indigenous resources whose reproduction had been severely hampered by settler encroachments. The disparity was quantitative not qualitative.[53]

It was also cumulative. As settler encroachment took over land and resources, and meted out genocidal violence against the Indigenous population, the latter was displaced and, in the process, increased pressure on other Indigenous populations' land and resources. Simultaneously, the increased accumulation of wealth based on this dispossession facilitated the arrival of more settlers, which allowed the settlements to expand even further, thus re-energising the infernal cycle.

To make matters worse, English settlers developed new forms of social organisation, based on purportedly innate differences to justify both the enslavement of Africans and the dispossession of Indigenous peoples – that is, racism. In doing so, they were able to attract even more Europeans to their settlements. The latter, made available by the spread of capitalist social relations and the accompanying peasant dispossession across the European continent, were now called upon to abandon national or religious differences and to think of themselves as White (see chapter 3). If the Spanish had been hamstrung by their continued reliance on Catholicism and religious orthodoxy in the recruitment of settlers, from the early eighteenth century onwards, the emergence of a supposedly White race effectively made unlimited numbers of settlers available to the (now British) settlements.[54] This, in turn, further accelerated the dispossession of Indigenous land.

It is also striking that it is in these colonies that the first secession by settlers from the metropole took place. While feelings of resentment towards what settlers considered to be unfair taxation and restrictive political control by the home country were broadly felt by settlers across the world, it was in the 13 British colonies that the first successful settler uprising took place. In his book *Settler Capitalism*, Donald Denoon argues that this success should largely be understood as emerging from the settlements' economic structure.[55] The latter was not solely based on the export of specific cash crops or natural resources to the metropole, extracted through enslaved Indigenous and/or African labour – although this was undoubtedly also part of its economic structure, especially in the South. Nor were these settlements dependent on Britain for the import of food or goods, as the Caribbean settlements were. Instead, the North American settlements developed as 'copies' of the British metropole and therefore also as increasingly independent economic competitors, for example, in shipbuilding. They could therefore secede and remain economically viable, while benefiting more directly from the wealth accumulated through slavery and Indigenous dispossession.

Whilst the specificities of these settlements should be underlined, it is equally true that important continuities remain. Genocidal violence unleashed against Indigenous people, theft of land, enslavement of Africans, and the continuous desire to expand the frontier, continued to be the guiding principle of settlers in North America (see chapter 2). In fact, it was the growing demands by settlers to accelerate the process of Indigenous dispossession, and London's perceived reticence to facilitate it, that finally led to American revolt and secession.

INTENSIFICATION AND EXPANSION OF THE SETTLER WORLD

In the nineteenth century, many of the processes discussed above reached the pinnacle of their development. This led to the ever-greater integration of the world market, the increasingly rapid circulation of goods, people and wealth across the globe, and the intensification of industrial development in the West. While it is not possible to do full justice to these processes here, a few general points can be made.[56] The first industrial revolution, which took place roughly from the mid-eighteenth to the mid-nineteenth century, was fed by the growing input from colonial exploitation and dispossession, as well as the workforce made available through the expanding enclosures. It was characterised by the development of mechanised production (primarily in textiles), the growing use of steam-powered engines, and communication acceleration through the discovery of electricity. Steamboats, railroads and telegraph lines connected not only the metropoles to their colonies, but also increasingly allowed communication and travel between the different settler colonies. The basis of the colonial economy shifted from sugar to cotton, and increasingly from enslaved to indentured labour.

These transformations also altered the balance of forces on a global scale between European and non-European empires. Throughout the century, lands across Africa and Asia, that had so far been impossible to colonise or subjugate, fell under the pressure of the growing economic and military might of the European powers, which was itself based on previous accumulation of wealth through colonial dispossession. This point is worth underlining. While European powers – first the Portuguese, then the Dutch, then the English – traded in enslaved Africans from the fifteenth century onwards, and built American colonial economies on the back of their labour, there is a danger of overstating their power in relation to the African states they encountered. To do so would be to read history backwards, and risk presenting European dominance as inevitable or innate. Here again, the comparative backwardness of European powers, which propelled their seaward expansion from the mid-fifteenth century onwards, should be remembered. Indeed, as Anievas and Nişancıoğlu point out:

> … in the 16th century when Europeans first began to develop the transatlantic slave trade, West African states held numerous geopolitical and economic advantages over Europeans … Although European states would eventually subjugate the continent from the 18th century onwards, prior to that period African states proved very effective in repelling European territorial encroachments. Moreover, in terms of trade, Europe offered very little to Africa that it did not already produce or obtain from elsewhere.[57]

They further point out that European attempts, for example, to establish on the West African coast the kind of colonial plantation economies that would come to define the Caribbean and Brazil, were repeatedly repelled by the existing African states they encountered. The trade in enslaved Africans between European and West African powers was then the outcome of the impossibility to resolve the tension between European maritime and African territorial power. It was only in the course of the eighteenth century that the cumulative effects of an ever-growing European demand for slaves so weakened the West African states' social structure, that it became possible for the former to push inland. The numbers speak for themselves:

> From 1501 to 1650, a period during which Portuguese elites, at least until about 1620, and then their Dutch

peers, held a dominant position in delivering transatlantic imports of captives: 726,000 Africans were dragged to the Americas, essentially to Spanish settlements and Brazil. By way of contrast, from 1650 to 1775, during London's and Paris's ascendancy and the concomitant accelerated development of sugar and tobacco, about 4.8 million Africans were brought to the Americas. Then, for the next century or so, until 1866, almost 5.1 million manacled Africans were brought to the region, at a time when the republicans in North America played a preeminent role in this dirty business.[58]

It was during the nineteenth century then that European colonialism rapidly expanded across the globe, reaping the benefits of centuries of colonial accumulation and the cumulative weakening of the states and empires it encountered. Military defeats were followed by forced trade agreements, which in turn opened new markets to European exports. Mass-produced industrial goods would flood local economies and destroy local manufacturing capacities, which in turn further weakened the ability of targeted societies to resist Western encroachment. While collaborating elites accumulated wealth as Indigenous agents of the colonial powers, hunger, disease and abject poverty were the outcome for the great majority.[59]

The Chinese Opium Wars of the mid-nineteenth century represent these changes well. While not formerly colonised, the attempt by the Chinese imperial power to ban the import of opium into the country by the British East India Company was met with overwhelming military action. Not only did these military campaigns bring the

Chinese empire to heel, they also led to the British occupation of Hong Kong and the opening of free-trade ports, including in Shanghai. Both areas continue to operate separately from the Chinese state, under heavy Western influence, to this day. China was not formerly occupied, nor were its shores populated with British settlers to displace the local population and create a new White state in East Asia. Instead, control was established through the dual violence of the bullet and the market.

In addition, these changes took place very much under the banner of British power. The defeat of Napoleon on the European mainland ended over half a century of nearly continuous war on a world scale between France and Britain. France was evicted directly and indirectly from North America (in 1803, it sold its colonies to the United States in the Louisiana Purchase) and India, which led it to turn its attention to Northern and Western Africa. From 1830, for example, France colonised increasingly large tracts of land in Algeria and encouraged their settlement by French and Southern European populations. The low availability of settlers, the sustained struggle by Algerian resistance movements, and the densely populated nature of the arable coastal plains, however, led to the development of an economy based, much like Spanish colonial holdings in Central and South America, on cheap, highly exploited Indigenous labour for the export of cash crops to France.

At the same time, Britain increased its control over the Caribbean and the maritime trade routes to India. From the late eighteenth century onwards, it initiated the colonisation and settlement of both Australia and New Zealand, which intensified throughout the nineteenth century. These new colonies replicated the eliminatory logic of settlement in North America and were used as outlets for the growing populations in the metropole, which were a direct outcome of their industrialisation. Britain would also wrestle control of the Cape of Good Hope, in today's South Africa, from the hands of Dutch colonists in 1795 and again in 1806. Under its rule, southern Africa's colonisation would intensify throughout the century. The empire also worked to establish a land corridor all the way to Egypt in the north of the continent. Its rule was further strengthened through the settlement of White populations throughout this area, such as in Kenya, Zimbabwe (then Southern Rhodesia) and South Africa.

THE END OF SLAVERY?

As the end of the eighteenth century neared, so did that of the transatlantic slave trade, which had been so central to the colonial economies that connected West Africa, the Americas and Europe, and on the back of which both settlers and the metropoles accumulated such vast amounts of wealth.

There is an element of historic justice – as far as such a term can apply – in the fact that the slave economies' death knell rang on one of the islands where it had first been developed in the immediate aftermath of Columbus' invasions. In Haiti, in 1791, the enslaved rose up. There had, of course, been slave revolts before. In fact, they were endemic to slave economies and continuously haunted slave-owning settlers, who remained stuck between their

unquenchable greed and their terror at being so outnumbered by a rebellious majority.[60] Chapter 3 will return to
the fact that rebellion was a continuous feature of plantation societies and led to the development of different
forms of social control – central amongst them racism.

The Haitian revolt turned into a twelve-year-long revolution, which would defeat both slavers and the numerous
armies sent to crush it. Not only did the uprising lead to
the establishment of the first Black independent republic,
but also, in time, to the end of slavery all together.[61] If it
took until the end of the nineteenth century to see the
institution of slavery end across the Americas – at least
officially – it was in Haiti that the enslaved masses demonstrated the founded nature of slave-owners' fears across
the Americas: successful revolutions by the enslaved
were possible. Indeed, under the pressure of the Haitian
revolution – and the uprisings that followed it on other
islands like Barbados and Jamaica – it became increasingly clear to plantation owners and colonial officials that
economies built on the back of majority-enslaved populations presented a real danger of revolution and, therefore,
to their continued successful extraction of profits.

The nineteenth century saw, then, slavery's official end
in the British empire in 1833, in the French empire in 1848,
and the United States in 1865. Brazil, the world's largest
slave economy, abolished slavery in 1888. The official end
of slavery did not, however, translate to an end of unfree
labour. Different legal remedies were put in place to
guarantee continued exploitation – and therefore profits –
in the plantations. For example, formerly enslaved people
were barred from owning appropriate land for their own

subsistence, or trapped in so-called 'apprenticeships' in the Caribbean that kept them on the plantations. The emergence of Jim Crow segregation in the US South was another way to legally bar Black people from achieving full political and economic rights.

Simultaneously, as formerly enslaved populations were denied full freedom, plantation owners and settler states started importing indentured East and South Asian workers who were to serve as a buffer between the White and Black populations in the Caribbean. As Lisa Lowe documents in *Intimacies of Four Continents*, while not formally enslaved, these workers were often transported, housed and exploited in extremely similar conditions to those of enslaved African workers before them. John Bellamy Foster, Brett Clark and Hannah Holleman make a similar point in a passage that is worth quoting at length:

Over ninety thousand Chinese workers were shipped to Peru during the heyday of the guano trade — approximately 10 percent died in passage due mainly to poor treatment and malnourishment. The most unfortunate unfree laborers were sent to the guano islands, where the total workforce fluctuated between two hundred to eight hundred workers at any given moment, but where lives were used up rapidly — considered of less value than the guano that they dug up. Only men were sent to these islands, where over 'one hundred armed soldiers' kept guard, preventing workers from committing suicide by running into the ocean ... Eye-witness accounts noted that these Chinese workers were treated as expendable, regularly flogged and whipped if they did not fulfil the demanding work expectations. They laboured in the hot sun, filling sacks and wheelbarrows with guano, which they then transported to a chute that loaded the boats. Guano dust coated their bodies and filled their lungs. The smell was overwhelming. One account described the conditions as 'the infernal art of using up human life to the very last inch,' as the lives of the workers were very short. Several British shipmasters were 'horrified at the cruelties ... inflicted on the Chinese, whose dead bodies they described as floating round the islands.'[62]

Lowe also points out that between 1834 and the end of the century, 'half a million Asian immigrants made their way to the British West Indies, in the context of tens of millions going to Latin America, North America, Australia, New Zealand, and South East Asia.'[63] There, they were met not only by horrendous working conditions, but also with violent opposition by settler labour movements.

In addition, these population movements were closely related to the industrial revolution. Steamships and the greater internal connection within the empire facilitated the mass transport of populations from one colonial locale to another. These movements, as Lowe has emphasised, also connected franchise colonies in Asia to settler colonies in Africa and the Americas, where Asian workers were often mobilised as cheap, captive labour to build the railways that were so central to settlement, colonialism and trade.

East Asian workers built much of the lines in the US West for example, where they faced sustained racism from White workers and where increasing anti-migration policies targeted them towards the end of the century.[64] The British empire similarly exported large amounts of Indian workers to its African settler colonies, where they served – much as in the Caribbean – as buffer populations between White settlers and Black Indigenous populations. The Ugandan railway, connecting Mombasa to Lake Victoria, was laid by such labour, for low wages and in horrendous conditions. Thousands died in the process. Not to be left out, the Dutch also turned to the transportation of indentured Asian workers to Suriname in the aftermath of slavery's formal abolition.

RAILWAYS AND PORTS

The industrial revolution, as well as British global economic, maritime and military dominance, did more than accelerate the expansion of empire. It also impacted the nature of settler colonial expansion and control in a number of crucial ways. Changing patterns of exploitation, as discussed above, encouraged the development of what were until then peripheral settlements, and delivered the military and mechanical means for settlers to intensify Indigenous dispossession and deepen their control over the lands so conquered.

First, the expansion of world trade, facilitated by steam engines on land and sea, and the rapid growth of industrial exports from the metropole to the colonial dominions, led to a dual increase in the demand for infrastructural development as well as natural resources in the European settler world. Larger ports that could sustain the more frequent and bigger ships passing through were developed in key strategic points, such as those in the Cape and Buenos Aires. In his classic study *Settler Capitalism*, Donald Denoon showed that, as the port cities grew, so did the need for commerce and basic industry to sustain their expanding populations.[65] This, in turn, led to a greater demand for agricultural output to feed the settler populations, encouraging further expansion of agricultural settlement – and Indigenous dispossession and displacement – in the lands surrounding the port cities. These processes of growing settler expansion also increased the appeal of previously small and isolated settlement towns for the poor in the metropole.

Growing demand for wool, meat and precious metals in the centre of the empire also gave a boost to settler colonial economies in the Southern Hemisphere, spanning a corridor from Chile to New Zealand, passing through Argentina, South Africa and Australia. Just as the circulation of new steamships increased demand, they also helped meet it through the more regular connection of the settler world to the metropoles. This new technology also facilitated greater settler movement between the two, as well as between individual settlements. As chapters 2 and 4 will discuss respectively, it is through this greater integration of settler ports in the world economy that inward expansion accelerated in these areas, leading to the emergence of newly enlarged settler polities. It also led to the development of an imperial White working class, as noted by Jonathan Hyslop,[66] which moved regularly between the different settler colonies in search for work – for example, between the mining sectors of England,

Australia, Southern Africa and South America. These more regular transport connections and settler flows facilitated the movement of ideas, forms of organisation and methods of Indigenous dispossession. It is through these networks that the reservation as a form of Indigenous dispossession and control travelled between the US, South Africa and Palestine, and that labour campaigns in the defence of Whiteness were replicated between Australia and South Africa.

Second, technical developments also facilitated the intensification of settler expansion and control. The mechanisation of warfare on the one hand, and the more effective infrastructural integration of the colonial frontier into imperial networks of circulation on the other, further disadvantaged Indigenous populations and facilitated settler domination. The importance in this period of the railway, so vaunted as a supposedly positive colonial legacy by today's defenders of empire, cannot be overstated:

In 1845, outside Europe, the only 'underdeveloped' country which possessed even a mile of railway line was Cuba. By 1855 there were lines in all five continents, though those of South America (Brazil, Chile, Peru) and Australia were hardly visible. By 1865 New Zealand, Algeria, Mexico and South Africa had their first railways, and by 1875, while Brazil, Argentina, Peru and Egypt had around a thousand miles or more of track, Ceylon, Java, Japan and even remote Tahiti had acquired their first lines. Meanwhile by 1875 the world possessed 62,000 locomotives, 112,000 carriages and almost half a million goods wagons, carrying between them, so it was estimated, 1,371 million passengers and 715 million tons of goods, or about nine times as much as was carried by sea each year (on average) during this decade.[67]

Railways would be especially important in the Anglo settler colonies where they facilitated conquest and population transfer: 'In 1875, the top five nations in terms of rail miles per capita were the United States (with 1,922 miles of rail per million people), New Zealand (1,350), Canada (1,159) Australia (998) and Britain (527).'[68] Throughout the nineteenth century, existing settler states expanded rapidly, through sustained warfare against Indigenous populations, the colonisation of Australia, Canada and the United States being cases in point. In the span of a century, massive amounts of lands were annexed and settled, while Indigenous populations, their economies, and land rights, were decimated. Indentured workers – often South and East Asian – were enlisted and shipped across the world, to lay the tracks in appalling and often murderous conditions. This process should be understood, in the words of Manu Karuka, as 'railroad colonialism: territorial expansion through financial logics and corporate organization, using unfree imported laborers, blending the economic and military functions of the state, materializing in construction projects across the colonized world'.[69]

In 1830, for example, the US government, under President Andrew Jackson, passed the Indian Removal Act, initiating the forced displacement of the Cherokee, Chickasaw, Choctaw, Creek and Seminole peoples to the lands west of the Mississippi River. This violent expulsion led to the death of tens of thousands. The next chapter will return to this process in detail, but for now it suffices to say that these mass displacements laid the foundation for the increasingly rapid expansion of settlement westwards. Although as Roxanne Dunbar-Ortiz points out:

> Traversing the continent 'from sea to shining sea' was hardly a natural westward procession of covered wagons as portrayed in Western movies. The US invasion of Mexico was carried out by US marines, by sea, through Veracruz, and the early colonisation of California initially progressed from the Pacific coast, reached from the Atlantic coast by way of Tierra el Fuego. Between the Mississippi River and the Rockies lay a vast region controlled by Indigenous nations that were neither conquered nor colonised by any European power, and although the United States managed to annex Northern Mexico, large number of settlers could not reach the Northern California goldfields or the fertile Willamette Valley region of the Pacific North-west without army regiments accompanying them.[70]

Total continental conquest was officially announced to be completed in 1890, with the so-called 'closing of the frontier', following the massacre of hundreds of Lakota Indians at Wounded Knee. This did not, however, signify the end of Indigenous dispossession at the hands of settlers and their state, as chapters 2 and 5 will discuss further. For example, 'Native American communities in the Great Plains Dust Bowl region lost some 90 percent of their remaining landholdings between 1890 and 1933 and had among the highest poverty rates in the country'.[71]

Central to this expansion was the introduction of the railways in North America in the 1830s and 1840s, which allowed the rapid movement of soldiers and settlers, as well as the strategic fragmenting of Indigenous land. In the 1860s, as the dispossession of Indigenous people continued to gather speed, federal land grants were distributed to industrialists and financiers (as well as universities) to develop settler infrastructure and accelerate land acquisition: 'The Pacific Railroad Act provided private companies with nearly two hundred million acres of Indigenous land.'[72] Mass expropriation, alongside the parcelling out of Indigenous lands to individual homesteaders, sparked large-scale Indigenous revolts so extensive that they momentarily halted settlers achieving statehood in 'Colorado, North and South Dakota, Montana, Washington, Idaho, Wyoming, Utah, New Mexico, and Arizona.'[73] Here again, the railway was key. Dunbar-Ortiz notes that:

> The federal land grants to the railroad barons, carved out of Indigenous territories, were not limited to the width of the railroad tracks, but rather formed a checkerboard of square-mile sections stretching for dozens of miles on both sides of the right of way. This was land the railroads were free to sell in parcels for their own profit.[74]

The tracks and the surrounding privately owned land ran through and divided Indigenous nations from each other. They also facilitated the arrival of settlers and soldiers, which in turn allowed for more rapid and deadly assaults against Indigenous people. This infrastructure would also be mobilised to allow the US Army to massacre between 10 and 15 million buffalo, bringing the animal to near extinction in the space of two decades, in order 'to destroy the basic economic base of the Plains Nations'[75] and hasten their elimination and dispossession.

So central were the railways to settlement that, as Deborah Cowan points out, they were both the necessary precondition and the requirement for Canadian unification. They 'literally, materially made the Canadian state possible … Delegates from the provinces of Nova Scotia and New Brunswick made the construction of the "Intercolonial rail" a condition of their entry into Confederation.'[76] The railways connected disparate tracts of land and distant settlements, while facilitating the control and dispossession of the Indigenous populations. Similarly in Russia, the construction of the Trans-Siberian Railway from the late nineteenth century onwards facilitated the deepening integration of lands colonised in the two previous centuries and the transfer of settlers into Siberia. In return, growing amounts of wheat flowed westwards.[77]

In South Africa, as gold-mining emerged in the Rand in the closing decades of the nineteenth century, railway development would become of central importance both to extract the rich minerals as quickly as possible, and to facilitate the movement of goods and settlers towards the mining area. The whole business further facilitated accumulation. James Belich notes that:

Between 1886 and 1892, the Rand was supplied from the Transvaal and Natal by ox wagon. The rail line from Cape Town arrived in 1892, that from Durban in 1895. A third line, from Delagoa Bay in Portuguese Mozambique, arrived in 1894. These ports competed desperately to complete their railways and plug into the Rand.[78]

In other locales in southern Africa too, the railway played a key role in spreading settler power and assaulting Indigenous populations. When, in 1904, the Herero rebelled against German rule, the latter

> ... used railroads that had been built by forced Herero labour to rapidly move troops. Facing down a troop train armed with machine guns, insurgents sabotaged the tracks in several places after intense fighting, and the train was unable to lift the Herero siege on Okahandja. The fighting persisted for four years, until the Germans had destroyed the basis of independent Herero political leadership and Herero landholding, through mass executions and forced-labour concentration camps. Herero prisoners of war, regardless of gender, were forced to work on railroad construction from Lüderlitz to Aus. Upon completion of the Otavi railway line, surviving Hereros (including children) were then redistributed among settler farmers.[79]

If the railways were central to Indigenous dispossession and the aggressive expansion of settler rule, they were also sites of struggle and of resistance – both military and industrial. Mass strikes by railroad workers travelled up and down the tracks, challenging the violence of both exploitation and dispossession. In 1867 during the construction of the Central Pacific Railroad, Chinese workers went on strike, demanding higher wages, shorter hours, the right to resign, and an end to whipping. Karuka also reads possible interactions between Chinese railroad workers and Indigenous Paiute populations during the strike, in the rumours circulated about the latter at the time.[80] Railway workers and the communities that the tracks dispossessed played a key role in a variety of anti-colonial uprisings and movements, including the Boxer Rebellion, Indian anti-colonial agitation from the late nineteenth century onwards, as well as Egyptian, Rhodesian and Gold Coast liberation movements:[81] 'Railroads had become the sites of mass, organized unrest across the African continent by the end of the First World War.'[82]

Simultaneously, as these transformations facilitated settlement as well as intra-settler connections, alongside greater local economic development, the movements for settler independence grew stronger. Beginning with the United States in 1776, the century that followed saw the rise of settler independence struggles across Central and South America. Settler republics broke politically with the metropoles, while remaining integrated in international networks of accumulations centred on European economies, primarily Britain's. Throughout the century, British involvement in banking, mining and trade with Latin America increased.[83] Much of the railway construction across the world discussed above was, at least in part, financed by British capital. These revolutions, while transforming the world map, should not, as already pointed out in the Introduction, be confused with later processes of decolonisation or be described as opening a period of post-colonialism. On the contrary, they often went hand-in-hand with increased (or at least continued) dispossession of Indigenous populations by the now independent settler republics.

The nineteenth century was the century of the acceleration of European global dominance, under British leadership, primarily achieved through the technological and economic tools unleashed by the industrial revolution. This revolution was largely made possible by the dispossession, plunder, elimination and exploitation of the colonial world and its populations in previous centuries. Industrialisation, technical developments such as mechanised looms and steam engines, and the concomitant European military power on land and sea, accelerated colonial processes put in motion throughout the previous centuries. Millions were displaced. The steamboat and the railway became key tools in the dispossession of Indigenous peoples, the settlement of larger swathes of the globe, and the movement of largely Asian indentured labour to Africa and the Americas. Port cities grew in importance and increased the demand for agricultural production and labour, encouraging further settler expansion in previously peripheral areas of empire. However, while the speed of settlement and colonial expansion increased, it was fast approaching collapse across much of the globe.

OVERSTRETCH AND REVOLUTION

The turn of the twentieth century saw the further (and final) expansion of European (largely franchise) colonialism into the African continent and the Middle East, as well as non-European settler colonialism, chiefly that of Japan in Korea.[84] It is in the same period that the Zionist movement started settling Palestine, with the backing, from 1917 onwards, of the British empire. Whilst at first glance Zionism represented a departure from previous settler colonialism, because of its original independence from state support and the oppression faced by its settlers in Europe, the overview given in this chapter should point to much more striking continuities. Throughout the four hundred years under review here, political, religious, or social 'undesirables' have fled poverty and repression at home and become the vanguard of expanding settlement abroad. The much-vaunted Pilgrims were a persecuted minority in Europe who, in the course of their crossing of the Atlantic, became the carriers of English sovereignty into Indigenous lands in North America. The settlement process turned them from outcasts at home to heroes of the settler colonial project.

Much the same could be said for the Jewish Zionists, fleeing antisemitism and persecution in Europe, who established what Sir Ronald Storrs called 'a little loyal Jewish Ulster in a sea of potentially hostile Arabism', making obvious the link to other settler colonial settings.[85] More will be said about Zionism's relationship with the Indigenous Palestinian populations in chapters 3 and 4, and of Palestinian resistance in chapter 5. For now, it suffices to point out that Zionism's, and then Israel's, role in the region was part of a wider process of regional domination by Britain. The settlers were then, as captured in the Storrs quote above, to be an imperial outpost in the Middle East, which would be mobilised to confront anti-colonial uprisings, protect British pipelines, and secure one side of the Suez Canal. Placing Zionism and Israel in this larger colonial context also clarifies the continued support by Western states for its settler colonial project in Palestine.

It is also worth noting that the Nakba – the Palestinian catastrophe in which 700,000 Palestinians were expelled from their homes and over 500 Palestinian villages and urban centres were destroyed by Zionist militias first, and then the Israeli Army, between 1947 and 1949 – captures the way in which settler colonialism can intensify at the very moment when the colonial metropole retreats.[86] Indeed, it was Britain quitting Palestine, which opened the door for a large-scale assault by Zionist militias on Palestinian society and the establishment of the state of Israel. Much the same process will be discussed in the case of the United States in chapter 2. Across the African continent, similar attempts to establish independent settler states in the face of weakening colonial empires and strengthening Indigenous resistance took place throughout the century. Some were successful – at least for a time – as was the case in South Africa and Southern Rhodesia; others less so, as in the failed generals' coup in 1961 in Algeria.

In some cases, the twentieth century's simultaneous extension and collapse of colonial empires coincided in a striking manner. The Portuguese, for example, aimed to solidify their colonial hold on their African empire at the eleventh hour. In the aftermath of the Second World War, while colonial states and empires were being torn asunder by anti-colonial uprisings, mass strike and military insurrections, the Portuguese state accelerated the transfer of settlers to Mozambique and Angola. It continued to do so despite growing revolutionary war waged by liberation movements in both countries, committing growing numbers of troops to bloody repression. In the end, the anti-colonial struggle's steadfastness in the face of this violence, triggered a revolutionary uprising in the metropole, which brought an end both to the fascist regime and to Portuguese settler colonies: 'Within two years ... Portuguese who settled in Angola and Mozambique returned to Portugal in a tidal wave of some 400,000 civilians and 100,000 troops.'[87] The fate of Portugal's settler colonies was emblematic of the wider trend across the century, centred particularly on the Asian and African continents, during which Indigenous movements successfully rose up against a wide variety of colonial formations and achieved their independence.[88] That same struggle for liberation continues across much of the world today, as chapter 5 will discuss.

As this chapter has argued, no neat division can be made between capitalist development, colonial extraction, and settlement. They are part and parcel of one and the same historical process, and are co-constitutive. Enslavement, genocide and settlement became the holy trinity that made the accumulation of wealth possible on a global scale, into the coffers of European states, merchants and emerging capitalists. This process transformed the colonial nations' economies and facilitated the rise of a new bourgeois class to power. In turn, this new-found wealth and power accelerated the dispossession of the peasantry, which provided both industry and settlement with its needed labour power, accelerating settlement and dispossession once more.

At the root of this process lay unprecedented levels of violence, both in their geographic scale and intensity: the violence of the slave ship and the plantation, of genocide and dispossession, of displacement and indentured labour, of the machine and manufactured famine. Exploitation and elimination operated side by side throughout this process, at both ends of the same historical development, oiling the wheels of economic growth in Europe and across the settler world. By the early twentieth century, it had truly covered the globe in 'blood and fire'.

Simultaneously, as we have seen throughout this chapter, this violence was never passively accepted by those against whom it was unleashed. The enslaved and the colonised continued to rise up and fight back against their conquerors and oppressors. It is their resistance that brought an end to chattel slavery in the nineteenth century, and it is their resistance that achieved the wave of decolonisation that continued throughout the twentieth. The same dual process of settler violence and Indigenous resistance, continues to define the settler colonial world today.

CHAPTER TWO

Dispossessing the Native

Settlers settle. In doing so, they also dispossess. As the previous chapter has shown, settlers murder and displace Indigenous populations, in order to accumulate Indigenous peoples' land, resources and/or labour power. This process of dispossession, carried out on a global scale, requires gargantuan levels of violence. Roxanne Dunbar-Ortiz, writing in the context of the United States, explains:

> Settler colonialism, as an institution or system, requires violence or the threat of violence to attain its goals. People do not hand over their land, resources, children, and futures without a fight, and that fight is met with violence. In employing the force necessary to accomplish its expansionist goals, a colonising regime institutionalises violence. The notion that settler-Indigenous conflict is an inevitable product of cultural differences and misunderstandings, or that the violence was committed equally by the colonised and the coloniser, blurs the nature of the historical process. Euro-American colonialism, an aspect of the capitalist economic globalisation, had from its beginnings a genocidal tendency.[1]

Despite the almost obvious nature of this observation – to build a society where another already exists requires the latter's destruction, in one form or another, as well as the suppression of any resistance to that destruction – it bears repeating. Too often settler violence is obscured, relativised, or presented as one side of a vicious circle in which both Indigenous and settler populations play comparable roles.

Instead, as we will see in this chapter, settler violence is not only foundational, it is continuous. Dispossession is enacted, and repeated, as long as the settlement process continues. Indigenous populations are removed from the land through conquest – figuratively, through the denial of their presence, and literally, through murder and displacement. Following conquest, this process continues. Indigenous people are submitted to many forms of control by the settler state and penned into open-air prisons, or 'prisoners of war camps' in Nick Estes' formulation,[2] variously called reserves, reservations, Bantustans, territories, or areas, depending on the context.

This, in turn, gives settlers ever greater access to Indigenous land as well as control over Indigenous people and their labour. While in certain settler colonies, Indigenous dispossession leads to their exclusion from the settler economy, in favour of settler labour, we will see that, in others, the same forms of dispossession and physical domination are mobilised to establish tight control over Indigenous labour, upon which the settler economy depends. In both cases, the necessary precondition for the process of accumulation, described earlier, is imposed on Indigenous peoples by settlers and their states: dispossession.

EMPTY LANDS EVERYWHERE

Settlers have systematically tried to obscure this fact of dispossession in a number of different ways. Most prominent amongst the discursive strategies used has been the denial that they encountered Indigenous societies at all. Even when settlers recognised the presence of Indigenous peoples and societies, they argued that these were so primitive as to be virtually undifferentiated from the local fauna and flora, which in turn justified their subjugation, or even their elimination, by Europeans. Juan Ginés de Sepúlveda, the sixteenth-century Spanish theologian, in his famous defence of the Indigenous populations' enslavement in the Americas, argued:

> In wisdom, skill, virtue and humanity, these people are as inferior to the Spaniards as children are to adults and women to men; there is as great a difference between them as there is between savagery and forbearance, between violence and moderation, almost – I am inclined to say – as between monkeys and men.[3]

This assertion was then used to justify unleashing great violence against the inhabitants of newly conquered lands, to kill them, subjugate them, and put them to work on the land and in the mines from which the empire grew rich. Sepúlveda was certainly not alone in this. He was, in many ways, simply re-stating the dominant doctrine that directed Spanish empire building and settlement.

The so-called 'Doctrine of Discovery', which would be so central to this process, emerged from a series of Papal Bulls from the mid-fifteenth century onwards. It granted the Catholic monarchies of Portugal and Spain the right to claim lands they 'discovered' – first in West Africa and later in the Americas. In doing so, the stage was set for the emergence of a key idea that underlies much of settler colonial expansion: that Europeans could claim to 'discover' lands, which were already inhabited, cultivated and/or home to existing societies. One hundred million people populated the Americas, living in its empires and city states. They built and travelled on its roads and canals, and agricultural production was key to their economies across the continents. Forests and grasslands were shaped and maintained by the peoples that inhabited them, in order to facilitate food production, travel and animal migration.[4] None of this, however, stopped European settlers from claiming rights of 'discovery' – rather than invasion – or from describing the environments they encountered as pristine and untouched.

Nor were settlers in the Western Hemisphere alone in constructing such narratives, which are ubiquitous across the settler world – from Southern Africa where settlers claimed to have found empty lands that were later invaded by African populations,[5] to Palestine where the Zionist movement talked about a 'land without a people for a people without a land'. The so-called '*Terra Nullius*' paradigm, which identified colonised lands as belonging to no one, formed a key justifying narrative for settler expansion around the globe. The claim of non-existing occupancy before 'discovery' was a central aspect when claiming ownership over land and removing the Indigenous peoples who inhabited it. The latter, turned into foreigners, migrants, or invaders, could then be fought ruthlessly by settlers in order to protect what was 'rightfully' theirs. In fact, this same principle remains central to denying Indigenous people the right to their land today, as we will see. Settlers, of course, have always known these claims to be vacuous. This is clear given the energy they expounded in developing and imposing the necessary forms of violence and domination that made possible the conquest, displacement and/or exploitation of the same Indigenous people whom they claimed were absent.

While the Doctrine of Discovery remained important in these processes – the US Supreme Court still referred to it in its rulings regarding the relationship with Indigenous nations in the nineteenth century – it was complemented from the seventeenth century onwards by liberal thinkers who developed further justification for colonial conquest, settler violence and slavery. Chief amongst these thinkers was John Locke, himself an active political and financial supporter of settlement in the Carolina Colony. In his *Two Treatises of Government*, Locke claimed that those who transgressed the law or those who were guilty of waging 'unjust' wars could be punished or killed.[6] This theory gave ideological cover to settlers, who could justify their massacres of Indigenous people through the fact that the latter had 'unjustly' attacked them or transgressed their laws. The cycle, which would define so much of settler colonial history, would unravel as follows: settlers lay claim on Indigenous lands, resources and people. The latter rebel, after which more settler violence is unleashed to punish the 'transgressors'. This, in turn, allows settlers to claim more Indigenous land, resources and/or labour.

The Jamestown settlers, in the early seventeenth century, for example, demanded that the Powhatan confederacy provide them with food, land and labour. When they refused, the settlers, led by John Smith (of later whitewashed Disney fame) unleashed war on the confederacy. Yet, a year into the conflict, the settlers could still claim to be taking revenge on the Powhatan by mass-murdering their children.[7] A decade later, when the Powhatan launched a new assault on the settlers to reclaim their lands, the settlers turned to the 'systematic destruction of all Indigenous agricultural resources'.[8] In the 1640s, settlers returned again, focusing on starving the Indigenous population into exile by destroying their food supplies. These confrontations, alongside the expansion of tobacco cultivation and the influx of more settlers, led to the colony's further expansion. By the mid-1670s, this led to new confrontations, this time with the Susquehannock people whose lands the planters were encroaching on. And so, the process continued. Settler expansion is dependent on taking over Indigenous land, increasing in the process the existential pressure on the Indigenous population and leading to conflict and displacement. Conflict then results in further encroachment on Indigenous nations' lands, whose existing social and economic systems have already been destabilised through settler influx and the displacement of other Indigenous peoples.

Locke's second contribution to the ideological justification for settlement was his argument that private
property was generated through improvement, by mixing
labour and land. Once land was claimed to be pristine
and untouched, all labour carried out on it by settlers was
seen as extracting it from its 'state of nature', improving
it through work, and in the same stroke, transforming it into settler property. Private property was the key
through which this distinction could be made. To own
land privately, in a way recognisable to European settlers,
was synonymous to being civilised. A failure to recognise
private property and the laws that enshrined it, such as
holding land in common, or simultaneous and overlap-
ping forms of property (see below), marked Indigenous
people, unable to recognise the settlers' laws, as savages
who could then be targeted through Lockean 'just war'.
Discussing the 1831 US Supreme Court's ruling, which
designated Indigenous people as 'wards' of the federal
government and their nations as 'dependent' on it, Jody A.
Byrd points out how Lockean approaches merged with the
Doctrine of Discovery:

> … the Court facilitated continued removals, forced
> diasporas, colonization, and assimilation through the
> establishment of a paternal relation between the United
> States and those peoples it deemed were its 'children' or
> 'wards'. The superior claim to land that [it] acknowl-
> edges … addresses the 'Doctrine of Discovery'; which
> gave Europeans and by extension their agents in the
> new world a claim to native lands by the physical act of
> discovery. So long as Indigenous peoples lived peace-

fully on the land, the question of title would not be forced; the only ways to cede title were through either treaty negotiations or 'just war'.[9]

In order to make these claims of ownership a reality, a wide range of approaches were used by settler regimes. While it is impossible to offer a detailed review of all these different methods of domination and conquest – across the globe and throughout the last five centuries – a number of key themes can be identified. These range from military conquest, ethnic cleansing and expulsion, to geographically confining Indigenous populations, forcefully assimilating them through the imposition of private property, and strengthening the rule of collaborating Indigenous elites. A key method in doing so was the imposition of the reservation.[10] This technique of control and domination travelled from Ireland to North America, and then across the settler world. Reservations are a key mechanism of dispossession, which facilitates, depending on the local circumstances, either Indigenous exclusion from, or controlled integration into, the settler economy. Before turning to an overview of the use of reservations across different settler regimes, a short discussion on the concept of dispossession and its application in settler colonial contexts is necessary.

PRIMITIVE ACCUMULATION

Dispossession is central to the functioning of settler colonialism. At the most basic level, in order to claim the land to settle on, settlers must first take control of it and declare it their own. Moreover, settlers undermine the existing social and economic structures of those Indigenous peoples that inhabit the land, which, in turn, both accelerates the settlers' accumulation of land and the destruction of Indigenous societies. Dispossession is not, however, solely a settler colonial process. It is a central aspect of the development of capitalism and its transformation of pre-existing social relations. Dispossession is also ongoing, through which land continues to be conquered and turned into a commodity that can be bought and sold in search of profit. In doing so, Indigenous peoples are dispossessed, ecological breakdown is accelerated, and colonial accumulation continues apace.

In order to make sense of this, it is useful to return to Marx's analysis of the role of accumulation and dispossession in the history of capitalism, already touched upon in chapter 1. He discusses the way classical political economy, developed by the likes of Adam Smith, imagined the origins of capitalism as an 'idyllic' past in which certain individuals – industrious and self-abnegating – accumulated wealth through hard work and financial self-discipline. This 'previous accumulation', in the words of Adam Smith, made the emergence of a new – capitalist – economic system possible through the investment of this accumulated wealth in new forms of production. This narrative, which Marx ridicules, imagines a profoundly ethical and laudable origin story for the birth of capitalism as well as for the emergence of economic inequality. The bourgeoisie's wealth is, then, not the outcome of structural inequalities and violence expended on a global scale, but of their (or at least their ancestors') hard work.

Against this imagined past, Marx puts forward a very different account of the emergence of capitalism and the nature of this 'so-called primitive accumulation', which he describes as 'nothing else than the historical process of divorcing the producer from the means of production', in order to make them available for exploitation by capitalists.[11] This historical process is illustrated in *Capital* through the process of enclosures in England, during which the peasantry was violently expelled from the land and forced to sell its labour power in the emerging urban manufacturing centres. Peasants not only lost direct access to land but also resources, such as forests or rivers, that were, until then, held in common. In so doing, peasants lost the ability to provide for their own subsistence and had no other choice but to look for employment elsewhere, as wage-labourers. At the same time, land itself was transformed into a commodity, to be bought and sold. Far from being the outcome of careful saving and hard work by those who would become capitalists, this 'primitive accumulation' that made capitalism possible, in Marx's account, was based on violence and coercion.

Marx did not stop there. He expanded his claims from this historical experience in England, to the violent accumulation of wealth through conquest, enslavement and looting across the colonial world. If this was an important acknowledgement of the ways in which the capitalist order was born through a global process of plunder, it was also a partial one. Marx recognised the importance of colonialism to the accumulation of bourgeois wealth and power in Europe and to the development of capitalist social relations, but did not provide a specific analysis, as he did with the English enclosures, of how these colonial forms of dispossession took place and what their consequences were for the populations so targeted. Moreover, there also remain questions about how Marx made sense of the temporal and normative nature of this process of primitive accumulation. Was it, as for the classical political economists, something which was done once, violently drawing land, resources and people into the emerging global market? Or was dispossession conceived as continuous, alongside exploitation, for example, which remained a structuring characteristic of capitalism? And did Marx consider this process to be historically necessary, despite its violence?

Both these questions have occupied an important place in debates surrounding colonialism and its consequence. Perhaps most famously, Edward Said argued in *Orientalism,* based primarily on his reading of Marx's early writings on the colonisation of India, that the latter considered European colonialism necessary, because it drew more backward forms of economic and social life into the modern capitalist world.[12] In this reading, Marx saw primitive accumulation as both limited in time, an early phase in capitalist accumulation, and necessary, as a stage in a teleological historical movement that inexorably advanced towards socialism.[13] Another reading focuses on Marx's intellectual evolution over time and his engagement, towards the end of his life, with different forms of social organisation in Russia, Algeria and the Iroquois confederacy (Haudenosaunee). This reading argues that Marx came to see how pre-capitalist social formations, which continued to value and defend collective relations to nature, property and decision making, could form the basis for anti-capitalist struggles and communistic alternatives.[14] In this view, Marx's ideas evolved and came to reject earlier assumptions about the linear development of human history through capitalism and towards socialism. Instead, Marx saw how Indigenous social formations could serve both as effective forms of resistance to colonial and capitalist encroachment, as well as provide the basis for alternatives to it.

Similarly, the issue of primitive accumulation's temporal nature is important in making sense of its relevance to settler colonial dispossession, as well as capitalist development. Indeed, starting with Rosa Luxemburg's writings on imperialism in the early twentieth century,[15] an alternative reading of dispossession emerged within the Marxist tradition. Instead of seeing primitive accumulation as original and limited in time, this approach focused on the continuous nature of capitalist dispossession and its drive to incorporate, continuously and violently, non-capitalist resources into the market, turning the stuff of life into commodities to be bought and sold. Perhaps most famously, David Harvey described this continuous aspect of capitalist expansion as 'accumulation by dispossession', doing away with the specific temporal aspect that the use of *primitive* accumulation can imply.[16] Authors in this tradition reject a reading that imagines the process of violent dispossession as progressive or necessary. Instead, they see in it a continuous process of struggle between the expansionist tendency of capital, aiming to subsume all things to the logic of accumulation and profit, and the needs of those being dispossessed, fighting to maintain collective non-commodified forms of life.

If the global process of violent incorporation of people, land and resources into the market is a key aspect of the capitalist order, then resisting this tendency becomes key to anti-capitalist praxis. This matters because, as we saw in the Introduction, there is a tendency to view Indigenous liberation movements as so particular that they have no relevance to wider struggles for systemic change. Understanding the co-constitutive nature of settler colonialism and capitalism, as chapter 1 outlined, as well as the potential alternatives to the latter contained in the struggles against the former, foregrounds their universal significance.

INDIGENOUS DISPOSSESSION AND ELIMINATION

These issues are also central to Indigenous political thought, for which the protection of land and resources from the encroachment of settler colonial expansion and capitalist extraction is key. Theorists of Indigenous thought and politics point to land and place as central to Indigenous modes of existence, forms of knowledge and world views.[17] They counterpose this place-based mode of existence to claims made by European settlers, which normalise colonial encroachment, murder, theft and destruction through narratives of linear progress and development. As such, they theorise Indigenous resistance against settler capitalism, as a defence of place against the market's totalising and abstracting logic, measured through time, which is imposed on Indigenous people and land through the advance of capitalist social relations.[18]

Building on these insights, Glen S. Coulthard has developed a corrective to Marxist approaches to dispossession from the perspective of Indigenous peoples in North America. His critique functions on two levels.[19] On the one hand, Coulthard challenges approaches to primitive accumulation that assume either a temporal limit or its progressive developmental nature – in echoes of the debates mentioned above. Arguing from the perspective of settler colonial encroachment of Indigenous land and life in Canada, Coulthard shows primitive accumulation to be both continuous and continuing. He illustrates this point through the current struggles by Indigenous peoples against the Canadian state's attempt at imposing oil extraction from, and pipelines through Indigenous lands. On the other hand, Coulthard also rejects any notion that this process might be progressive or developmental. Instead, he shows that it is based on the destruction of Indigenous life, as well as nature, and the genocidal removal and elimination of Indigenous people by the British and Canadian states.[20] This final point leads him to make an important distinction between Marx's analysis of primitive accumulation in England and the process of dispossession and accumulation in Canada.

While the former was based on the violent removal of the peasants from the land in order to integrate them into the nascent urban manufacturing centres, the latter was limited to violently expelling Indigenous people from the land. The principal aim was not their integration into the workforce but their removal from the land. Although some forms of Indigenous exploitation did take place in Anglo-settler contexts, they never became the dominant form of settler rule.[21] Settlers from England, France and other European states, themselves made mobile through the process of dispossession in Europe, populated the land, and worked in the settler colony's industries. This in turn allowed for the acceleration of the British and Canadian states' genocidal policies against Indigenous peoples, made 'redundant' to the process of accumulation once they had been separated from the land. Coulthard demonstrates that the link between dispossession and proletarianisation is neither automatic nor present in the eliminatory context of the Anglo-settler world.

Echoing Coulthard's view, Robert Nichols argues that in the context of Anglo settlements – Canada, New Zealand/ Aotearoa, the United States and Australia (CANZAUS) – the relationship between dispossession of the Indigenous population and proletarianisation does not occur along the lines developed by Marx. He then turns this empirical observation back on the Marxist account of primitive accumulation to argue that what Marx observed was not one process, called 'primitive accumulation' – but four interrelated ones: dispossession, proletarianisation, market formation, and the separation of agriculture and industry.[22] These four processes do not necessarily need to occur simultaneously, in the way that they did in the context of seventeenth-century England. In fact, by dis-aggregating them, Nichols argues that specific forms of dispossession can be observed more accurately across the globe, in different periods. This also helps resolve the argument about primitive accumulation's temporal character. While Marx identified a specific historical development in England, which laid the foundation for the birth of capitalism there, his observation does not preclude continued processes of dispossession in other locales, at other times.

Nichols builds on this insight to discuss what might at first sight appear as a contradictory claim, made by Indigenous nations in their struggle for liberation. On the one hand, Indigenous people reject the imposition of private landed property as antithetical to their collective forms of social organisation prior to settler invasion. On the other, they demand the restitution of the land, based on their prior occupancy. The question that then emerges is, how can something that is not owned be stolen? And even more poignantly, how can something which was not owned be returned to its original owner? Here Nichols makes a double move. He argues that any society's relationship to land is a particular one, which denotes the way that society understands and organises its relationship to the earth and its natural environment. Societies without private property, who produce collectively, and understand their relationship to the earth in reciprocal ways do not, then, develop concepts of private ownership of land nor an abstract concept of land that can be measured, parcelled out, bought and sold.[23]

Nichols is then able to identify an important specificity in the process of dispossession: it is one in which private ownership is imposed while simultaneously being transferred. It is not because something is property that it can be stolen, it is because it is being stolen that it is turned into property – hence his book's title: *Theft is Property!*.

The claim made by Indigenous people for the return of land is then not contradictory at all. Instead, it accurately describes the consequences of settler dispossession: a simultaneous capture of land and imposition of a new form of ownership over it. In fact, Nichols goes further. He shows that in the course of dispossession, Indigenous people are marked by settlers and their states as private owners who can only be alienated from their property. To be Indigenous is to have the 'right' to sell – or be stolen – while to be a settler is to have the right to acquire. Dispossession is – literally – foundational to the conflict between settlers and Indigenous populations. Nichols illustrates how this played out in New Zealand/Aotearoa.

In the case of New Zealand/Aotearoa,[24] unlike in other contexts, the British recognised that the Indigenous Māori population had proprietary rights over the land, which they cultivated extensively. The myth of an empty land, waiting to be settled, was largely absent from the British colonial claims on the island – unlike in Australia. However, the rights that Māori people held were not compatible with those the British were familiar with. Individuals did not own land or resources as their own, unalienable, property but could lay claim to the use of a specific plot of land or resource, for a particular purpose, for a specified period of time. For example, individuals or families could lay claim to the 'right to fish from *this* stream, or collect fruit from *that* tree, at this time of year, and so on. Since proprietary interests were functional in this way, they overlapped and coexisted in the same geographic space.'[25]

This state of affairs frustrated settler desires for control, as it challenged their ability to parcel, enclose and claim plots of land and the resources found within its bounds. Thus, from the 1840s onwards, the British went about imposing a much more restrictive form of landownership – limited to land that was enclosed and farmed – on the Māori, as well as the 'right' of individuals, rather than collectives, to sell. Simultaneously, they claimed a monopoly on land transactions, which allowed them to control the market and subsidise settler purchases, while imposing higher tariffs on Māori sellers.

When the Indigenous population rebelled, the British armed those Māori who had been willing to sell their land, in order to encourage civil war and strengthen the side it favoured to win. They then launched a full military assault against the dissenters and 'restored the peace' – that is, an orderly market for land, tilted in favour of the settlers. As Nichols points out: 'In less than one hundred years, British colonisers had managed simultaneously to convert the underlying property regime of Aotearoa and transfer ownership to it.'[26] If the transfer itself was organised through a formal system of buying and selling land, the establishment of the market itself was dependent on the imposition of force and war – echoing the claim made by Dunbar-Ortiz at the beginning of this chapter.

It is important to underline once again that these processes – of dispossession and violence – are also deeply gendered. Chapter 1 already showed how Spanish settlers enforced patriarchal rule while imposing dispossession upon Indigenous peoples in the Americas. Local collaborating elites were selected among the men of the colonised societies, and women were particularly targeted for repression. Property was made synonymous with masculinity and patriarchal power. Also in Europe, the imposition of private property in the countryside and the clearing of the commons, went hand-in-hand with the dispossession of women and the collective degradation of their social position.[27] As we will see below, this process played itself out across the settler colonial world. As Indigenous populations were dispossessed, expelled from their lands, and contained in reservations, settlers systematically imposed patriarchal power relations by selecting exclusively male collaborating elites from among the dispossessed Indigenous societies. Much like other forms of dispossession, this required prodigious amounts of violence – including the systematic use of rape, child theft and murder.[28] Aileen Moreton-Robinson makes the point that the property relations in the settler colonial world were premised on both racism and patriarchy – simultaneously excluding women, the enslaved and the Indigenous from the right to possess, ascribing to them the role of being possessed instead.[29]

INDIGENOUS DISPOSSESSION AND EXPLOITATION

Some settler states did forcefully integrate Indigenous peoples into the workforce after dispossessing them, as attested by Indigenous miners in Bolivia and South Africa, or indentured agricultural labourers in Mexico and Algeria. For example, as the Spanish conquered and destroyed the Inca, Maya and Aztec empires in South and Central America, they repurposed existing forms of tribute payment to draw Indigenous people into producing for the settler economy. The *encomienda*, first used in the Iberian Peninsula after the conquest of Muslim-controlled lands, gave settlers management rights, in perpetuity but in the name of the Crown, over land and (a portion of) the labour of the Indigenous people who inhabited it. In practice, it became a form of totalising control over Indigenous land and labour, not much different from slavery. In the second half of the eighteenth century, the *encomienda* system was replaced by the *haciendas*, large private estates, run by settlers, which relied on Indigenous labour to tend to cattle or crops.[30] This system accelerated in the aftermath of Mexican independence from Spain in 1810. Across Latin America, while mass Indigenous participation in the wars of independence opened up the possibility of a fundamental transformation – and overthrow – of settler colonial relations, the newly independent states rapidly imposed breaks on these processes. They turned to accelerated European migration throughout the nineteenth century in order to reverse the shifts in the balance of power and to stabilise settler rule.[31]

As M. Bianet Castellanos has argued, in the context of the Yucatán Peninsula, there is a direct connection to be drawn between the historical use of debt in the *hacienda* economy, in order to dispossess Maya Indigenous farmers from their land and draw them into the labour market, and the present. The Yucatán Peninsula is important in this process, as it was the theatre of war between Maya peoples and the Mexican state, which lasted for most of the second half of the nineteenth century, and led to settlers leaving in large numbers. This process was reversed after the Mexican Revolution, when farmers from neighbour-

ing states were re-settled in the peninsula.[32] Although
the post-revolutionary state gave greater access to land to
Indigenous communities, through the partial expropriation of *haciendas* and the creation of the *ejido* system – a
form of collective community control over land use and
output, while land ownership remained in the hands of
the state – these limited gains were undermined in the
neoliberal era.[33]

Starting with the North American Free Trade Agreement
(NAFTA) in 1994, land redistribution programmes were
halted and effectively reversed through granting rights to
individual *ejido* holders – undermining the *ejido*-holding
communities' collective decision making – 'to sell, rent,
sharecrop, or mortgage land parcels to foreign capital'.
Bianet Castellanos further notes that the 'primary outcome
of land reform after NAFTA was to displace Indigenous
peoples from their land, making them readily available
as surplus labour'.[34] This is the same process which led
to the Zapatista uprising mentioned in the Introduction.
Bianet Castellanos shows how the contemporary housing
market, and the state's drive to encourage Indigenous
workers in the city of Cancún to indebt themselves in
order to buy 'affordable' housing in the city, is playing
a very similar role. It further distances Maya workers
from their communal lands, makes them available to the
(largely tourist) urban industry, and encourages them to
sell their *ejidos* shares.

Although no two historical processes are identical,
the Mexican case fits much more closely to the traditional account of primitive accumulation, as developed
in *Capital*, than that of dispossession without subsequent

proletarianisation described by Coulthard in Canada. As collective forms of labour and land occupancy were destroyed, regained and undermined again, Indigenous populations were drawn into the settler economy as dispossessed labourers, needing to sell their labour power to survive. The insights developed by Coulthard are important because they lead us to pay careful attention to different historical processes of dispossession and to recognise that there is no automatic connection between dispossession and proletarianisation in the settler colonial context. In those settler states that focused on excluding the natives from the labour market, the connection between the two processes is anything but assured.

The parallels, as well as the differences, between the examples drawn from the history of Māori dispossession in Aotearoa and that of Maya dispossession in Mexico are worth drawing out briefly. Both processes of dispossession are made possible through military violence, first in conquest and then in the suppression of Indigenous resistance against settler land encroachment. In addition, in both contexts, this extra economic violence lays the groundwork for the formal transfer of land to the settler state and population. In this process, Indigenous 'rights' are limited to that of disposing of their claims to the land, as Nichols argues. This takes place in strikingly similar ways, whether in the nineteenth century or in the aftermath of NAFTA at the end of the twentieth. The aims, however, diverge. While in both locales the Indigenous population is dispossessed, in one case this dispossession aims at their elimination and their replacement by a settler population, while in the latter the goal is primarily their (further) integration into the workforce.

CONSTRUCTING AND CONTAINING INDIGENEITY

One aspect that emerges from the account of Indigenous dispossession discussed above is the importance for settlers and their states to construct and impose specific identities and characteristics on those they aim to dispossess. In Nichols' account, for example, this distinction is made concretely between those populations that can be dispossessed and those that can do the dispossessing. Being Indigenous, as perceived by the settler state, is to be marked for alienation from the land, to have the 'right' to be dispossessed. To be a settler means the opposite. This political distinction is important. It is the settler state that creates the dual political identities of settler and Indigenous, as totalising material realities that do away with the distinctions between nations, origins and societies. The right to land, to violence, and to life are granted to the former and simultaneously withheld from the latter.

The imposition of this reality and its reproduction are not automatic, however. They necessitate conquest and control, which is to say violence, meted out systematically and over long periods of time. Kevin Bruyneel summarises it as follows:

Only after centuries of European-based conquest, colonization, and settlement in North America did terms like Indian or Indigenous gain any meaning at all by setting the collective identity of people such as the Cherokee, Pequot, Mohawk, Chippewa, and hundreds of other tribes and nations into contrast with the emerging Eurocentric settler societies. It was not until the 1700s that 'tribal groups in the East were beginning to see themselves as having something in common together as opposed to the Europeans' ... the words Indian and American Indian, like Native American, aboriginal, and Indigenous, emerged as a product of a co-constitutive relationship with terms such as colonizers, settler, and American.[35]

This project of imposition, however, is not all-encompassing. As Bruyneel attests, Indigenous resistance movements have also turned these impositions into strategies for collective identification, solidarity and resistance. However, their origins are located in the dispossessing logic described above, and emerge from the destruction of pre-existing forms of Indigenous life and social organisation. As the next chapter will show, the process of racialisation also played a crucial role in this regard.

Mahmood Mamdani, writing about the global transformation of British 'native policy' in the mid-nineteenth century following large-scale revolts across the empire from the Caribbean to India, similarly notes that 'the native is the creation of the colonial state: colonized, the native is pinned down, localized, thrown out of civilization as an outcast, confined to custom, and then defined as its product.'[36] He goes on to identify, in Henry Maine's writings, the outline of what he calls a theory of Nativism:

... if the settler was modern, the native was not; if history defined the settler, geography defined the native; if legislation and sanction defined modern political society, habitual observance defined that of the native. If continuous progress was the mark of settler civilization, culture was best thought of as part of nature, fixed and unchanging.[37]

This fundamental opposition between settler and native necessitated, Maine argued, fundamentally different forms of government for both groups. If this was not an innovation as such, the importance of his contribution to colonial governance was to call for a double distinction. On the one hand, settler and natives were to be separated and ruled through different legal orders. On the other, amongst natives themselves, differences needed to be 'recognised' and local elites should be empowered to rule through 'customary law'. These differences, rulers, and customs were not, however, to be left to the natives themselves to determine, but were to be codified, imposed and policed by the colonial power. Mamdani has described this process as 'Define and Rule'[38] – the seemingly contradictory ways in which colonial states imposed both overall distinctions between natives and settlers, while simultaneously imposing and policing differences within the Indigenous population in the name of their 'self-rule'.

While Maine wrote in the context of India, his ideas were studied by colonial officials throughout the empire, and applied, for example, across Southern and Western Africa.[39] Nor was this form of rule limited to the British. In Algeria, the French similarly set about, after conquest, to both separate the Indigenous population and settlers on the one hand, and divide the Indigenous population through ethnic and geographical markers.[40] The first objective took its most lasting form through the Indigenous Code of 1881, which made Algerians French nationals but not citizens. It further set out the different laws and courts that would apply to the *Indigènes*, and would differ from those available to the settlers. The second objective was secured through the administrative codification of the difference between Indigenous Algerians – most importantly those between Arabs and Berbers, as well as between different Berber groups – and the eventual extraction of Jewish North Africans from the Indigenous population all together, as discussed in the next chapter.

Simultaneously, the French imposed strict geographic divisions between the Indigenous population, creating militarily imposed cantons. The Indigenous population was administered in each zone by 'Arab bureaus' from the 1840s to 1870, after which they remained in place only in the south. Run by French Orientalists, who supposedly understood and sympathised with the local populations, the bureaus effectively ruled over Algerians despotically. 'Local "chiefs", conservative figures invested with "aristocratic" authority, were sought as the natural allies' of the French,[41] who could serve as intermediaries between the colonial state and the Indigenous population. These 'chiefs' were later demoted to '*qa'id* ("caïd"), an essentially clerical functionary, as the sole, and sorrily denigrated, interlocutor between Algerians and the [French] administration'.[42]

The French policy was thus three-fold: control the Indigenous population through geographic containment

and separation, emphasise and institutionalise supposedly innate religious and ethnic differences between different Indigenous groups, and create a handpicked 'Indigenous elite' to whom the day-to-day running of settler rule could be outsourced – always under the settler state's tight supervision. Such a policy allowed simultaneously for the stratification of Indigenous society, undermining alternative forms of organisation and resistance, and securing settler rule in the process. Emerging first in the second half of the nineteenth century in the United States, the form that native policy would take in the Anglo-settler world to achieve similar goals, was a particularly brutal and totalising form: the reservation.

ETHNIC CLEANSING AND THEFT

First used in Ulster, in the north of Ireland, reservations were designed to tame the 'wild Irish' after policies aimed at their elimination had failed. At the turn of the seventeenth century, the territory was divided into six counties (which are still occupied to this day, and part of the United Kingdom) and the Indigenous population was forced into a network of reservations. Local chiefs were put in charge of their day-to-day administrative running, under British supervision, while their children were taken from them to be educated in English schools and many local customs were banned.[43] Later that century, a form of reservation was also imposed on the Pequot Indians, after their military defeat at the hands of the settlers. However, it is not until the 1850s that the system would become a central aspect of the US's 'Indian policy'.

Key to the system were two interrelated procedures: one was military conquest of Indigenous nations, and the other was the removal of Indigenous populations from the land to make way for the settlers. The reservation emerged from treaties, imposed after the military victory, in which Indigenous nations were forced to accept 'a narrowed land base from a much larger one in exchange for US government protection from settlers and the provision of social services'.[44] These 'agreements' were reached through murder, ethnic cleansing and forced displacement. As Nick Estes has pointed out, reservations might better be understood as 'prisoners of war camps'.[45] The scale of the violence meted out against different peoples in the century or so following secession from Britain cannot be done justice to in the space available here.[46] It is perhaps sufficient to note Dunbar-Ortiz's assessment of the reasons for the US's ability to conquer such wide stretches of Indigenous lands in this time period, reasons which were '[n]either superior technology nor an overwhelming number of settlers ... the chief cause was the colonialist settler-state's willingness to eliminate whole civilizations of people in order to possess their land'.[47]

One such example might be drawn from the 1830s, following the election of Andrew Jackson to the US presidency. Jackson was a land speculator and a veteran of the wars fought against the Muskogee and Seminole nations, having been made Major General in the US Army by President James Madison in recognition of his exploits. These included 'his troops fashion[ing] reins for their horses' bridles from skin stripped from the Muskogee bodies, and ... [seeing] to it that souvenirs from the corpses were given "to the ladies of Tennessee".[48] Jackson sponsored the Indian Removal Act, which led to approximately 70,000 Indigenous peoples being expelled from their lands east of the Mississippi to what was called 'Indian Territory', west of the river. The removals culminated in the 1838 expulsion, known as the 'Trail of Tears', of the 'five civilised nations'. In this process, at least half of the 16,000 Cherokee exiles died as they were 'force-marched in the dead of winter out of their country ... The Muskogees and Seminoles suffered similar death rates in their forced transfer, while the Chickasaws and Choctaws lost around 15 percent of their people en route.'[49] Similar programmes of ethnic cleansing would follow the discovery of gold in California, or the conquest of the Great Plains in the 1860s. The outcome was always the same: after military violence came forced displacement, making land available to settlers and speculators.

The reservation was first used in California as something more akin to a concentration camp, as noted by Mamdani, and was a central tool in the mass murder of roughly 70,000 out of 100,000 Indigenous people there, between 1845 and 1870.[50] While the reservation system was later stripped from its immediate murderous role, it remained a mechanism for the consolidation of settler violence, dispossession and ethnic cleansing. President Lincoln, for example, under whose leadership the removal policy accelerated in order to make space for settlers and railroads to the West, announced to Congress that through war, treaty making and displacement into reservations, nearly 3 million acres of land had been made available in

1863–64 alone.[51] Nor was displacement into reservations the end of settler violence against Indigenous nations.

There, while nominally living under self-rule, Indigenous people were considered wards of the federal government and submitted to the policies of the Bureau of Indian Affairs (BIA), which aimed to 'civilise' them through a mixture of Christian missionary activity and the banning of expressions of Indigenous religion and culture. 'Indian police' and later 'Courts of Indian Offences' were imposed to implement BIA rule, employing collaborating Indigenous staff, while thousands of children were sent to boarding schools to be alienated from their languages and cultures. These re-education programmes' philosophy was captured starkly in the motto of the Carlisle Indian Industrial School's founder, Captain Richard Henry Pratt: 'Kill the Indian, and save the man.' The school was modelled on Pratt's earlier re-education experiments with Indigenous captives at Fort Marion Prison.[52] Moreover, until the 1920s, mobility between reservations was highly limited and a pass system, copied over from the slave plantations, was implemented which gave BIA agents the right to grant or restrict the right of movement to Indigenous people in the reservations.[53]

As defeated Indigenous people continued to be expelled into Indian Territory, and with the so-called 'closing of the frontier' – a euphemism for full continental military conquest – the US government attempted to rid itself of its 'Indian problem' once and for all. The General Allotment Act of 1887 aimed to disappear Indigenous nations and their collective land claims through assimilation, by parcelling out reservation lands into individual allotments.

In exchange for these plots of lands, individuals had to renounce their tribal memberships. What were labelled 'unassigned' lands were then parcelled out to settlers. A decade later, the land of the five southern tribes, expelled from the south-east by Andrew Jackson, were targeted for allotment by the Curtis Act, with 'surplus' land again parcelled out amongst settlers. The combined effect of both Acts, alongside the creation of the state of Oklahoma in 1907 on what was left of Indian Territory, was the privatisation of 'half of all federal reservations, with a loss of three-fourths of the Indigenous land base that still existed'.[54] Moreover, allotted land did not necessarily remain in the hands of individual Indigenous farmers. On the contrary, the latter were actively encouraged to lease or sell, creating more opportunities for settlers to take over previously inaccessible land.

This programme of allotment was stopped by the 1934 Indian Reorganisation Act (IRA), although not reversed. The IRA also called for the formation of 'tribal governments', which led to a situation where 'English speaking Native elites, often aligned with Christian denominations, signed onto the law and formed authoritarian governments that enriched families and undermined communal traditions and traditional forms of government'.[55] The IRA was important because it recognised, at least in theory, the possibility for some form of Indigenous self-rule.[56] However, its extent remained very limited. Major decisions by tribal governments remained dependent on approval by the Secretary of the Interior, while the BIA's control was not weakened but merely staffed by more Indigenous officers.[57] This oscillation between elimination through assimilation and control through reservation continued to define US policy for the rest of the century. Between 1954 and 1970, for example, the US government moved to 'terminate' Indigenous tribes and reservations altogether, before reverting to the previous order under the Nixon presidency.

TRAVELLING TECHNOLOGY OF DISPOSSESSION

This version of settler rule and theft of Indigenous land – through forced displacement and the imposition of 'self-rule' on considerably shrunk land-bases – crossed the Atlantic, after a settler delegation from newly independent South Africa visited the US and Canada on a fact-finding mission. Three years later, in 1913, the South African government published the Natives Land Act, which 'declared 87 percent of the land for whites and divided the remaining 13 percent into tribal homelands for the native population. These homelands were called reserves.'[58] The pass system later also became a cornerstone of racial and geographic segregation in South Africa, controlling Indigenous South Africans' movement in and out of their so-called homelands. The policy was not only a North American import, however. From the mid-nineteenth century, the British had imposed a similar system in the colony of Natal, where the 100,000-strong, majority-Zulu, Indigenous population was restricted to ten 'locations'.

Each location was put under the administrative control of a 'chief'. Local chiefs were appointed by the 'supreme chief' – the British Lieutenant Governor of the colony – who could 'forcibly move any "tribe, portion thereof," or individual to any part of the colony. He could "amalgamate" or "divide" tribes. He had "absolute power" to call upon all "natives" to supply labour."[59] Here, an important difference between North America and Southern Africa emerges. Whereas the former forced Indigenous populations into reserves to separate them from the settler populations, take over their land, and attempt to disappear them altogether, through a mixture of murder and assimilation, in the latter case, settlers aimed to take over Indigenous land, but they also remained dependent on Indigenous labour in farms and mines.

Moreover, the chief system not only provided dictatorial powers to the Lieutenant Governor, it also aimed to redraw Zulu social relations by vesting a (subordinate) totalitarian and patriarchal power over each village in the hands of a male chief. The latter ruled absolutely and had wardship over all minors. Women were included in this category and denied any form of property or access to income.[60] This interconnection between settler power and the imposition of gendered power structures was a key aspect in the reshaping of social relations across the (settler) colonial world. Not only did these new power relations depend on imposing the rule of compliant and collaborating elites on the Indigenous majority, it was also profoundly connected to the imposition of structural sexism and the rule of men.

In the 1920s, these two forms of settler control – through geographic and political separation of the Indigenous population – merged in an attempt to undermine the growing militancy of Black labour movements, especially in the mines. The 1927 Native Administration Act, for example, vested the Governor General with the powers of 'supreme chief', an amplified version of those held by the Lieutenant General in Natal. The Governor General could now create new tribes, as well as areas that required passes in order to control Indigenous movement.[61] At the same time, all native South Africans were brought under 'customary' law – that is, the law imposed on Indigenous tribes by the settler state – even if they did not live in a designated homeland. This way the South African state could combine its three goals: conquest of land, political control over the Indigenous population, and the simultaneous accessibility of their labour. Apartheid would also emerge out of this process. The reserves led to the later Bantustans, which were similarly unsustainable homelands – even though the Apartheid regime would go as far as to claim that they were independent states. Instead, they represented a form of political control over the Black population through settler-controlled chiefs. They made Indigenous people politically dependent on specific geographical areas, while – given the inadequacy of land availability in the reserves – making them economically dependent on labour outside of those areas, in the settler economy.

This approach would travel again, northwards this time, in the context of the Zionist colonisation of Palestine.[62] The Zionist focus, before the creation of the Israeli state in 1948, was to avoid a South African situation where the settler economy would be dependent on Indigenous labour.[63] Instead, the Labour Zionist movement focused on 'conquering labour', which concretely meant the exclusion of Palestinian labour (and produce) from the economy of the Yishuv (the Jewish community in Palestine before 1948). During the Nakba, this full exclusion came close to being accomplished, through a combination of factors. First, and most importantly, Zionist militias expelled at least 700,000 Palestinians from their land (roughly three-quarters of the Indigenous population within the newly formed Israeli state's borders) and destroyed around 500 Palestinian villages and urban centres. The expulsion was followed by a series of administrative moves that facilitated Palestinian land expropriation. Most cynically, the Absentee Property law allowed the state to claim land from which owners, as the name suggests, were absent. That the latter were made 'absent' through expulsion or military rule did not alter the process:

> Altogether, approximately 4.5 million dunams [1 dunam = 100 sq. m.] of cultivable land were confiscated from absent, present, and 'present-absentee' Arabs, increasing the area available to Jewish farmers by 250 percent ... The UN Refugee Office estimated the value of abandoned Arab movable and real property at nearly £120 million (greater than Israel's total domestic capital formation from 1949 to 1953).[64]

Second, those Palestinians that managed to avoid expulsion were placed under military rule, unable to leave their areas (largely but not exclusively in the Galilee and the Negev/Naqab) without explicit permission from the settler state.[65] Third, existing labour shortages that could not be filled by Jewish workers were dealt with by distributing passes to Palestinians, allowing them to travel to and from their workplace for the duration of their employment only. In this sense, the Zionist movement combined both the reserve system in North America, based on eliminating the Indigenous population from the settlement, and, in a much more limited way, the South African system, based on exploiting Indigenous labour in the settler economy.

This contradiction would be further intensified in the aftermath of the whole of historic Palestine's occupation, alongside the Sinai Desert and the Golan Heights, in 1967. Labour shortages had already led to the lifting of military rule on the Palestinians inside the state, in the mid-1960s. After 1967, and especially from the 1970s onwards, the Israeli economy became increasingly dependent, in specific sectors, on Palestinian labour from the West Bank and the Gaza Strip (WBGS). These Palestinian workers were controlled, just as their predecessors, through a mixture of military rule and a pass system, which remains in place to this day. From the 1990s onwards, after the first intifada and the creation of the Palestinian Authority (PA), the nominally self-ruled Palestinian territories were further fragmented in zones controlled by Israel, by the PA, and those under 'joint rule'. In practice, while Israel continued to develop settlements and remained in control of the whole of the territory in question, elements of everyday administration and – crucially – policing were outsourced to the PA.[66] Still, the PA has no army, no control over its borders, and no way to control Israeli actions, including in its supposedly 'sovereign territory'.

Leila Farsakh has described this process as 'bantustanisation', referring specifically to the South African situation. In both contexts, settlers created economically unsustainable enclaves, separated from each other and under nominal Indigenous control, which facilitated settler access to Indigenous land and labour. However, the latter is, in the case of Palestine, a peripheral outcome of the primary focus on land. As Farsakh points out:

> The process of 'bantustanisation' in the WBGS is distinct from the case of South Africa in so far as the Israeli state's motivation behind labour control and its policy of territorial domination is different. Unlike white South Africa, Israel is not interested in the economic resources of the WBGS per se, nor has it created specific 'bantustans' to help sustain the supply of cheap labour that would ensure economic growth in the settlers' sectors. Palestinian labour, while important in Israeli construction, did not represent more than 7 per cent of the overall Israeli labour force, whereas 'natives' in South Africa formed more than 65 per cent of the working population.[67]

This situation is not limited to the WBGS. It continues apace within the borders of the Israeli state as well. In the south, for example, Palestinian Bedouin populations continue to be targeted by successive displacement policies, which attempt to relocate the population into an ever-shrinking geographical area. One such attempt at forcefully transferring up to 70,000 Palestinian Bedouin from their land – the Prawer Plan – was defeated by a mass Palestinian social movement in 2013.[68] However, the programme of dispossession continues. For example, numerous Palestinian Bedouin villages – home to around half of the Bedouin population in the Naqab – remain 'unrecognised' by the state. This means that they have no access to basic infrastructure (water, electricity, roads, etc.) and that their houses can be – and regularly are – destroyed by the state.

The process of dispossession is central to settler colonialism. It makes settlement possible, by accumulating land, while also laying the foundation for settler domination over Indigenous people by breaking up existing forms of social organisation. However, while dispossession is a crucial settler colonial process, it is also one which runs throughout the history of capitalism more generally. As we have seen already, it was the (settler) colonial planetary accumulation of land, labour and resources that facilitated and accelerated capitalist transition. The struggle against it is therefore also of wider systemic importance. Dispossession in the settler colonial world, as this chapter has illustrated, can lead to different outcomes. On the one hand, Anglo settlements in CANZAUS are primarily based on the elimination of the native. Indigenous dispossession leads to their exclusion from the settler economy and their replacement by proletarianised settlers. On the other, in contexts such as Mexico, Algeria, South Africa, or Ireland, Indigenous dispossession was a central aspect in breaking up existing Indigenous modes of subsistence in order to put Indigenous people to work in the plantations, mines and other settler economy industries. Zionist and Israeli settlements in Palestine have oscillated between these two models, with Palestinian labour remaining crucial in certain industries, such as construction.

While the different settler colonial contexts under review here all have their own specificities, they share characteristics that are important in order to understand the ways in which settlers dispossess. Crucial to their ability to do so, is the imposition of strictly differentiated identities between natives and settlers – that is, between those who can be dispossessed and those who can do the dispossessing. This identification that relies on a foundational denial of Indigenous claims over the land (or even Indigenous humanity), is imposed through war and conquest, and then policed through the Indigenous population's physical containment. The latter is achieved through a combination of physical violence, legal domination, and the destruction of alternative forms of economic and political life. The reservation, pioneered in Ireland by the British, and developed to its full extent in North America by the United States, combined these different elements. It placed Indigenous peoples beyond inclusion in the settler state, solidified their expulsion from the land, and – in some cases – made their labour available to the settler economy. In addition, by placing these Indigenous enclaves under the subordinated rule of hand-picked and highly constrained Indigenous (male) elites, colonial rule and violence could partly be outsourced and, in the process, normalised.

The reservation system also had a dual function regarding the identification of Indigenous populations. On the one hand, it imposed a unitary identity across national, geographic, tribal and other societal differences. To be targeted for dispossession and containment in a reservation was to be Indigenous, and to be Indigenous was to be targeted for dispossession and containment in a reservation. However, at the same time, it also served to divide Indigenous populations geographically – in different locales – and politically – under different leaderships, whose relationship was primarily directed towards the settler state rather than between different Indigenous populations. When those structures were challenged by Indigenous resistance, large-scale settler violence can be (was and is) deployed to re-impose order and separation. If Indigenous rule in the reservations was used to naturalise the settler colonial status quo, this was not the only method to do so. Another aspect of settler rule, which aimed to present colonial violence and control as the expression of immutable, natural realities, was racism, which divided – supposedly naturally – settlers, Indigenous and enslaved populations. We turn to this issue in the next chapter.

CHAPTER THREE

Racism as Social Control

The invasion, conquest and domination by European states over large swathes of the globe led to the development of a wide variety of forms of control that attempted to stabilise this order and allow accumulation to continue apace. As we have already seen, stabilisation was needed. Indigenous and enslaved population rebelled and fought for liberation from the moment Europeans set foot on their shores. An inordinate amount of violence was necessary to maintain the latter's rule over the former. However, alongside this continuous violence, other forms of social control emerged, which aimed to present this state of affairs as natural, immutable, and therefore unchallengeable. None was so powerful – and lasting – as racism.

By tracing the emergence of racism – from Spain and Ireland to the Americas, Australia, as well as South and North Africa – this chapter argues that racism is best understood as the ideological justification for the global process of accumulation, based on the dispossession of colonised land across the (settler) colonial world, and the exploitation, enslavement and/or elimination of the colonised. Different settler regimes, facing different social and economic realities, develop different forms of racist domination. All of them, however, have in common that they represent (settler) colonial power as natural and immutable. Much like chapter 1 argued with regards to capitalism, this chapter will point to the co-constitutive relationship between settler colonialism and racism.

Racism remains a powerful – and murderous – global reality, which continues to shape social relations across the board. One outcome of anti-racist social movements in the Global North and anti-colonial national liberation struggles across the (settler) colonial world, has been that formerly dominant ideas of inherent White superiority, biological racial differences, and their concomitant hierarchical classification have been considerably weakened. It has become an intellectual commonplace to say that 'race is a social construct.' Despite the worrisome remobilisation of 'race science' under new guises, such as 'replacement theory', popular discourse tends to recognise that 'race' does not correspond to a biological reality. It is generally accepted (and scientifically demonstrated) that there are no fundamental genetic differences between human beings from different geographic or ethnic origins, let alone differences that could point to different evolutionary paths, physical attributes, or intellectual capabilities.

Yet, as Karen E. Fields and Barbara J. Fields explain, to acknowledge the social constructed nature of 'race' is only half the battle:

> The right-minded teaching that 'race has nothing to do with biology, but is merely a social construction,' is true but misleading. For one thing, there is nothing 'mere' about a social construct. From the days of Thomas Jefferson, what Americans believe in as biological race has always been, at the same time, embodied and disem-

bodied, visible and invisible. For another, discovering the independence from biology of what Americans call race opens the way to investigating social construction itself, as thought and action.[1]

They further point to the common practice of, in the same breath, identifying 'race' as a social construct while simultaneously continuing to presuppose its verifiable material existence in the world. They argue that this contradictory move tells us something about the ideology of racism, as well as about ideology itself. Ideology, which in their view is best understood as a 'distillate of experience',[2] functions as a seemingly accurate description of the world that surrounds us and is therefore reinforced by experience. In fact, if an ideology is to survive, it must be 'constantly created and verified in social life; if it is not, it dies.'[3] The apparent contradiction then between 'race' being acknowledged as socially constructed and its continued use in describing and understanding society can be untangled. While the idea of 'race' has been debunked scientifically, the social reality of racism continues to structure the world around us. Access (granted or denied) to education, work, healthcare, housing, migration, justice, or life, to name but a few, continue to be conditioned by racism's structural impositions.

The task at hand, then, is to make sense of the issue without reproducing an analysis that presupposes what it tries to explain: the emergence of racism. In the words of Cedric J. Robinson:

Racial regimes are constructed social systems in which race is proposed as a justification for the relations of power. While necessarily articulated with accruals of power, the covering conceit of a racial regime is a makeshift patchwork masquerading as memory and the immutable. Nevertheless, racial regimes do possess history, that is, discernible origins and mechanisms of assembly. But racial regimes are unrelentingly hostile to their exhibition.[4]

Fields and Fields similarly raise the importance of looking beyond the supposedly immutable or natural, to discern the specific social relations that give birth to racism, as a mode of justification for existing forms of power and domination. In their critique of the dominant analyses of slavery in the Americas, which describe the institution primarily in terms of 'race relations' or 'segregation', Fields and Fields point towards an alternative approach. The chief business of slavery, they remind their readers, was not race relations or segregation – nor even racism. It was 'cotton, sugar, rice, and tobacco'.[5] Similarly, in making sense of racism's varied forms as constructed and imposed by settlers and their states across the globe, it is necessary to understand the varied forms of dispossession and exploitation that underlined them.

In addition, it is important to proceed with caution as the analysis moves between different forms of racialisation involving European settlers, enslaved populations, and Indigenous nations. As Jody A. Byrd has argued, there is a danger in subsuming Indigenous struggles for liberation in the language of racism alone. While racism is one of the modalities of settler rule, the language of anti-racism in isolation from a broader acknowledgement of the colonial relationship between settlers and Indigenous peoples, risks normalising the settler colonial state, by demanding greater inclusion of Indigenous people *within* it – instead of highlighting their continued struggle for liberation *from* it. Byrd writes, in the context of the US, that the

> ... cacophony of competing struggles for hegemony within and outside institutions of power, no matter how those struggles might challenge the state through loci of race, class, gender, and sexuality, serves to misdirect and cloud attention from the underlying structures of settler colonialism that made the United States possible as oppressor in the first place.[6]

Indigenous people were colonised, dispossessed, eliminated and/or exploited by settlers and their states. The process of bringing an end to the racism that justifies this state of affairs, cannot be separated from ending the underlying process of domination that gave birth to it. Only by ending the social reality of settler domination can the ideology that normalises it die.

In this chapter, we look at some of the ways in which racism emerged during the settlement process, first by discussing the 'prehistory of racism', in two starting points already introduced in this book: the Spanish *Reconquista* and English rule in Ireland. We then move on to discuss the emergence, during the process of colonisation and enslavement, of a global ideology of racism, and how this process was, in the image of settler colonialism itself, both global in its reach and dependent on local social relations in its forms. This chapter highlights how racism evolved from attempts to stabilise the social order in the settler colonial world and quell revolts against settler elites. We then explore the emergence of 'scientific racism' in the nineteenth century, in relation to blood quantums and the attempts by settler states to measure and quantify Black and Indigenous blood. Finally, we will examine the way settler states also 'de-racialised' certain populations in order to integrate them into the settler and 'diminish' the Indigenous population.

SPAIN AND THE PURITY OF BLOOD

It was only by the turn of the nineteenth century that racism became a global, increasingly 'scientific', ideology of difference. However, this was the outcome of much longer processes of racialisation, directed towards constructing an ideological scaffolding that could explain colonial power relations and slavery, as well as Indigenous dispossession and genocide.[7] As Europeans came to rule over much of the world, they increasingly understood themselves as united by a fundamental set of characteristics that set them apart from, and above, those they ruled. No longer the outcome of plunder, war making, and – as chapter 1 has shown – chance, Europe's rise to global domination was viewed as a practical demonstration of its people's superiority. Equally, the enslavement of Africans or the colonisation and dispossession of Indigenous people was the demonstration, in practice, of their inferiority. The development of these ideas can be traced through a variety of threads, perhaps best thought of as the prehistory of racism: ideas and practices that were distinct from racism itself, but necessary for its emergence. Chapter 2 has already pointed to the dehumanising logic of the Doctrine of Discovery and the *Terra Nullius* paradigm, as one important such thread.

Another one begins, as we saw earlier, in the Iberian Peninsula at the end of the fifteenth century. Before this point, difference – and the oppression of minorities – had primarily been religious. This meant that although unspeakable violence could be meted out against other religions and those considered heretical, oppression had a practical limit: conversion. This would, at least in theory, remain the Church's official doctrine. In addition, for over seven centuries, the Iberian Peninsula had largely been under the rule of Muslim dynasties, which vied with each other, as well as with Christian lords, for power and influence. In this period, the Iberian Peninsula experienced relative religious tolerance, where Jews, Muslims and Christians made up sufficiently large populations that different rulers needed, in order to maintain social order, to protect the rights of each. This order crumbled under the *Reconquista* and the unprecedented forms of state repression it unleashed.[8]

To accept the official narrative of this process at face value – that Spain was literally 'reconquered' by its rightful Christian heirs – would be a mistake. Instead, the *Reconquista* is best understood as a prolonged civil war, during which different rulers, from different faiths, fought each other, built and broke alliances, and attempted to impose their rule. Out of these conflicts, with the support of the

Papacy, what were called the Catholic Monarchs emerged victorious. They inaugurated their rule by expelling hundreds of thousands of, first, Jews, then Muslims. Not content with their victory, they unleashed the Spanish Inquisition to discover those whose conversions to Christianity had been insincere. Marranos and Moriscos – Jews and Muslims, respectively, who had converted to escape exile and repression, and continued to practice their faith – would be persecuted for centuries, laying the groundwork for numerous forms of racism that are still with us to this day. For example, in the seventeenth century, a conspiracy theory emerged about a cabal of Jewish elders in Salonica, plotting to bring down the Spanish empire and reverse the religious 'purification' of Spain.[9] This bears more than a passing resemblance to the twentieth-century Russian antisemitic conspiracy theory of the *Protocols of the Elders of Zion*.

Another development of this period, which closed the door more decisively on conversion as a strategy to escape oppression, was the emergence of a quasi-biological concept to justify the expulsion and subsequent hunt for hidden Jews and Muslims: *la Limpieza de Sangre* (cleanliness/purity of blood). In discussing this phenomenon, Dunbar-Ortiz explains that this pure blood ideology led to the formation of a new cross-class Iberian national unity, based on the redistribution of lands confiscated from expelled Muslims and Jews, the identification of Christian peasants with their rulers in the war against the 'impure', and the stabilisation of the economic and political system. In doing so, it therefore also, ironically, ensured the peasants' continued submission to seigneurial power. In addition, she points out that 'Before this time the concept of biological race based on "blood" is not known to have existed as law or taboo in Christian Europe or anywhere else.'[10] Although it would be a mistake to fully equate the talk of blood purity in the fifteenth and sixteenth century with more modern concepts of biological race, the ideological connections between this and later 'race science', as discussed below, are unmistakable.

Indeed, one should be careful to not overstate the equivalence between varying forms of difference, and therefore their stability. Different forms of domination require different forms of imposed difference. To make sense of how these ideas develop is therefore important. For example, Jack Forbes, in his *Africans and Native Americans*, traces the use of the word 'Mulatto' across the settler colonial world. One might assume that, at all times, the word would describe, as it did in the language of colonial racism, a person of mixed European and African descent. Instead, Forbes shows that the term, along with many other descriptors of colour, origin and 'blood', was used in a wide variety of ways – including to describe Indigenous, Jewish, or Muslim people with no known African ancestry at all, or simply the children of parents from different religions. By tracing the evolution of the classifications of difference through the colonial archive, Forbes points to the evolution of a system of difference based on religion – in which Jews, Muslims, and other 'heretics' were the prime target for repression and dispossession – to one where racism emerged to justify Indigenous and African dispossession and exploitation. Forbes' work points to the fact that it took time for racist colonial ideologies to develop and settle, as it were, on their targets.

Another indication of the lack of equivalence between early forms of racialisation and later racist regimes is the greater level of instability within the former. A powerful example of this, already touched upon in chapter 1, is the Spanish empire's relationship to Africans during the sixteenth century.[11] On the one hand, the empire became increasingly dependent on enslaved labour, drawn largely from the Portuguese West African trade. As Indigenous populations rebelled against the settlers, were murdered, or worked to death, and without access to the large flows of settlers that would later be available to primarily Anglo settler colonies, the empire continued to increase its reliance on enslaved African populations. At the same time, the Spanish continued to rely on religious difference as their primary selection method for settlers, barring at different times Jews, Protestants and Muslims from their colonies in the Americas.

Africans could, however, be incorporated into the military and settler population, as long as their Catholicism could be vouched for. There were then 'so-called Black Conquistadors' such as 'Juan Garrido, instrumental in the creation of "New Spain" or Mexico, and Sebastian Toral, who obtained his freedom because of his role in the siege of Yucatan, and Juan Valiente, who helped to conquer Guatemala, then settled in Chile'.[12] At the same time, enslaved Africans were leading revolts against the same settlers, often alongside Indigenous populations, throughout the century. For example, 'in Cuzco in Peru, enslaved Africans and indigenes – in contrast to the Black

Conquistadors – formed a rebellious contingent led by an indigene, Francisco Chichima. Due north in Vera Cruz, a citadel was formed in the 1580s by Nanga (Yanga), possibly of Akan or West African origin,[13] which forced the settlers into negotiating a treaty. Clearly, modern racist regimes were not yet dominant, even if the preponderance of enslaved African labour in the empire was clearly paving the way for it.

A further way in which early forms of inherent difference and, crucially, inferiority emerged, was in the Catholic Church's theorisation of justified war against the heathen – that is, against Muslim empires. In this context, the Pope ordained, in the fifteenth century, that Spanish and Portuguese rulers were justified in enslaving and dispossessing 'all Saracens and pagans whatsoever and all other enemies of Christ wheresoever placed'.[14] This edict was not only targeted at encouraging those fighting Muslim rulers in the Iberian Peninsula but also at giving free rein to Portuguese colonisation, as they developed settlements along the coast of the African continent. By 1537, Pope Paul III would legislate that this edict did not apply to the Indigenous peoples in the Americas, who were not to be enslaved. The cat was of course already out of the bag, and the Pope's claims 'not only failed to accord with the actual practices of the conquistadors but was also strongly challenged on intellectual grounds'.[15] For example, 13 years later, an infamous debate would pit the Dominican friar Bartolomé de Las Casas against the Spanish jurist Juan Ginés de Sepúlveda. Their argument centred on the so-called 'rational souls' of Indigenous peoples in the Americas – that is, their capacity to be converted to Christianity – and whether or not they could therefore be enslaved.[16] The latter argued that enslavement was justified for 'persons of both inborn rudeness and of inhuman and barbarous customs'. What is more, in de Sepúlveda's view, if those so naturally disposed refused to be enslaved by their colonial masters, 'they may be forced to obey by arms and may be warred against as justly as one would hunt down wild beast.'[17]

The outcome of the debate is unclear. It appears that no final decision was made by the judges. This seems, in a sense, adequate, given the fact that in practice Indigenous peoples were already being dispossessed, enslaved, and worked to death by Spanish settlers in the Americas. However, the debate points to the move away from the assumption that, at least in theory, all humans could be included in the Church – and therefore avoid persecution. Instead, a new ideology of fundamental difference was emerging, which justified domination, enslavement and dispossession of the oppressed at the hands of their masters as natural and therefore inescapable. Here a new concept was being added to the *Reconquista*'s 'impure blood' category: the 'savage', which not only stood in direct opposition to the 'civilised', but also needed to be ruled, tamed and brought into the remit of civilisation. This language of a 'civilising' mission would remain a central aspect of the ideological toolbox of subsequent European empires, in justifying both racialised and gendered oppression.[18] It would serve to justify conquest, enslavement and domination, as well as the worst genocidal crimes carried out against Indigenous peoples across the globe. If the Indigenous in the Americas were being worked to death in the silver mines, for example, it was not only the natural order of things, but a crucial step towards their integration, through their labour, into the halo of European civilisation. Quite a civilisation indeed.

SAVAGERY AND THE COLONISATION OF IRELAND

The concept of savagery is another important thread in the prehistory of racism. It is not only to be found in Spanish debates over the treatment of Indigenous populations in the Americas. The English conquest and subjugation of Ireland gave rise to similar narratives and claims. In the same way as the previous concepts discussed above, the idea of the 'savage' starts to move away from a form of oppression based on religion. Indeed, the 'savages' could be Christians – and phenotypically alike to their colonisers for that matter – as the Irish were, and still be considered to be outside of the bounds of civilisation. In fact, English lords desirous of settling Ireland repeatedly compared it with the 'Indies' being settled by the Spanish, and the Irish with the Indigenous people of the Americas. Theodore Allen gives the example, from the late sixteenth century, of Robert Dudley, the First Earl of Leicester, whom he calls an 'early English conquistador'. For Dudley and his contemporaries, Allen points out, the 'Irish were "a barbarous people" … and the English should deal with them as other Christian colonizers did with barbarians elsewhere in the world.'[19]

In 1609, as the English began imposing the plantations of Ulster and the province's concomitant settlement by

Scottish settlers,[20] they appealed to the Spanish Crown, as a fellow civilised nation, to refuse to aid the Irish resistance. Sir Charles Cornwallis told the Spanish Lords of Council that, the 'Irish were "so savage a people" that they ... deserved the same treatment "used by the Kings of Spain in the Indies [Americas], or those employed with the Moors".[21] Cornwallis further argued, that just as the Spanish had done with Muslims and Indigenous peoples, the English would expel the Irish from their lands – 'scattering them in other parts'.[22] It also appears that the Spanish, despite their shared Catholic faith, also used the language of savagery when referring to the Irish. For example, a Spanish mariner, shipwrecked off the coast of Ireland in the process of a failed invasion of England, wrote that his men had been attacked by 'two thousand savages and Englishmen'.[23] The fact that no further qualifiers were needed to explain who these 'savages' were, suggests that it would have been widely understood as referring to the Irish.

Around the same time, Sir John Davies, the English attorney general for Ireland, argued that the backwards nature of Irish society led to the destruction of the land on which they lived, otherwise so fertile. He illustrated the lack of Irish civilisation through a number of factors, such as the absence of the death penalty, the equal inheritance of land by all heirs (including 'bastards'), and the lack of stable Irish family structures.[24] Nearly two centuries later, British colonial officers would make similar claims about the need to civilise Egyptian society by reforming the family – that is, the social position of women. The British Controller-General in Egypt, Lord Cromer, for example, wrote that '[t]he position of women in Egypt is a fatal obstacle to the attainment of that elevation of thought and character which should accompany the introduction of European civilisation.'[25]

The connection made by Davies between the supposed barbarous nature of the Indigenous inhabitants and the destruction of the land would also remain of central importance in arguments justifying colonisation and settlement. That is, Indigenous inhabitants' forms of land use and cultivation lacked what the English and later British colonisers considered to be acceptable, such as private landed property and agricultural exploitation beyond subsistence needs. Faced with such wanton misuse of the rich Irish soil, what else could the English possibly do, but invade and settle? There is a striking parallel in fact between the language of colonisers supposedly needing to 'save' colonised women from colonised men's barbarous practices, and that of needing to 'save' the land from its inhabitants' barbarous practices.[26]

In discussing the work of William Petty, who was appointed in 1654 to survey – and later parcel out – the land in Ireland, Brenna Bhandar has argued that he played a crucial role in developing this connection between the productivity of the land and the productivity of its people. Bhandar shows how Petty set out to calculate 'objectively' the value of both Irish land and Irish people. The latter he found, perhaps unsurprising, to be lacking. Petty's solution was to 'forcibly [transport] up to a million Irish from their native land',[27] redistributing it to the conquerors to settle, as well as intermarrying the English and Irish – further underlining the gendered character of settler domination.

This argument for miscegenation (to which we return below) between the Irish and English was supposed to 'produce a more industrious and disciplined population', by – once again – 'mixing their blood'.[28] Much like in the case of Spanish ideas of 'pure blood', there is here a noticeable slide towards a biological concept of alterity and the idea that there are fundamental, ingrained and hierarchal differences between populations. It is, as Bhandar points out, 'akin to the method an agricultural scientist might utilise in the interbreeding of plant species to improve yield'.[29]

There is, then, a direct link, as Bhandar demonstrates, between the abstracting logics of commodifying land and turning its inhabitants into productive labourers on it – or expelling them to make room for others. Both land and people must be 'improved' for the market's sake. The development of racism is co-constitutive of a logic that abstracts the human into another unit of production to be measured, used and exploited – or discarded if it cannot (or no longer can) be used. It is this same logic that was so important in the settling of North America and the genocidal dispossession of its inhabitants.

Between the fifteenth and seventeenth century, emerging (settler) colonial powers developed a new ideology of difference that justified taking and settling land, as well as expelling or exploiting its inhabitants. In the process, they moved from a justification of war, oppression and dispossession on the basis primarily of faith, to one based on characteristics imagined to be fundamental, such as the blood or the innate nature of those who were being brought under their rule. These processes should be understood as the prehistory of racism. These new characteristics imposed on Jewish and Muslim populations as well as the Irish, before crossing the Atlantic, served to justify their murder, dispossession and/or enslavement.

Another outcome of this process was to develop new forms of cross-class cooperation, which stabilised the unequal social order under which, for example, the vast majority of 'pure-blooded' Old Christians in the Iberian Peninsula continued to live. As Dunbar-Ortiz points out, 'The ideology of White supremacy', here still in its early stages, 'was paramount in neutralizing the class antago- nisms of the landless against the landed and distributing confiscated lands and properties of Moors and Jews in Iberia, of the Irish in Ulster, and of Native American and African peoples.'[30]

RACISM AND RESISTANCE

It should be clear by now that the emergence of different narratives of innate difference and inferiority represent the emergence of an ideology of conquest, subjugation and colonisation. The more European nations were able to impose their power over peoples and lands across the world, the more necessary – and possible – it became to explain this order in ideological terms that would natural- ise it. On the other hand, it is also important to underline the relational nature of this emerging ideology of racism. As it defined particular populations as naturally inferior, and therefore justified their dispossession and subjugation, it also defined others as naturally superior and therefore justified their rule. This relational logic continued to play itself out in racism's emergence throughout the settler colonial world. In the Americas, three groups interacted: European settlers, Indigenous peoples and enslaved African populations. As Wolfe notes, 'subjugated populations are racialised in distinct but complementary ways that together sustain the overall dominance of European colonisers.'[31]

In their varied ways, all colonial powers – Portuguese, Spanish, French, Dutch, English – were involved in this process of dispossession and subjugation, which would, in time, give rise to an idea of a White 'race', giving biological content to European rule. Cheryl I. Harris has described this process in her essay 'Whiteness as Property', which traces the construction of Whiteness, from conquest up until the present, in North America. Harris argues that:

> The racialization of identity and the racial subordination of Blacks and Native Americans provided the ideological basis for slavery and conquest. Although the systems of oppression of Blacks and Native Americans differed in form – the former involving the seizure and appropriation of labour, the latter entailing the seizure and appropriation of land – undergirding both was a racialized conception of property implemented by force and ratified by law.[32]

She further points out that Whiteness and property, therefore, are constructed around similar properties, central amongst which is the right to exclude. As discussed in the previous chapter, Aileen Moreton-Robinson makes a similar point in relation to Indigenous peoples' colonisation and dispossession in Australia, as she identifies the 'possessive logics' which continue to justify and normalise, through racism, the 'theft and appropriation of Indigenous lands in the first world'.[33] Criticising much of the literature on Whiteness for failing to address Indigenous dispossession alongside the enslavement of African populations in racism's emergence and reproduction, Moreton-Robinson points to the triple colonial relations at the heart of this process: 'from the sixteenth century onward race and gender divided humans into three categories: owning property, becoming propertyless, and being property'.[34]

The differences between the treatment of Indigenous and African populations in the Americas, while real, should also be discussed with a few caveats in mind. First, it is important to remember that, as Robin D.G. Kelley points out, African populations share a history of colonisation by European nations from the fifteenth century onwards, with their counterparts in the Americas. It is the same global process of Indigenous dispossession, on both sides of the Atlantic, albeit in different circumstances, which leads to the capture and transport of Africans to the Americas.[35]

Second, as already discussed, many Indigenous people in the Americas were also enslaved by European colonisers – and were from the very moment Columbus landed in the Caribbean. In fact, in much of the Spanish-controlled Americas, Indigenous peoples' forced labour in the mines and on the land would form the basis for the economy. This also laid the foundations for racialised forms of stratified social control, comparable to those developed in the Caribbean slave economies (see below), which placed European settlers on one end, Indigenous peoples on the other, and an intermediary class of those racialised as mixed (labelled *mestizos*) between the two.[36] While not the same as the hereditary, lifetime and transportation slavery imposed on Africans and their descendants, these forms of unfree labour were just as constituent of the racist order in the Americas. In the words of Jack D. Forbes, 'the term *mestizo* in both the Spanish and Portuguese Empire[s] reflects the kind of caste-like and racialist social orders which evolved in the colonies.'[37]

Third, and connected to the last point, Indigenous peoples in the lands that became the United States were also enslaved and put to work, often alongside African and European bonded workers, in the first century of settlement. While we return to these issues below, it is worth pointing out, as Forbes does, that there is much evidence to suggest that the social reality of Indigenous-African (American) relations diverges very much from that imagined by racist discourses, which defines both populations in very much separated terms.[38] Remarking on the gendered nature of this process of separation, Wolfe points out that the racist structure constructed by slavery imposed Blackness on all children of a Black parent – and primarily those of a Black mother. This imposition was key to the construction, discussed below, of the insolubility of Blackness and the dissolubility of Indigeneity. He writes:

Thus Black women are not only barred from having White children. Along with Black men, they are barred from having any children other than Black ones. For our purposes, a significant consequence of this rule is that Black people cannot have Native children … In its consequence for descent, the exclusive racialisation of Black people doubles as an eliminatory policy when it comes to the (non-)reproduction of Natives.[39]

Whether through the collective experience of enslavement or – crucially – that of resistance to it, both by escaping the plantations and developing free communities of formerly enslaved peoples, the relations between Indigenous and African populations diverge from, and undermine, the ideas of neat separation developed by the colonisers. Free maroon communities existed across the Americas, everywhere where people were enslaved. In some cases, the maroon communities would force their former slavers to sign peace treaties with them, as under the leadership of the elected King Bayano in Panama, while in others they continued to conduct raids against plantations to free more people, as in the republic of Palmares.[40] Not only did the republic's inhabitants continue to fight both Portuguese and Dutch settlers for nearly all of the seventeenth century, but they also built a free state that the Portuguese accounts described as:

… embrac[ing] some 99,000 square miles, an area about the size of Wyoming or Nevada, with a population of from 15,000 to 20,000 in ten major settlements. The elected king of Palmares, called Ganga Zumba [Great Lord], and most of the ruling element were native Africans, although among the leaders named in a 1677 Portuguese report there was one, Arotirene, presumed to have been an Amerindian.[41]

The fact of mixing between African and Indigenous peoples – through capture, forced labour and resistance to both – in the Americas is an important corrective to accepting as simple truth the racist classifications imposed by settlers to justify their power. It also raises questions about the neat differentiations made, even to the present day, between Indigenous and African-American populations, for example, in the US. To these points should be added, as Harris reminds her readers, those who 'disappeared' into the White population because of their ability to go unnoticed, to 'pass', in the racist language of the time, amongst the settlers.[42] These divergences from the racist script point to a crucial aspect of the story of racism's emergence, namely the continuous resistance by those upon whom bondage and dispossession was imposed. This resistance would not only bring the institution of chattel slavery to an end and defeat settler regimes across the world, it also helps to explain why racism became necessary for settlers, who tried to impose and maintain domination over extremely large groups of Indigenous and African peoples.

BONDED LABOUR – EUROPEAN AND AFRICAN

Although unfree and slave labour was certainly not invented in the settler colonial world – it played an important role in numerous societies across the globe throughout different periods of human history – but the form of racialised, lifelong and hereditary enslavement imposed on African peoples and their descendants in the Americas was specific to settler colonies. Its emergence is connected to the emergence of racism itself. The process is most frequently illustrated through the development, in the last quarter of the seventeenth century, of a new equation between Black and slave, in response to growing social unrest. It would, in the aftermath of Bacon's Rebellion (see below), be inscribed in the law of the English settlements in North America. In the process, it did away with European bonded labour, creating a new caste-like separation between White and Black as a stand-in for free and unfree. Several caveats are important to note, however, in order to grasp how important was the change taking place in this period.

First, the English colonies in North America were the destination of many unfree labourers, including Europeans. Nell Irvin Painter summarises the situation:

> ... before an eighteenth-century boom in the African slave trade, between one-half and two-thirds of all early White immigrants to the British colonies in the Western Hemisphere came as unfree labourers, some 300,000 to 400,000 people. The eighteenth century created the now familiar equation that converts race to black and black to slave.[43]

She points out that in early English settlements, 'Britons ... outnumbered Africans in American tobacco fields', a reality which would endure as late as the mid-seventeenth century.[44] Similarly, in his classic study of the role slavery played in the emergence of capitalism, Eric Williams points out that in 1683, 'White servants represented one-sixth of Virginia's population. Two-thirds of the immigrants to Pennsylvania during the eighteenth century were White servants; in four years 25,000 came to Philadelphia alone.'[45] The conditions in which these indentured servants and convicts were shipped to, and treated in, the plantations in the Americas, were both horrendous and deadly. Williams reflects bitterly on arguments that locate the planter's choice, in time, for African rather than European bonded labour in the 'humanity' the former felt for his 'fellow countrymen'. 'Of this humanity', Williams writes, 'there is not a trace in the records of the time.'[46] It is important to raise this point, not to equate – as some White supremacists and their ideological bedfellows have attempted – early European indentured labour and later African chattel slavery. It is, instead, to point out the latter's significance as it emerged.

Some (although by no means all, as discussed in chapter 1) chose, more or less freely, to indenture themselves – a freedom never granted to Indigenous or African enslaved people – paying for their passage with several years of bonded labour for settler landowners in the Americas. Their hope was to become free, landowning settlers in the 'New World' at the end of their service. However, for much of the century, this issue was relatively mute for all unfree labourers, European as well as African, as only very few survived their tenure at all. It is only when this 'morbid arithmetic',[47] in the words of Fields and Fields, changed that mortality rates improved, and that demands for freedom and access to (Indigenous) land would start to be raised more insistently. However, between the needs for labour in the Americas, the profits to be made by transporting bonded labourers, as well as the English ruling class's desire to do away with 'surplus populations' – religious nonconformists, Irish rebels, or simply the urban poor – forced exile of Europeans to the colonies continued. Williams points out that, in the aftermath of Oliver Cromwell's campaigns to crush the Irish revolt, so many Irish were sent to the West Indies that 'an active verb was added to the English language – to "barbadoes" a person.'[48]

The second caveat is that, in the early 1600s, there is no evidence of a systematic equivalence between African, Black and unfree in the English settlements, as would emerge by the next century. Undeniably, there was, in the same period, a greater control and punishment meted out against Africans, as well as growing arguments in favour of their lifetime and/or hereditary enslavement. The case of the African John Punch is an important such example. After Punch and two fellow – but European – bonded labourers ran away and were caught, in 1640 in Virginia, the General Court punished him and him alone with lifetime servitude. Twenty years later, when the limit on bonded servitude was legislated, it applied to those of Christian nations only – that is, to Europeans.[49] At the same time, however, free Africans, as well as their descendants, could, for example, own land, marry Europeans, challenge them in court (including to be freed when their terms of bondage had been fulfilled), or even own, buy and sell them as bonded labourers.[50] Allen illustrates the starkness of the difference between this period and that of chattel slavery thus:

In Northampton County in 1666, 10.9 percent of African-Americans and 17.6 percent of European-

Americans were landholders. This disparity is no more than normal considering that 53.4 percent of the European-American landholders, but none of the African-Americans, came as free persons … the ratio of farm ownership among European-Americans was 46 percent less in 1860 than … in 1665. But the fact that the proportion of the African landholding population was 95 percent less in 1860 than it was in 1666 was the result … of racial oppression. Let it be noted in passing that the proportion of European-Americans owning land in Virginia in 1860 was less than the proportion of African-American landowners in 1666.[51]

How, then, did the situation change? It was in response to a joined European and African revolt, known as Bacon's Rebellion, which demanded greater rights to settle Indigenous land, that the large landowners moved to impose the new social order.

INDIGENOUS LAND, ENSLAVED LABOUR

Bacon's Rebellion was ignited in the aftermath of a war waged against the Susquehannock people. Settlers attempted to take over more land for their tobacco plantations and were defeated by the Indigenous nation and their allies. In the aftermath of defeat, both settler landowners and bonded labourers rose up and 'took into their own hands the slaughter of Indigenous farmers with the aim of taking their land'.[52] As Dunbar-Ortiz points out, while the emergence of racism as a tool of social control in the rebellion's aftermath is important, it should not obscure the fact that it also marked the emergence of an alliance between landowning and poor settlers in the struggle to dispossess Indigenous nations of their land.[53]

The uprising's original goal had been to force the governor of Virginia's hand in regards to the speed (rather than the fact) of Indigenous dispossession. However, in doing so, the planters who had stoked the uprising, including Nathaniel Bacon, inadvertently created a space for the expression of the political demands of – both European and African – bonded labourers. The latter, already in arms and in direct confrontation with Governor William Berkeley, demanded tax reform, access to land, and an end to their terms of servitude, radicalising the revolt in the process. Allen notes:

> English poet and parliament member Andrew Marvell reported on 14 November 1676 that a ship had recently arrived from Virginia with the news that Bacon had 'proclam'd liberty to Servants and Negro's'. A letter written from Virginia in October seemed to suggest that a class differentiation had occurred among the rebels: 'Bacon's followers having deserted him he had proclaimed liberty to the servants and slaves which chiefly formed his army when he burnt James Town.'[54]

Although the rebellion survived the death of its eponymous instigator, it was defeated militarily by Berkeley's ships in January 1677. Its long-term impact would not be the weakening of settler landowners' power, but the reverse. Under pressure of continued uprisings (and the threat thereof) by both European and African unfree labourers in the decades that followed the uprising, the settler planters would develop – in Virginia and elsewhere – increasingly rigid laws that racialised Europeans and Africans by making freedom synonymous with Whiteness and servitude with Blackness.

In 1691, the Virginia General Assembly moved beyond allowing owners of African bonded labourers to freely 'use and abuse' them, when it forbade that they could be set free.[55] In 1705, the revised Virginia code limited the levels of violence that could be meted out against 'Christian White' bonded labourers, gave them recourse to the law in cases of excessive abuse, and specified in law the 'freedom dues' that they were owed at the end of their term.[56] At the same time, African bonded-labourers' livestock was confiscated, while lifetime bonded labourers, increasingly African only, could also not expect freedom dues.[57] In 1723, a new Act was passed, with the expressed purpose of 'directing the trial of Slaves … and for the better government of Negros, Mulattos, and Indians, bond or free'.[58] It is important to note that the Act no longer applied to differentiating between bonded Europeans and Africans, but between all – free or bonded – Whites and Blacks, clearly pointing to a racist system of oppression. It is also worth underlining that Indigenous populations were also being targeted, further reinforcing the relational process described above. The Act, which had to be read out to the public twice a year in church and once a year in court, legislated 'for the first time' that:

> … no free African American was to dare lift his or her hand against a 'Christian, not being a negro, mulatto,

or Indian' (3:459); that African American free-holders were no longer to be allowed to vote (4:133–134); that the provision of a previous enactment (3:87 [1691]) was being reinforced against the mating of English and Negroes as producing 'abominable mixture' and 'spurious issue' (3:453–454); that, as provided in the 1723 law for preventing freedom plots by African bond-labourers, 'any White person … found in company with any [illegally congregated] slaves' was to be fined (along with free African-Americans or Indians so offending) with a fine of fifteen shillings or to 'receive, on his, her, or their bare backs, for every such offense, twenty lashes well laid on' (4:129).[59]

Moreover, poor Whites were to serve as this system's enforcers, as members of what Allen calls the 'interme-diary stratum'. In doing so, they were drawn into the system of racial difference and oppression, by establish-ing social control over the Black enslaved population for the planters. Four years after the Act, for example, the so-called 'patrol' was established: a militia made up principally of poor Whites, often former bond labourers themselves, whose role was to prevent any 'dangerous' gathering of the enslaved. In other words, they were to quash further uprisings.[60] In drawing poor Whites into the system of domination, planters 'democratised' the imposition of slavery and broke up the alliances between unfree European and African labourers. By the mid-eight-eenth-century, White workers were actively campaigning for Black workers to be excluded from skilled trades,[61] a practice which would remain a pernicious presence in the American labour movement.[62]

Bacon's Rebellion and other social upheavals played an important role in focusing planters' minds and led them to develop a new system of social control. They enrolled poor Europeans (now Whites) into maintaining both slavery and Indigenous dispossession, while simultaneously imposing slavery in an increasingly systematic, perpetual and hereditary way on (now Black) Africans and their descendants. It is, however, also important to point out that a number of larger, global processes intervened in making this shift possible.

THE GLOBAL CONTEXT AND THE CARIBBEAN

Of course, these transformations, although crucial, did not take place in a vacuum. The growing British participation in, and dependence on, the slave trade also encouraged the shift away from bonded European labour, and towards enslaved Africans instead. These changes brought down the price of the latter, while falling mortality rates made lifetime (and hereditary) enslavement possible. As Fields and Fields point out, it is only in the second half of the seventeenth century that bonded and enslaved labourers started living long enough to give any real meaning to debates about limited or lifetime servitude. At the same time, intensifying wars between English and Dutch colonial powers decreased the number of Europeans who could be sent into bonded labour, while the British were increasingly able to directly transport enslaved Africans across the Atlantic, instead of depending on Caribbean and Brazilian transit.[63]

The growth in the direct and, by the mid-eighteenth century, no longer monopolistic transatlantic slave trade also made the African enslaved increasingly cheaper than European bonded labourers for English plantation owners – a direct reversal of the earlier trend in the previous century. Williams, for example, notes that enslaved Africans made up 'one-twentieth of the population [of Virginia and Maryland] in 1670' but 'were one fourth in 1730'.[64] He further points out that as the Royal African Company lost its monopoly over the trade in 1698, and the 'free market' took over, the number of enslaved Africans transported across the Atlantic boomed:

> The Royal African Company, between 1680 and 1686, transported an annual average of 5000 slaves. In the first nine years of free trade Bristol alone shipped 160,950 Negroes to the sugar plantations. In 1760, 146 ships sailed from British ports for Africa, with a capacity for 36,000 slaves; in 1771, the number of ships had increased to 190 and the number of slaves to 47,000. The importation into Jamaica from 1700 to 1786 was 610,000, and it has been estimated that the total import of slaves into all the British colonies between 1680 and 1786 was over two million.[65]

The scale of violence, exploitation and destruction is difficult to capture adequately here. However, it should be clear that while what the planters achieved through the population's racialisation was social control, it was not their only 'achievement'. They also set in motion one of the most murderous institutions in human history (alongside their other key contribution: Indigenous dispossession), all in the name of profit.

These changes also led to a transformation of the population in the British Caribbean, transforming these islands into majority-enslaved African societies. In Jamaica, for example:

> In 1662 the total population was 4,207: 3,653 Europeans and 554 Africans. By 1673—indicative of the manic energy of slave traders—the African population had grown to 7,768, loosely equal to the number of Europeans. But then the proportions began to shift dramatically in favour of Africans ... Imports of Africans jumped from 14,383 in the 1670s to 33,458 in the 1680s.[66]

As the balance of numbers between settlers and enslaved Africans changed, so did the intensification of the struggle by the enslaved to get free: 'Between 1673 and 1694 Jamaica experienced at least six major revolts of the enslaved, followed by eruptions in 1702 and 1704.'[67] This, in turn increased pressure on the settlers, who started moving in growing numbers to the mainland, where the balance of numbers seemed more in their favour, and land availability – based on the genocidal violence unleashed against the Indigenous population – served as an additional incentive. However, this further diminished the number of Europeans on the islands. In Barbados, a similar process played out, leading its settlers to establish

South Carolina, a 'colony's colony', in the words of Gerald Horne.[68]

While planters in the Caribbean also moved to set up White militias and establish laws mandating specific ratios of enslaved Africans to White overseers, they were unable to rely solely on poor Whites to play the role of an intermediary stratum. Instead, as Allen points out, the creation of a so-called 'free coloured' class was encouraged. This group was granted small plots of land and the right to own slaves, in order to recruit them into playing the role of social stabiliser, a post fulfilled by poor Whites on the mainland. In the case of Jamaica, in 1721, this group was literally positioned between the plantations and the mountainous territories controlled by the Maroons.[69] Allen notes: 'By the late 1770s, in Jamaica 36 percent of the free population was composed of persons of some degree of African ancestry; on the eve of emancipation, in 1833, they were a 72 percent majority. In Barbados in 1786, only 5 percent of free persons were persons of African ancestry; in 1833 they were 34 percent.'[70]

It is worth emphasising again that, given racism's role as a form of social control, it should not come as a surprise that different social relations generate different forms of racialisation. We have already seen, for example, that in the settler societies in the Spanish Americas what Allen calls the 'intermediary stratum', was assigned to the *mestizos*, racialised as a mixed group between Indigenous and Spanish settler populations. In that sense, they played a similar role to the so-called 'free coloured' class in the British Caribbean.

In the Dutch and Portuguese colonial empires, the lack of available settlers – which the English enclosures and subsequent industrialisation were unique in unleashing on the world in such large numbers – also led to the stratification of Indigenous and enslaved populations. Dutch colonial authorities, for example, encouraged the intermarriage, first in Indonesia and then in the Cape, between Dutch and Indigenous as well as enslaved women – giving further credence to Moreton-Robinson's argument that the possessive settler subject is patriarchal as well as White.

Fredrickson notes, that in the Cape Colony, while intermarriage with Indigenous Khoikhoi women took place, the settlers tended to marry imported slaves.[71] Their children were considered part of the settler population and could ascend to high office in the colonies, despite attempts from the late seventeenth century onwards to limit these practices. Only in the latter years of the eighteenth century, especially following the Cape's incorporation into the British empire in 1795, did more sharp racist stratification between White and Black emerge.[72] This tendency in Dutch colonialism should not, however, be read as a more progressive attitude amongst the settlers, but rather the expression of a different balance of forces between settlers, Indigenous, and enslaved populations.

To say that these different forms of racialisation were imposed by settlers as a form of social control, stabilisation of settler rule, and division, is not to say that they were, everywhere and always, effective. As we saw in chapter 1, revolts by Black majorities across the Caribbean, most notably in Haiti, overthrew settler rule and brought an end to the transatlantic slave trade. Not only does this highlight the ways in which stabilising tendencies have their limits, but also how the very revolts which had led to processes of racialisation in the first place, did not disappear after their imposition. In addition, it is equally important to acknowledge that these same struggles proposed alternative ways to organise social relations after their victory. For example, in the 1805 Haitian Constitution, promulgated by Jacques Dessalines, Blackness became a universal marker of citizenship, applied to all Haitians, regardless of their phenotype. The relevant articles read:

12. No whiteman of whatever nation he may be, shall put his foot on this territory with the title of master or proprietor, neither shall he in future acquire any property therein.

13. The preceding article cannot in the smallest degree affect white woman who have been naturalized Haytians by Government, nor does it extend to children already born, or that may be born of the said women. The Germans and Polanders naturalized by government are also comprized [sic] in the dispositions of the present article.

14. All acception [sic] of colour among the children of one and the same family, of whom the chief magistrate is the father, being necessarily to cease, *the Haytians shall hence forward be known only by the generic appellation of Blacks.*[73]

While the institutionalisation of patriarchal authority, in Article 14, underlines the continued gendered nature of power after liberation, the two preceding articles also point to the recognition by the newly independent government of both the White and patriarchal nature of settler power, as theorised by Moreton-Robinson (see above). Just as settlers could impose social identities to naturalise minority rule in the Caribbean, so the formerly enslaved developed their own to organise their society after liberation. To be Black in Haiti was to be free – whether one was formerly enslaved, or a Polish or German participant in the liberation struggle.

SCIENCE, REVOLUTION AND BLOOD QUANTUMS

A final element in the story of racism's emergence as a system of social control is the apparently contradictory intensification of processes of racialisation from the nineteenth century onwards, in the face of emancipation and the universal claims made by both the French and American revolutions. Indeed, from the late eighteenth century onwards, bourgeois revolutions claimed to install, in the words of the French revolutionaries, liberty, equality and fraternity amongst all men – and very much all *men*. In the case of the US, the settlers even found these principles to be self-evident. Yet the evidence points to, at the very least, a striking continuity between pre- and post-revolutionary denial of rights and liberty to the enslaved and the colonised. In fact, as already noted in relation to the transformations of the slave trade and the acceleration of Indigenous dispossession, these revolutions have tended to intensify modes of dispossession and exploitation on a global scale. The Haitian revolution stands out as the only uprising with genuinely universal aspirations, while the anti-Spanish revolts across the Americas led by Simon Bolivar (himself very much influenced by the experience in Haiti, where he spent two periods of exile) are a partial (and temporary) exception to the rule.

The dominant tendency, however, was the deepening of racism throughout the nineteenth century. Three inter-twined developments help explain this phenomenon.[74] First, the scientific revolution provided a new language to explain and naturalise difference. It became possible to claim that it was not because of racist practices, but because of racial characteristics – seen as inherent, genetic, evolu-tionary – that the promises of formal equality could not be met. 'Race enabled universality to presuppose distinction', in the words of Patrick Wolfe.[75] Second, the aftermath of the Haitian revolution led first to the end of the slave trade, and then the formal end of slavery itself. This had major consequences across the Americas. Not only did it open up the possibility of political freedom for millions of people across the hemisphere, but it also created a need to develop new forms of social control for the states and ruling classes that had so benefited from slavery until then. Third, the acceleration of conquest and Indigenous dispossession, made possible by the industrial revolution, pushed greater numbers of European settlers into the colonial world and provided them with new technologies to accelerate their conquests. As Anglo settlers 'closed the frontier', their policies towards Indigenous peoples shifted from intra-nation conflicts to internal 'management' within the boundaries of the state. In these conditions, a new language of racialisation emerged to explain and justify continued relations of domination, elimination and exploitation.

In his magnum opus, *Traces of History*, Patrick Wolfe shows how in the late nineteenth century the measure of blood quantums, as well as theories about the strengths and weaknesses of White, Indigenous and Black blood, emerged as key organising narratives of these processes. For example, in both the US and Australia, the 1880s would be a period of intense racialisation of the Indigenous populations. Wolfe shows how despite different racial descriptors – 'red' in the US and 'Black' in Australia – the processes in both countries were strikingly similar. Both aimed at disappearing Indigenous people in order to facilitate their further dispossession. 'Indigenous blood' was understood to be easily soluble into 'White blood', thereby making it possible to eliminate the Indigenous population by encouraging its assimilation into the settler population. The echo of earlier theories of 'civilising' through blood mixing in Ireland is, as Bhandar points out, striking.[76] Once thus eliminated, Indigenous claims to sovereignty, which by definition challenge those of the settler state, would disappear as well. If the theory of miscegenation is bad enough, its practice is worse.

Wolfe gives the example of the 1886 Aborigines Protection Act, which came to amend its 1869 predecessor, in the Australian colony of Victoria. In the latter Act, in a way strikingly similar to the imposition of reserves in the United States and South Africa, the government had given itself the right to impose 'the place where any aboriginal or any tribe of Aborigines shall reside'.[77] Similarly to both these settler regimes as well, the government also endowed itself with the power to define who was to be recognised as Indigenous. In 1886, the law was amended in two important ways. On the one hand, the new Act imposed racial definitions which differentiated between 'Aboriginals' and 'half castes'. The latter category included all 'persons whatever of mixed Aboriginal blood'.[78] The second important amendment excluded the so-defined 'half castes' from the reserves and missions where their families resided. Those so targeted were 'dispersed' into the settler population, and '[w]ithin the space of two decades, the other mainland colonies and, after 1900, mainland states of Australia followed suit'.[79] The policy's aim was clear: to diminish and disappear Indigenous populations and their collective claim to the land.

In 1936, in another echo of the US's practice, the policy of abducting Indigenous children into care homes would be coordinated on a national level and last until the 1960s. The logic was the same as that set in motion in Victoria in 1886: Indigenous people could – and should – be dissolved into the White population. This administrative elimination allowed the selling-off of land previously set aside for Indigenous reserves and missions, while limiting the use of state funds. The pecuniary argument was made repeatedly by those who supported the policy. All this is strikingly reminiscent of the US's allotment process, where blood quantum was (and continues to be) how the state recognises tribal membership. As Wolfe notes:

The coincidence is not merely chronological. In both Australia and the United States, concrete campaigns of Native assimilation commenced upon the ending of the frontier. In both countries, the cultural and biological aspects of assimilation fused inextricably, with blood quantum heuristically summarising a multidimensional engulfment.[80]

RACISM AFTER EMANCIPATION

While Indigenous populations were racialised in ways that allowed the settler state to make them disappear, and therefore further dispossess them of their land, a different logic was applied to Black populations in the Americas. For example, in the US, the infamous 'One Drop Rule' characterised 'Black blood' in terms that were diametrically opposed to that of Indigenous people. If the latter could be made to disappear through miscegenation with White people, the former had the opposite imagined properties. Even a singular drop of 'Black blood' – that is, the most distant African relative – would lead to the racialisation of a person as Black. This logic found its roots in the reproduction of the institution of slavery and the increase of the masters' property. Black women, as pointed out above, could not give birth to White or Indigenous children. Their progeny was doomed to enslavement. If Indigenous people needed to be made to disappear, in order to facilitate the theft of their land, the opposite was true for Black people. In slavery's dehumanising logic, more Black people meant more labour, and more labour meant more profit. Blackness had to be hereditary and inviolable.

The idea of 'passing', mentioned above, captured exactly this racist idea: someone could appear White to the naked eye, despite 'really being' Black – both categories were understood to be real biological facts. Strikingly, this racialisation of Blackness intensified from the late eighteenth century onwards, first in response to arguments about universal freedom, and then to the actual emancipation of the enslaved. In a sense, slavery solved the issue of who was and wasn't Black in practice: if someone was enslaved, or potentially could be, they were Black, and if someone was Black, they were, or potentially could be, enslaved. With the end of slavery, racism needed new structures and grounds to identify the target of political exclusion and hyper-exploitation. On the one hand, this was achieved structurally. The outcome of the counter-revolution in the American South, which pushed back against emancipation and Black reconstruction,[81] came to receive the collective title of 'Jim Crow' by the end of the 1880s – a series of laws which imposed segregation between White and Black and deprived the latter of the very civil, democratic and political rights that they had only recently acquired. On the other, the development of 'scientific' racism made available a new language to justify the inequalities between the two. If 'universal' rights were denied to Black people, and if White and Black were kept separate, it was because there were fundamental differences between the two populations that could not be overcome.

The continued exploitation of Black labour found new ideological clothes, and new forms of implementation. One such example are the extraordinary levels of violence directed at African Americans, such as the frightening normalisation of lynching, as punishment for Black people considered to be disrespecting racial hierarchies.

The mass character of those extra-judicial killings points to racism's continued social role in solidifying the caste-like separation between Whites and Blacks, which was dependent on unleashing unrestrained violence against African Americans in the wake of their liberation. This violence was, of course, maintained structurally by the state – as the famous case of *Plessy v. Ferguson* demonstrates. In 1896, the Supreme Court found against Homer Plessy, who was legally considered Black despite appearing to be White, and who had refused to sit in the carriage for Black passengers on a segregated train. In doing so, segregation in the South was legally enshrined at a federal level. As Wolfe points out, the case also helped move racist discourse 'steadily in the direction of what came to be known as the "one-drop rule", in which any evidence of any African ancestry whatsoever, no matter how far back or remote and regardless of phenotype, meant that one was qualified as Black.'[82] In 1924, the same logic would be applied when Virginia's anti-miscegenation law defined a White person as 'someone who had "no trace whatsoever of any blood other than Caucasian" or more than one-sixteenth American Indian blood.'[83] The colour line had to be maintained in order to salvage the American social order, as the revolutionary potential unleashed by the Civil Rights and Black Power movements in the second half of the twentieth century would demonstrate once more.

DE-RACIALISATION AS SOCIAL STRATIFICATION

There are, of course, many other examples, which point to different material realities faced by settler states, in their ongoing attempts to stabilise and naturalise social relations of dispossession and exploitation. In the regions of Brazil, where African enslavement had underwritten the plantation economy from the second half of the sixteenth century all the way to the 1880s, Portuguese settlers were largely outnumbered by Africans and their descendants. As slavery ended in the country, it became necessary – as it had been in the US – to find new ways to maintain the social order. The strategy followed was the polar opposite of that chosen in North America. While encouraging the increased immigration of Europeans to 'Whiten' the country, Afro-Brazilians were actively de-racialised. Instead of a one-drop rule, which imposed a monolithic and inescapable Blackness on anyone with any traceable African ancestry at all, the Brazilian case saw the multiplication of colour descriptors that fragmented an otherwise Afro-Brazilian majority that could threaten the reproduction of minority rule – just as the large-scale slave revolts in Brazil had done. One author identified over three hundred (and up to nearly five hundred) different such terms, twelve of which are the most frequently used.[84] This system of gradation, which assumes a sort of linear evolution from Black to White, also excludes the Indigenous population which is, as in the US, 'disappeared' in the process. Here racism functions through denial – what Wolfe calls 'a cumulative demography of dispossession'[85] – that is, the simultaneous disappearance of an African majority and of the Indigenous population.

Another process of de-racialisation in the second half of the nineteenth and first half of the twentieth century, was one by which Indigenous peoples were included into the White settler population, thereby bolstering the latter's numbers. One such process, famously studied by Noel Ignatiev, was the inclusion of Irish migrants into the White majority in the United States.[86] This transformation can appear extraordinary given the centrality of Ireland's colonisation by the English, in developing both forms of Indigenous dispossession and racialisation. Moreover, as the Irish arrived in the US, they were racialised in terms that likened them, as Nell Irvin Painter points out, to Black people.[87] The response of the Irish in America, in direct opposition with the strong abolitionist traditions of the republican struggle back in Ireland, was to distance themselves from African Americans by supporting the institution of slavery and the exclusion of Black workers from the labour movement. The strategy proved efficient, as demonstrated by the surprise elicited in most people today, so accustomed to the presumed obviousness of race, at the suggestion that there might have been a question about Irish people's Whiteness. The gradual inclusion of the Irish into the 'White race' was, for Ignatiev, 'both a strategy to secure an advantage in a competitive society'[88] and 'an alliance with capital on the basis of a shared "Whiteness"' which has been 'the greatest obstacles to the realisation of [the] possibility' of anti-capitalist working-class action in the United States.[89] We will return to this issue in chapter 4.

In Algeria, the French followed an even more striking course of action. Faced with their inability to overwhelm the Indigenous population through mass White immigration – as the British had – French settlers sought different ways to bolster their numbers. On the one hand, other (largely Southern) Europeans, who at first had been treated suspiciously by the settlers, and seen to be diminishing the quality of settler stock, were integrated, in time, into the settler population. On the other, in 1870, the French state announced that the Algerian Jews were to be French citizens. The Crémieux Decree, named after the minister who promulgated it, marked the beginning of an important – and tragic – aspect of French colonisation in North Africa.[90] Indeed, at the same time as Jews were 'lifted out' of their Algerian status, and granted new (and better) educational and professional opportunities, the majority Muslim Algerian population was consigned to Indigeneity. Benjamin Stora, the foremost historian of modern Algerian Jewry,[91] describes the Crémieux Decree as the first Algerian Jewish exile, which forcefully excised it from the body of Algerian society.[92] The move was followed by the imposition of the Indigeneity Code (*Code de l'Indigénat*), which formalised the different rights granted settlers and Indigenous populations, and further facilitated the dispossession of Indigenous lands. In practice, the code set up a system in which Algerians were both dispossessed of their land but kept on it as a cheap and captive workforce for the settler economy.

In this arrangement, Algerian Jews were erected as a barrier between the settler and Indigenous populations, to serve as Allen's 'intermediate stratum', so central in stabilising the settler colonial order. Relabelled from Indigenous to French, at the stroke of a pen, the Jewish population of Algeria would find itself increasingly stuck between a rabidly antisemitic French settler society, and an Algerian national movement that, at best, did not know how to make sense of their Jewish countrymen's place in the colonial order. While the National Liberation Front (FLN) made calls to Algerian Jews to join the anti-colonial struggle,[93] the material realities that had inscribed Algerian Jews as belonging to the settler society proved too strong to overcome. There were, for example, several cases where Algerian Jews were targeted as part and parcel of settler society by the FLN's military operations. At the same time, even those Jews that sided with the FLN against settler rule found themselves socially cut off from Algerian society after nearly a century of, albeit interrupted, integration into French society.[94] In the end, the near-totality of Algerian Jews left for France at independence, in 1962.

While forms of colonial racialisation can survive the process of anti-colonial struggle, it does not necessarily need to be this way. In South Africa, for example, Steve Biko, a key leader in the struggle against Apartheid and the theorist at the heart of the Black Consciousness Movement, fought vehemently against accepting the colour lines imposed by the settlers. He rejected official divisions between so-called Africans, Coloureds and Indians, arguing that these different identities had been imposed by the Apartheid state to divide the Black majority – understood as being made up of all three groups. He wrote: 'What we should at all times look at is the fact that: 1. We are all oppressed by the same system. 2. That we are oppressed to varying degrees is a deliberate design to stratify us not only socially but also in terms of the enemy's aspirations'[95] – that is, to say that racist segmentation was a key aspect of White minority rule. Instead, Biko argued, 'being black is a reflection of a mental attitude. Merely by describing yourself as black you have started on a road towards emancipation, you have committed yourself to fight against all forces that seek to use your blackness as a stamp that marks you out as a subservient being.'[96] Similar to the case of the Haitian 1805 Constitution discussed above, Biko argued that to build a different social order – in struggle and after liberation – settler methods of social control and division needed to be transformed radically. If the settler world was to be turned on its head, so settler forms of domination needed to be overthrown as well.

Throughout the settler world, as conquest gave way to direct rule, and as Indigenous and/or African labour became the backbone of its economies, a new grammar of domination and social control emerged. Building on earlier ideologies of domination and difference, developed in the early wars of conquest and colonisation in Spain and Ireland, which targeted Jews, Muslims and the Irish, settlers developed new methods of social control, which normalised and naturalised their power. Different forms of racialisation represent(ed) different social realities and balances of forces. However, what they all have in common, is that they mystified domination, accumulation and dispossession into the expression of a supposedly natural hierarchy. In the process, they erected social barriers between settlers, Indigenous and enslaved people that created caste-like social divisions, and undermined possibilities for effective joint revolt.

The settler poor, once White, could be won over to the reproduction of slavery and the imposition of racist differences. The intermediary strata, 'elevated' as a shield between minority settler societies and Indigenous or enslaved majorities could also be brought around to stabilising settler rule and the social order's active reproduction. The world appeared to confirm the racist narratives constructed by settlers, and were reinforced by race 'science' from the late eighteenth century onwards. This was true, at least, until new forms of social organisation were thrown up in the process of anti-colonial uprisings and revolutions. The latter's ongoing existence points to the limits of racism as a social stabiliser. Outside of these moments of revolt, however, it facilitates the reproduction of the social order, even when the material possibility for its destruction exists. This reality, and the role of settler labour movements in the reproduction of settler power, is the subject of the next chapter.

CHAPTER FOUR

Striking Settlers

'Workers of the World, Unite and Fight for a White South Africa!' This slogan was raised during the 1922 Rand Rebellion, during which White miners struck, rioted and took up arms. They were revolting against redundancies and the threat of greater numbers of Black workers being integrated into semi-skilled jobs. The strike laid the groundwork for the election of an alliance between the Labour Party and the National Party, which in the longer term, would lead to the implementation of Apartheid. The slogan raised by the miners captures the particular nature of social relations within settler colonies, shaped by the racism previously discussed. Striking settlers could make claims of internationalism and workers' solidarity, while in the same breath demand greater Indigenous exclusion and dispossession. Black workers, in this case, were not 'of the world' as the settlers saw it. In fact, they were a threat to it.

Far from challenging the process of settler expansion, settler workers repeatedly played a key role in intensifying racial segregation and Indigenous dispossessions. Settler class struggle was fought simultaneously against settler bosses and Indigenous workers. Settler labour movements demanded both an increase in their share of value extracted from their own labour power, as well as from the colonial loot extracted through the dispossession of Indigenous peoples. From Australia's labour-led 'White-Australia' campaign to the French labour movement's near-unanimous opposition to Algerian independence, across the colonial world, settler workers fought for the exclusion and dispossession of Indigenous and racialised people, and did so while deploying socialist, communist, or even internationalist rhetoric.

In previous chapters, we looked at the central role of labour regimes in the organisation of settler colonies, the treatment of Indigenous populations, and the process of racialisation. Here we discuss the specific nature of settler labour movements and their relation to both (settler) capital and Indigenous workers. This chapter highlights the central role played by settler workers' movements in the expansion of settlement, as well as in the Indigenous workers' exclusion from the settler economy – in part or in full. This process accelerates especially from the late nineteenth century onwards. As long as settler workers could exclude Indigenous workers from competing for the same jobs, they found material advantages in siding with the settler state and fighting for a greater share of the colonial pie within its structures. Moreover, access to Indigenous land being a precondition for the existence and expansion of settlement leads to powerful unifying tendencies within the settler population vis-à-vis Indigenous peoples. In chapter 3, we have already seen how unfree labourers in the Americas in the seventeenth century fought not only for greater freedom from their masters but also greater access to stolen land.

Here, these processes will be illustrated through the campaign for Hebrew Labour, led by the Labour Zionist movement in Palestine, and the White labour movement's campaign for a White South Africa. Both struggles led to new political realities in 1948, which reflected the specific outcomes of both settler assaults on Indigenous societies, and internal settler-class struggle in the preceding half-century. While the Labour Zionist movement's rise to prominence laid the foundations for the Palestinian Nakba, a stalemate between settler labour and capital led to the establishment of the Apartheid state in South Africa. Both outcomes were imposed on the back of the Indigenous populations, through greater dispossession of land and greater exclusion from the labour market.

SETTLER WORKERS

If the late eighteenth and nineteenth century saw the rise of a new social order, powered by steam, mechanised and spanning the entire globe, it also became the stage for intensifying confrontations between labour and capital. Throughout this period (and into the twentieth century), workers' movement grew in numbers, organisation and strength. Already in the first half of the nineteenth century, workers' movements arose demanding not only better pay and conditions but also more fundamental social transformations.[1] Chapter 1 already pointed to the ways in which African and Indigenous peoples' revolts in the New World's plantations and mines, pointed to the emergence of mass struggles at the point of production, which brought an end to both slave economies and the world market's reliance on silver.[2] In Europe, the 1848 revolutionary wave which swept across the continent, similarly signalled the entry of the working class onto the historical stage. One of the labour movement's most influential pamphlets – *The Communist Manifesto* by Karl Marx and Friedrich Engels – powerfully captures some of these important social changes.

By the end of the nineteenth century, what had been close networks of activists in more or less spontaneous revolts became increasingly formalised in mass worker organisations. Political parties and trade unions brought together hundreds of thousands of members across the world's industrial centres – particularly in Europe and its settler colonies. In time, their campaigns would achieve such things as curtailing the working day, imposing limits on the working age, and later still, paid holidays, sick leave, and welfare services. However, as we saw previously, the accumulation of wealth under capitalism does not only take place through exploitation, but also through dispossession. It will suffice here to remember how this process was central to capitalist development as natural resources, land and people were violently dragged into the world market. Indigenous peoples were displaced, murdered and enslaved across the colonial world, in order to facilitate wealth accumulation in the metropoles and within settler colonies.

This dual process placed settler labour movements in a contradictory position. Indeed, as industrial centres developed in the settler world, so did the settler working classes. While their size and strength varied, all settler societies, by their very nature, developed internal social relations, including class differences. Settler colonies based on the elimination of Indigenous population and the mass settlement of Europeans, such as in North America and Oceania, were naturally more dependent on the work of other settlers than those based on the exploitation of imported, enslaved and/or Indigenous labour. Settlers exploited settlers and this, much like in the colonial metropoles, led to class-based confrontations and the formation of workers' organisations.

In fact, these organisations were often particularly radical and well organised in the settler colonies, partly because of the social role that the colonies played. Indeed, political undesirables could be dealt with by ruling classes in Europe through deporting them to the settlements, thus playing the dual role of beheading domestic social unrest by depriving movements of their leaders, while continuing to furnish the settlements with new arrivals. For example, in the aftermath of the Paris Commune in 1871, as the French state repressed the revolutionaries, many were deported to Algeria. Similarly, the Tolpuddle Martyrs, after organising agricultural workers in England in the early 1830s, were arrested on trumped-up charges and deported to New South Wales. The six were repatriated after mass protests in England.

However, a number of the martyrs would later decide to settle – voluntarily this time – in Canada. In doing so, they also represented another important aspect of the formation of settler labour movements: the regular movement of workers between settler colonies, as well as between settler colonies and the metropole, in search of work. As Jonathan Hyslop has shown in the case of miners in the British empire of the late nineteenth and early twentieth centuries,[3] a White imperial working class emerged through these migratory waves, which exchanged and spread both political and organisational practices. This played a crucial role in the development, for example, of the White labour movement in South Africa. Much like persecuted minorities could become, in the process of emigration and settlement, the vanguard of colonial expansion, so could those who fought for the tearing asunder of the bourgeois order in Europe become its staunchest defenders in the settler colonial world, through a similar social alchemy.

While facing the settler bourgeoisie, by whom they are exploited, settler workers do not stop simultaneously facing Indigenous peoples, whom they dispossess. Settler class relations should be understood through the prism of this dual tension. Settler labour movements develop their institutions and political traditions through their struggle for a greater share of the value they create, as well as their simultaneous struggle for a greater share of the colonial loot which they participate in accumulating.

Indigenous societies then face, as we will see in this chapter, settler assaults within the labour market as well as being dispossessed of land and resources. Within the labour market, settler workers treat Indigenous workers as competition – as racialised, unskilled and 'cheap', which is to say highly vulnerable and violently disciplined.[4] The latter are exposed to state repression, little legal protection (if any) from employers, and low wages. When settler labour working in the same industries as Indigenous workers, as was the case in British Mandate industries and citrus groves in Palestine, or the mines of South Africa, it experiences these workers as downward pressures on their own – considerably better – living and working standards. Employing Indigenous workers was regarded in both cases as a betrayal of settler workers by settler capitalists who, they argue, should afford the former better conditions in the process of building the new nation.

On this question, settler capital and labour can become bitterly divided. In both examples discussed in this chapter, employers preferred the more profitable use of Indigenous workers over their settler counterparts. If the latter were to be hired at all, it should be on 'competitive' wages. In response, settler labour movements organised to force employers to provide higher pay and better conditions to them and them alone. Indigenous workers were to be excluded from workplaces – or at least from the more highly skilled and better-paid jobs – in order to give employers no choice in the matter. The outcome of these struggles was more often than not an agreement between settler labour and capital, which took the form of a division of the workforce, policed through a colour bar, with skilled and unionised work monopolised by settlers, rather than the full exclusion of Indigenous workers.[5]

These processes meant that in the settler colonial context, far from fighting alongside Indigenous workers or defending the ideas of solidarity or the 'unity of labour', the workers' movement tended to be at the forefront of political demands for greater racial segregation, Indigenous exclusion and expulsion. These behaviours certainly have echoes in racist labour campaigns outside of settler contexts, for example, surrounding the threat of migrants to national workers' wages. However, whereas workers' self-organisation has been and continues to be able to challenge these discourses on the basis of raising migrant wages rather than excluding them from the workforce, the material benefits available to settler workers – crucially Indigenous land – have tended, as shown below, to be too great to make these progressive challenges effective.[6]

BALANCE OF FORCES AND SOCIAL DEMANDS

The need for settlers to keep the settlement project alive in the face of Indigenous resistance, made capitalists vulnerable to settlers' political and economic demands. Indeed, the construction of housing and industry, as well as travel and communication infrastructure, are both crucial for the well-being of settler working classes and the settler colony's development. As the settlement expands, it establishes firmer control over Indigenous land. As seen in chapter 1, infrastructure plays a central role in policing Indigenous populations, isolating different populations from each other, and further moving the balance of forces to the settlers' advantage. A similar observation can be made about the distribution of the settler populations on ever-expanding tracts of land, who play both the role of occupiers and potential military enforcers. Much the same is true for the demands of settler women and feminist organisations. As Patricia Grimshaw has shown in the cases of Australia, New Zealand and Hawai'i, settler women were able to impose their political interests – such as suffrage – more effectively and rapidly in the settler colonial world, because in doing so they participated in imposing settler dominance over Indigenous peoples and land.[7] Far from indicating settler societies' enlightened or liberated nature, the greater integration of settler women in the polity reflects the basic material needs of settler societies locked into conflict with the Indigenous populations they aim to dispossess. All hands, as it were, on deck.

If the need for personnel makes capitalists vulnerable to the economic and political demands of settler workers' (or women's) movements, their ability to distribute material advantages such as cheap (or free) land and housing to settlers serves as an effective tool to mitigate internal social strife, while also deepening the colonial process. Settlers demanding better social conditions or greater redistribution of wealth can therefore be integrated in the colonial process through distributing greater amounts of Indigenous resources to them. Furthermore, the settlers are dependent on the state's military power and protection to continue making these resources available, which puts a limit on how far they are prepared to rock the boat. This leads to a certain settler quietism, considerably limiting how far internal social contestation is prepared to go in challenging the state: demanding a greater share of the pie without ever losing sight of the infrastructure and resources necessary to keep eating the pie.[8] In the previous chapter, we have already seen this issue illustrated in the case of Bacon's Rebellion. While poor settlers rebelled against the landowners, they did so on the basis of demanding greater and more rapid expropriation of Indigenous land. The movement was broken by an imposition of differences between European and African rebels, but also through the further expansion of settlement, achieved through military conquest.

While this process will be further illustrated below in the case of both Palestine and South Africa before 1948, it is also worth pointing out these processes continue to be relevant today (see chapter 5). In 2011, for example, when Israeli protestors marched and occupied squares in their hundreds of thousands against expensive housing and growing inequality, the government was able to resolve the crisis through accelerating settlement building and continuing the displacement of Palestinians in Jerusalem and the Negev/Naqab.[9] Strikingly, the key organisations involved in supporting the movement and providing it with its organisational infrastructure emerged out of the Labour Zionist movement, and its social base was rooted primarily among white-collar and young precarious workers. No public rejection of the government's plans was formulated and throughout the movement Palestinian demands, on either side of the Green Line, were ignored.[10]

As demonstrated in both the Zionist and South African cases, the settler workers' movement played a key role in structuring the colony's labour market, its policy towards Indigenous peoples, and its economic programme. These examples show again that a settler colony's specific structure is not set in stone, but can change over time in response to new political and economic realities. The Labour Zionist movement shifted the Yishuv (the pre-state Jewish community in Palestine) away from a model based on the exploitation of the Palestinian population by a settler minority, and towards the attempted creation of an exclusively settler economy. In South Africa, the White workers' movement confronted the push by the Anglo-Saxon settler bourgeoisie to move the settler economy in the opposite direction. While their resistance failed, it did achieve the segregation of the labour movement and the institutionalisation of a colour bar.

COUNTER-TENDENCIES

A word should also be said, however, about those who fought for a different world. Often emerging from communist or syndicalist traditions, some groups of workers within the settler population participated in the establishment of joint unions alongside Indigenous workers, and took part in struggles for decolonisation.[11] They often did so under the influence of international political developments and movements, such as the formation of the Industrial Workers of the World, the Russian Revolution, and the emergence of the Third International. Just as colonial ideas and technologies travelled across the settler world, so revolutionary ideas could spread through these same networks. In the early twentieth century, syndicalists fought across Southern Africa against colonialism and for joint Black and White unions; in Morocco (largely Southern) European workers participated alongside their Moroccan counterparts in growing industrial unrest during the lead-up to independence, while the Palestine Communist Party (PCP) strove to bring Jewish and Palestinian workers together in opposition to British rule, as well as Zionism. The latter did so with a level of success – organising workers in mixed industries and even achieving important scores in elections during the 1920s. As the Zionist movement became more powerful in Palestine, from the end of the decade onwards, its pull became increasingly felt, also in communist circles. This process eventually led to the PCP splitting along national lines, with its majority-Jewish wing abandoning its previous internationalism and espousing Zionism's state-building aspirations.[12]

It is striking that what these movements had in common was a broader opposition to capitalism and the state. By fighting for systemic change, they were able to convince settler workers to participate in alliances with their Indigenous counterparts and commit to ending colonisation. Within the confines of the existing order, settler workers had access to forms of colonial accumulation to improve their lot. By pointing to a more fundamental transformation of society – doing away with exploitation and oppression altogether – communist and syndicalist organisers were able to win over sections of the settler labour movement. In earlier periods, Indigenous societies could represent a similar systemic challenge to settler economic and political structures. For example, as English settlement was taking off in North America in the early seventeenth century, in the Chesapeake area, the Indigenous Algonquian confederation acted as a powerful pull for poor and exploited English men and women. Indeed, the confederation was 'nourished upon a better all-around diet than the Europeans', functioned 'without classes, without a state', and 'was organized around matrilineal descent ... both men and women enjoyed sexual freedom outside marriage [and t]here existed no political/military bureaucracy'.[13] By running away, indentured workers could – just as the enslaved – escape exploitation as well as gendered oppression. As long as settler power had not managed to conquer Indigenous societies, nor unify the settler population through racism and Indigenous dispossession, escape could serve as a powerful anti-systemic alternative.

However, while the political commitment of those fighting together for a way out of settler colonialism should be acknowledged, it is also important to point out that they repeatedly failed to outflank the settler labour movement's exclusionary currents. The argument presented in this chapter is that these failures should not be understood as the outcome of personal shortcomings by those involved, but as the consequence of structural elements within settler societies. As long as colonial loot – land, resources, but also access to better working conditions and greater political power – can be redistributed amongst the settler population, forms of solidarity between Indigenous and settler workers can be powerfully undermined. Strategies that are available to take on racism amongst workers outside of the settler colonial context, are undermined by the real and immediate material gains that settler workers enjoy through the defeat and dispossession of their Indigenous counterparts – first and foremost amongst which is access to the latter's land. Where successful joint struggle did occur – even in limited numbers – such as in the case of minority White (largely communist) participation in the Southern African or Algerian struggles for liberation, this emerged out of the revolutionary dynamics generated by mass Indigenous resistance and revolution, and not on the basis of a fundamental shift within settler societies.[14]

THE CONQUEST OF LABOUR

The Zionist movement in Palestine was riven by complex class contradictions from the start. The movement's leaders were middle- to upper-class Europeans who, confronted with growing antisemitism in Europe and the rejection by their gentile counterparts, turned to a colonial solution for the so-called 'Jewish question'. Their approach, ironically, demonstrated their deep integration into European culture. Faced with the rise of nation states on the one hand, and the European tendency to solve internal social crises by exporting them to the colonial world on the other, the Zionists resolved to build a colonial state in Palestine, with the support of the European empires. This, they further argued, would be attractive to the latter as it would both rid them of their Jewish populations at home and facilitate expansion abroad. Theodore Herzl, the Zionist movement's most prominent figure in the late nineteenth century and its key theoretician, was therefore confident when he wrote in his book *The Jewish State* that 'honest Anti-Semites, whilst preserving their independence, will combine with our officials in controlling the transfer of our estates',[15] and again in his diaries: 'The anti-Semites will become our most loyal friends, the anti-Semitic nations will become our allies.'[16] Moreover, the establishment of a settler colony in Palestine would allow the European empires to expand their control over the Middle East, its trade routes and resources. This political vision led to the foundation of the Zionist Organisation (ZO) in 1897, in Basle.

The majority of the world's Jewish population, however, were concentrated in the rapidly expanding industrial centres and small towns of the Pale of Settlement in the Russian empire (roughly today's Lithuania, Poland, Ukraine and Belarus). Their response to the double pressure of proletarianisation and antisemitic repression was only rarely Zionism. Many emigrated to North America (and to a lesser extent the UK and Western Europe) or joined the ranks of the increasingly militant labour movement. Trade unions, political parties such as the Bund and the other factions of the Russian Social Democratic Party, all saw a massive intake of Jewish workers.[17] These further played a key role in repeated uprisings and revolutions, the most important one being that of 1917.

These political and class differences within European Jewry would profoundly impact the Zionist movement's development in Palestine also. For one, these differences generated a chronic difficulty in attracting new settlers to Palestine, a situation which would continue to undermine the colonial project until the late 1920s/early 1930s. By then, the deepening world economic crisis, the rise of fascism, and the closing of US and UK borders compelled increasing numbers of Jews to seek refuge in Palestine. Until this period, it was common for many Jews to treat the settlement as a pit-stop in a longer journey across the Atlantic.[18] To this structural weakness two separate responses emerged – both, once again, based on class lines.

Important figures within the Zionist movement's higher echelons, such as the French Baron Edmond de Rothschild, had envisaged the development of a settler colony modelled on the French settlements in North Africa.[19] A minority of Jewish landowners would rule over a majority of Indigenous Palestinians and would compel the latter to provide cheap labour for their agricultural holdings – principally citrus groves – providing cash crops for export to the European market. Low numbers of settlers would then not be an issue. They would largely remain concentrated in urban populations and as supervisors in the fields.

Against this position, the Labour Zionist movement emerged. It made a wholly different claim: for the settlement project to survive, and to avoid Indigenous resistance shutting down its economy as it had done in other settlements, it was necessary to construct a separate economy, free from dependence on Palestinian labour and produce.[20] This, they argued, would both undermine the dangers of Indigenous workers' militancy, attract more Jewish settlers to Palestine and, crucially, retain them. Only by offering better wages and working conditions to Jewish workers than those available in Palestine in the early twentieth century could these goals be met. This necessitated, so the nascent Labour Zionists argued, eliminating competition from cheaper Palestinian workers – that is, their exclusion from Jewish-owned farms and workplaces.

To achieve this goal, the Labour Zionist movement launched its campaign for the 'conquest of labour'. Targeting both Jewish employers and Palestinian workers simultaneously, Labour Zionists picketed citrus groves and companies that employed Indigenous labour, organised boycotts of products made by Palestinian workers, and targeted Jewish-owned businesses that sold them.

The aim was to make it more costly for Jewish farmers and bosses to continue to hire cheap Palestinian workers than to provide higher wages and better working conditions to Jewish workers – effectively forcing them to subsidise the 'Hebrew economy'. It is through waging this campaign for 'Hebrew Labour' that a number of the key institutions of the Yishuv and, later, the Israeli state, were born. It is also through these colonial institutions that the Labour Zionist movement was able to establish its political dominance over the Yishuv and the Zionist movement more generally.

First, and perhaps most emblematic amongst them, was the kibbutz.[21] Well-known in the West as proto-socialist collective farms, the kibbutz was where workers lived, toiled and made decisions collectively without managers or owners. In the 1960s and 1970s, it was common for young European and North American progressives to spend a summer on a kibbutz to experience its 'liberated' atmosphere. What is less often acknowledged, however, is that the kibbutz emerged out of the campaign for Hebrew Labour, as the first agricultural settlement that had successfully excluded Palestinians, following a strike by Jewish workers in Kinneret in 1908. They had opposed the introduction to their farm of Palestinian workers. The end of the strike was negotiated by the ZO on the basis of the creation of a new farm, the first kibbutz, in Degania. The ZO would own the land through the Jewish National Fund (JNF),[22] and the workers would collectively run it. In the process, the beginning of an alliance between Labour Zionism in Palestine and the ZO abroad was born, which was premised on the dispossession of Palestinian land and the exclusion of Palestinian workers. This alliance would define Zionist and Israeli politics until the end of the 1970s.

Second, and as a direct consequence of the development of agricultural settlements in Palestine, the Labour Zionist movement organised its own militias. Replacing Arab guards, whom many settlements had used thus far, these militias served both to expand land control, 'settle disputes' with Palestinian farmers, and defend the settlement from Indigenous revolt and retaliation – much like the settlement militias in the occupied Palestinian territories (oPt) today.[23] These militias, alongside their Revisionist counterparts,[24] would play a central role in repressing Palestinian resistance and the Arab revolt, carrying out the ethnic cleansing of Palestine during the Nakba, as well as forming the backbone of the new Israeli Army.

Third, in 1920, the Histadrut was founded.[25] Officially a trade union federation, it played a much more expansive role in the Zionist movement's history. Its tasks throughout the pre-1948 years can best be understood as consisting of three main areas:

1. Organising the Hebrew Labour campaign across the Yishuv, centralising its efforts, and taking on those groups of workers who failed to respect its principles – including those communist and joint union initiatives mentioned above.[26]

2. Developing key infrastructure and institutions for the state to come. It owned, for example, a construction company (Solel Boneh) as well as a bank (Bank HaPoalim).

3. Providing the basis for a separate settler economy, within its own workplaces and industries, serving as a key employer – something it would do until the 1990s.

The Histadrut has often, with good reason, been described as the Israeli state-in-waiting and many of its pre-1948 leaders (such as David Ben Gurion, Yitzak Ben Zvi and Golda Meir) later played key roles in the political life of the Israeli state.[27] From its foundation, its role was to mobilise workers for the creation of the settlers' state. Its constitution stated clearly that it aimed to 'unite all the workers and labourers in the country who live by their own labour without exploiting the labour of others, in order to arrange for all settlement, economic and also cultural affairs of all the workers in the country, so as to build a society of Jewish labour in Eretz Yisra'el'.[28]

A decade after its founding, it became clear that although the Histadrut had not managed to exclude Palestinian workers as such – they remained, for example, employed in much larger numbers in key colonial industries such as the railways, the oil industry and the ports – it had created a separate economic sector in Palestine, and positioned itself at the head of the Zionist movement.[29] Its organisations laid the foundations for a future state, its representatives were in close contact with the British colonial authorities, and as greater numbers of Jews fled the rise of fascism in Europe, it was through the Histadrut's institutions that they were integrated, housed and employed. International donations to the Yishuv were received through Bank HaPoalim and its military power was primarily concentrated in the Hagana – the Labour Zionist militia.

The repression of the Arab Revolt (1936–39), which opposed both Zionist expansion and British rule, demonstrated the strength of Labour Zionism as well as its commitment to the conquest of labour. The revolt started with a six-month-long Palestinian general strike (potentially the longest general strike in history) in which the Palestinian Arab Workers Societies played a key role. It then turned into a military uprising, in which the Palestinian revolutionary movement managed to take control of the majority of the country's cities. In 1938, Palestinians controlled Jaffa, Beersheba, Gaza, Jericho, Bethlehem, Ramallah and the old city of Jerusalem.[30] In the words of one British official at the time: '[T]he situation was such that civil administration and control of the country was, to all practical purposes, non-existent.'[31] Only extraordinary military violence unleashed by the British empire, including aerial bombardments of entire villages, alongside the betrayal by its landowning figureheads, managed to behead the movement and defeat the revolution.[32] In the end, '10 percent of the adult male population was killed, wounded, imprisoned, or exiled.'[33]

The Labour Zionist movement was an active participant in this process. The Histadrut organised strike-breaking units to keep key sectors of the colonial economy running, especially the railways, the ports and the oil industry. This mobilisation undermined the strike's effectiveness and allowed the British to keep vital industries running. After the revolt, the Mandate authorities rewarded the Histadrut by increasing the Jewish representations within state industries.[34] This was particularly significant because it was there that the campaign for Hebrew Labour had been least effective. At the same time, the Histadrut also supported the creation of special night squads, which were trained by the British to guard key infrastructure, primarily railways and pipelines, against sabotage by the revolutionaries.[35]

In 1939, as the Palestinian national movement emerged defeated, divided and politically beheaded, the Labour Zionists had increased both their military capacity and their influence over key strategic industries. A full expulsion of Palestinian workers from the economy was not possible, but Labour Zionism improved its position in the colonial balance of forces. Its opportunity emerged in 1947–48, when the unilateral retreat of British Mandate forces from Palestine gave the Zionist movement the green light to unleash unrestrained violence against the Palestinian population. The Nakba, in this perspective, is not an accident of history or of war, but the outcome of several decades of struggle for the implementation of exclusionary policy by the Labour Zionist movement. In the aftermath of the ethnic cleansing, the remaining Palestinians within the new state's borders were put under military rule and forbidden from leaving their villages. In this period, the aim of achieving a fully separated economy was most closely achieved. Further territorial expansion, however, in 1967, as well as important labour shortages in the Israeli economy, would undermine the policy of Hebrew Labour and tens of thousands of Palestinians would be integrated into the Israeli workforce.[36]

This necessarily brief historical overview demonstrates the central role played by the Labour Zionist movement in fighting for segregation and the elimination of the Indigenous Palestinian population from the settler economy – and from the settlement altogether. In addition, it illustrates how settler class struggle in the Yishuv played out simultaneously between settler classes as well as against Palestinian workers. The nature of the Yishuv's (and later the Israeli state's) relationship to the Palestinian population was therefore not set in stone, but was the outcome of both internal struggle amongst settlers and the struggle between settlers and the Indigenous population. We now move on to discuss settler class relations in pre-1948 South Africa. While settler class struggle laid the groundwork for ethnic cleansing in Palestine, in South Africa it achieved the institutionalisation of a rigid colour bar, stratifying the labour force along racial lines. It did so despite the defeat of the White workers' movement by the bosses and the state, in the conflict over the organisation of the settlement and its economy.

TOWARDS APARTHEID

The South African case is, in many ways, very different from the Palestinian one, not least because of its longevity. The presence of White settlers in South Africa pre-dates the arrival of their counterparts in Palestine by a number of centuries. Yet here also settler class relations played themselves out on the back of Indigenous populations and shaped the settlement's political and economic trajectory. We will see two examples of this process here. First, the clash between Boer smallholders and British industrialists in the early nineteenth century, when the Cape Colony passed into the hands of the British empire. This confrontation ended with the smallholders migrating inland and considerably expanding the amount of land under settler control. This example also demonstrates that settler social relations are not exclusively played out between capital and labour, but also between other social classes. We then look at the struggles over the labour market's organisation after the discovery of diamond and gold in the second half of the century. Both examples once again demonstrate the dual nature of social relations within settler societies – pitting different classes of settlers against one another, as well as against the Indigenous population, over the distribution of surplus value as well as colonial loot.

Between 1795 and 1806, the Cape Colony repeatedly changed hands between both the Dutch and British empires, after which it remained firmly in the hands of the latter until South African independence. In this period, Southern African territories were integrated into the empire's trade routes through the Cape's ports. This process accelerated considerably after the discovery of gold in the Witwatersrand in 1886. Both periods of transition came with intense military conflict and social strife, which focused repeatedly on the organisation of labour, the place of Indigenous peoples in the settler economy, and wealth distribution amongst different settler groups.

Integration into the British empire also meant integration into the industrial revolution centred on England. The demands of the metropole's markets and industries significantly accelerated world trade, which in turn led to the expansion of strategic ports and their industries. The Cape Colony was no different. Not only did several thousand English settlers join their Dutch and French Huguenot counterparts – as well as their enslaved workers, who outnumbered them – but the growth of international traffic and trade also drew increasing numbers of sailors, traders and military personnel towards the settlement, further developing the port city and its industries once again.

If these changes already meant an important transformation of what had been, until then, a settlement made up primarily of small landowning farmers, the integration into the British empire also meant growing tensions regarding the enslaved population's political rights. This was not out of any deep British humanitarian feeling towards the latter, but was rooted in the growing need for labour in the colony's industries, which could best be serviced by a formally free labour force. This same process of industrialisation and integration into the world market also led to growing economic pressures on the settler population. Settlers, as George Fredrickson points out in his book *White Supremacy*,[37] experienced proletarianisation as a process of racial degradation, given that most artisanal and manual work in urban centres had been carried out by enslaved workers before the arrival of the British.

The situation came to a head in 1834 when the colonial government outlawed slavery and later offered limited suffrage to the Indigenous population.[38] The smallholding settlers rebelled and, faced with the British empire's overwhelming power, moved further inland, beyond the frontier of the Cape Colony. This 'Great Trek', as it became known, laid the foundation for the creation, just over a decade later, of the independent Boer Republics: the Orange Free State, the South African Republic, more commonly known as the Transvaal, and (briefly) the Natalia Republic. These settler states, in turn, secured the preservation of slavery in Southern Africa until the end of the century. Moreover, in migrating, the Boers considerably expanded settler control over Indigenous lands and came into conflict with numerous Indigenous people.

In fact, as Donald Denoon has pointed out, the gradual advance of the settlers had important – and devastating – consequences for Indigenous agriculture and society.[39] As they advanced, the Boers pushed Indigenous populations into the lands of others, where their arrival caused greater stress on available resources and destabilised existing social relations. In doing so, settlers effectively facilitated their future expansionary movements by undermining Indigenous socio-economic relations and their ability to fight back effectively. The Boers' advance into the interior, accumulating land as they went, was finally stopped by the Zulu, who successfully held the settlers' advance in check until the Zulu's defeat at the hands of the British. The Boers, while escaping British rule, expanded the settler colonial realm in Southern Africa, imposing – once again – private property rights over the land, and disorganising Indigenous social relations.

The clash between the British and the Boers was a clash between expanding industrial capital and smallholding farmers, as well as one between industrial capitalism's expanding demand for free – that is, flexible and movable – labour, and the slave labour regime of the Dutch settlers.

This conflict was – temporarily – resolved through the Boers' movement inland and their dramatic conquest of large swathes of Indigenous territory. In doing so, rivalry between the British in the Cape and the Boers in the 'free states' drew to a temporary stalemate, achieved through Indigenous dispossession and the geographical displacement, rather than the abolition, of slavery. Once more, the conflicts emerging within settler social relations were resolved through an intensification and expansion of the colonial process. Much as the metropole resolved its own social tensions by deporting them to the settler colonial world, so it was within settler colonies as well. In doing so, the Boers laid the groundwork for further British expansion. Indeed, it was in these newly settled territories that large deposits of precious minerals would be discovered, from the late 1860s onwards. As Denoon points out, '[l]egend has it that the Afrikaner trekkers into the interior were limiting their ties not only with an odious British colonialism, but also with the market. On the contrary, they were [at] the cutting edge of both.'[40]

The period leading up to the unification of the Union of South Africa, as a British Dominion in 1910, saw a further rapid and dramatic transformation of the settler colony's social relations. Three key factors were at play. First, the discovery of gold and diamonds in Kimberly and Witwatersrand (especially the latter, in 1886) led to the development of new industries, needed to service the growing populations around the mines, and the construction of infrastructure linking the mines to the coast. By 1890, '[t]he [diamond] mines had a market valuation of over £23 million and sold about £3,717,000 worth of diamonds each year.' At the same time '[t]he labour force had been whittled down from 3,100 white and 17,000 other miners, to a mere 1,272 white and 6,830 black workers.'[41] In the gold-mining sector, 'The precise volume of capital invested in the Witwatersrand mines is difficult to determine; but Frankel suggests £35 million by 1895, £60 million by 1900, and over £100 million by 1910 ... At full capacity these mines employed over 100,000 black and 12,500 white workers.'[42]

These changes then facilitated the transfer of settler and Indigenous workforces to these newly expanding mining centres. Workers came not only from the Cape and the surrounding area, bur from across the British empire. Indeed, Southern Africa's growing industries were serviced by workers drawn from a number of places.[43] Numerous miners, who were central to the South African economy, came from Cornwall and Australia, where the mining industry had entered a period of decline. The Australian connection in particular would play an important role in the years to come, as workers who had been involved in the creation of the Australian Labour Party, and its campaign for the 'White Australia' policy, would play crucial organising roles in establishing the South African Labour movement. The institutions that emerged in this period – whether trade unions, trades and labour councils, or the emergence of the Labour Party – would overwhelmingly reflect these same traditions. As the Israeli labour movement learned the lesson from its counterparts in South Africa, so had the latter learned from the Australian experience – a veritable Settler International.

Second, the discoveries of precious minerals also led to increasing conflict over the control of the inland territories between White settlers and the Indigenous populations, as well as between Boers and the British Crown. As the British moved eastwards, they waged war on the African nations that stood in their way, most famously the Zulu population. Once these military victories had been secured, British attention turned to the Boer republics, leading to the two Boer Wars, in 1880–81 and 1899–1902 respectively. These conflicts brought the South African republics under British control and facilitated the centralisation of resources, capital and labour necessary for the mining industry's development. The Union of South Africa, in 1910, represents the institutionalisation of this process.

Third, the 'closing of the frontier' and the creation of Indigenous reserves by the British, led to a shift amongst the Boer settlers from external expansion to internal land accumulation. In this period, within the Boer population, a growing polarisation emerged between large landowners on the one hand, and landless agricultural workers on the other. The latter were, to some extent, employed on the larger estates. However, most importantly, they were pulled into the mining and industrial centres, where settler labour was confronted with mixed workplaces employing both Black and White workers. The very issue of proletarianisation and integrated work places, which had led the Boers to move eastwards nearly a century earlier, was thereby brought back to the forefront of the political arena in the late nineteenth century.

Again, the mining sector was particularly important in this regard. A key concern of mine owners was to keep costs down and to rely on cheap labour for the extraction of gold and diamonds, to be sold on the world market. In practice, this meant the development of a complicated network of laws, taxes and repressive measures aimed at removing Indigenous workers from the land, so as to make them dependent on employment in industry. The workforce in the mines, made possible through this process of dispossession, was highly segregated. Skilled labour was the preserve of White workers. Dynamite, for example, could not be handled by Black workers – for obvious reasons – effectively creating a Whites-only section of the workforce.[44] The vast bulk of unskilled work on the other hand was carried out by Black workers. Skilled – that is, White – workers earned up to five times as much as their unskilled – that is, Black – counterparts.[45] This existing division of labour is important because, as Fredrickson points out, the struggles by White workers in the 1910s and 1920s were not waged over the segregation of the workforce as such, but over its extent and severity.[46]

The first mass campaign for White Labour in South Africa was waged against the importation of Asian workers, in the early twentieth century. Asian workers were being drafted in to address growing Black labour shortages, caused by the Boer Wars. The campaign, which was ultimately successful, underscores the close relation between the South African and Australian cases. The White Australia policy was similarly fought for by settler labour against the introduction of Asian workers, while anti-Asian campaigns played a central role in the US labour movement in the late nineteenth century.[47] Similar to the example of Palestine discussed above, workers mobilised the labour movement's tools and institutions to expel cheaper, racialised workers, instead of organising them. There were two important differences: they did not fight for a full exclusion of Indigenous labour but for the intensification of segregation, and they did not develop state-building institutions in doing so. Unlike in Palestine, these already existed and the workers appealed to, and were at times repressed by, them.

However, while the anti-Asian campaign was an important foundational step in the organisation of the White labour movement in South Africa, the real fight was over the control of semi-skilled and auxiliary work by White workers against their Black counterparts. In an attempt to increase their profits, employers moved to increase the hiring of Indigenous labour in semi-skilled jobs, especially in the mines, where working conditions were horrendous – across the board. Disease and accidents were common, and both Black and White workers grew increasingly militant in those years, demanding better pay and conditions. The White Labour movement's racism served, however, to keep these two strands of labour militancy apart. Tensions increased and led to growing industrial conflict, with especially important strikes in the mining region of the Witwatersrand culminating in the 1922 Rand Revolt. In the words of Lucien Van Der Walt: '[T]he Rand Revolt was only one episode in the regional wave of class struggles, and only one of a series of dramatic confrontations between white labour and white capital.'[48]

The last strike of comparable magnitude had been put down through violent military repression and the leaders' deportation to Britain in 1913. The First World War calmed down the situation, as men were mobilised to the Front. Subsequent labour shortages also strengthened labour's hand. However, in the aftermath of the war, a drastic collapse of gold prices on the world market led mine managers to return to the offensive by cutting wages and attempting to increase the proportion of Black workers in semi-skilled work. In addition, the previous period had also seen important mobilisations of Black workers against colonial control through the pass system, and for improved working conditions. Two years earlier, up to 70,000 Black workers had gone on strike, but were forced back to work through extensive military repression.[49] White workers saw their position in the industry beset on all sides – by the pressures of capital and Indigenous workers' demands. In this context, Keith Breckenridge has argued that their strike should be understood not only as a workers' uprising against bad working conditions but as 'a deliberate, violent assault on the political organisation of their African working-class peers'.[50]

The immediate spark that lit the powder keg was the move by the Chamber of Mines to cut 2,000 semi-skilled White jobs, and the fear by White workers that this represented the beginning of a larger assault on the colour bar in the industry. What started as a local strike, turned into a two-month-long general shutdown – and ended up as an armed uprising. It brought together White workers and armed rural Boer commandos, which certainly resisted the state and the employers, but also carried out repeated pogroms against Black workers. They demanded not the end of exploitation but the agreement of the former in keeping the latter in their (lower) place. As such, this was a struggle waged by White farmers and workers against both capital and Black labour, in defence of a 'White South Africa'. No alliance of the 'workers of the world', or even simply of the mines, was to be seen – despite the uprising's slogan quoted in the opening line of this chapter. Brecken-ridge summarises the rebels' goal: 'They sought to restore a less comprehensively capitalist environment than that in which the Afrikaner workers now found themselves. But it was also a world in which white men ruled by force of arms, and Africans knew their place.'[51]

The uprising was crushed ruthlessly by the South African state, which spared no military power to break the resolve of the miners and the commandos. In the end, aerial bombardments were even used, leaving at least 150 dead. While the uprising itself was defeated, the strikers' political demands were met three years later. In 1924, an alliance of the Labour and National parties – that is, the same alliance between White farmers and workers that had led the revolt – won the elections. The following year, the alliance implemented a series of Acts that institution-alised the colour bar – first in mining, and then across a whole number of industries. White workers were also given access to healthcare and, later, education, while Black workers were consigned once and for all to the lowest, most dangerous, and worst-paid sections of the workforce. Once the militant organisation of both White workers and farmers had been defeated, settler bosses and the settler state were prepared to come to an agreement over the labour market's segregation, achieving social peace within the settler population, to the detriment of the Indigenous population in the process. This legalised segregation of the labour market laid the foundation for its full extension across society with the advent of Apartheid, in 1948.

In both Palestine and South Africa, intense and sometimes violent clashes emerged between settler classes over the nature of settler rule. These could be resolved, and indeed were, on the backs of Indigenous workers and communities, through the intensification of their dispossession, exploitation and/or expulsion. Both examples point to the specific character of social relations in a settler colonial context and their importance in making sense of the development of colonial policies. They further point to what has been called 'settler quietism' in this chapter: the fact that all settler classes, despite their internal social tensions and conflicts, depend on the Indigenous population's continued dispossession, as well as on the settler state to impose their dominance and distribute the colonial loot. Even when the situation escalates to internal military confrontation, peace can be re-established not through structural change but through the intensification of colonial violence, to the settler population's collective benefit.

Similar to the case of racism discussed in chapter 3, land distribution and economic advantages to settler workers serve as powerful tools for stabilisation of settler rule. They also facilitate the economy's continued functioning as well as the reproduction of both the settler state's and capitalist class's power. In that sense, settler workers participate in securing their continued exploitation, in exchange for land and comparatively better working conditions. While nothing is automatic in this process and, as discussed above, there are examples of settlers joining forces with Indigenous workers and fighting for decolonisation, this process does offer a powerful safety valve to settler ruling classes. The agency to end colonial rule lies, as the following chapter discusses, firmly in the hands of Indigenous people and their liberation movements.

CHAPTER FIVE

Liberation and Return

The aim of this book has been to introduce the reader to settler colonialism by giving an overview of its spread across the world from the late fifteenth century onwards, key aspects of settler rule, and some of the ways in which it has – and continues to – shape the global order. Many more issues, examples and areas could (no doubt should) have been covered to do the topic justice. But my hope is that the material discussed here, as well as the sources referred to, will serve as a springboard for readers who want to develop their knowledge on the subject further.

The book has been structured to help readers make sense both of settler colonialism's global reach and significance, as well as the particular ways in which European settlers and their descendants were able to impose and stabilise their rule. We started with looking at the different approaches to the study of settler colonialism, and an explanation of the book's choice of expanding conceptual boundaries somewhat, in order to incorporate processes of settlement in Africa and South America, which are often omitted from such accounts. Leaving aside different approaches that focus on ideal types of colonial formations, the book takes the presence of settlers – and therefore the conflict between settlers and Indigenous populations – as its starting point in defining settler colonialism. This has allowed the analysis to incorporate and compare more examples, while also pointing out the different ways in which settler regimes dispossess, eliminate and/or exploit Indigenous populations.

We moved from the issue of settler colonialism's conceptualisation, to an overview in chapter 1 of its expansion from 1492 onwards, attempting to provide a sense, not only of the magnitude of the settler enterprise and its cataclysmic consequences for the peoples it conquered and occupied, but also of its foundational role in the emergence of the modern global capitalist system. The violent extraction of Indigenous resources, labour power and land, first in the Americas and then across the world, allowed for unprecedented levels of accumulation of wealth in Europe. This, in turn, transformed social relations, and led to the rise of North Western European states and the development of new industries. This process of accumulation became the foundation upon which new political and economic powers emerged, and the altar upon which the world's Indigenous people were sacrificed.

Moreover, as European manufacturing centres grew, the emerging bourgeoisie in England increasingly expelled peasants from the land in order to make them available for industrial-driven labour. This process simultaneously made these dispossessed peasants available for exploitation at home and settlement abroad. By doing so, they consolidated settler control over Indigenous land and fed back into this deadly loop. To talk about settler colonialism is then to talk about the process of imposing and maintaining colonial power over Indigenous populations, as well as about its co-constitutive relation with capitalism's emergence across the globe. This also holds true in relation to the ecological catastrophe humanity is facing today, as a consequence of the unbridled and destructive extractive economies that emerged in this period.[1]

After this global overview of the link between settlement, the transition to capitalism, and the mutually reinforcing processes of dispossession on both sides of the Atlantic, we focused on dispossession in chapter 2. How do settlers dispossess, how does this process compare to its counterpart in Europe, and what are the consequences of the differences between the two? In order to respond to these questions, we first took a step back from the empirical evidence to discuss the critical engagement with Marx's theory of so-called 'primitive accumulation' in the field of Indigenous Studies. From the vantage point of North America (and the Anglo-settler world more generally), the connection between dispossession, proletarianisation and market formation does not appear so obvious. Indeed, as Coulthard has shown in the Canadian context, the consequences of dispossession for Indigenous people are not necessarily proletarianisation. In fact, settler dispossession can – and often does – lead to the *elimination* of the Native, to use Wolfe's formulation, rather than their *exploitation*. In those cases, the targets of dispossession in Europe were proletarianised in the settler colonies, while Indigenous people were murdered, displaced and spatially constrained, imprisoned in reservations, to make their lands available for settlement. In certain contexts – such as Mexico, Algeria, Ireland, or South Africa – we saw how Indigenous people were violently dispossessed, moved off the land, and spatially contained, in order to be exploited, becoming the backbone of the settler economy.

In chapter 3, we moved on to explore the different ways in which racialisation took hold across the settler world as a form of social control, naturalising the power relations between Indigenous, enslaved and settler populations. First, we looked at the ways in which settlers were able to draw on a 'pre-history of racism', developed in Europe, through early acts of invasion, conquest and domination both in the Iberian Peninsula and in Ireland. In the former, the Catholic conquistadors, who would later unleash their bloody thirst for power on Indigenous nations in the Americas, developed early methods of biologically inclined (if not yet systematic) exclusion, based on 'blood purity', first imposed on Jewish and Muslim inhabitants and their descendants. In the latter, English conquerors developed ideas of inherent Irish savagery, regardless of the latter's adherence to Christianity. This barbarian nature, it could then be claimed, demanded English intervention, control and miscegenation, in order to lift the Irish out of darkness, into the light of civilisation – and market relations. Both trends would have long afterlives across the world, for Indigenous peoples as well as enslaved Africans.

We then moved on to detail the ways in which racism developed in the English colonies in North America, as a response to joint revolts by European and African bonded labourers. We then pointed out how the very basis for this struggle was Indigenous dispossession and genocide. In the process, and through the settler state's structuring power, Blackness and slavery were made synonymous, giving birth to modern chattel slavery in which Africans' enslavement was imposed for life and made hereditary. We ended with a discussion of the transition to fully fledged biological justifications for racism, and the ways in which different populations were racialised, depending on the social role assigned to them by different settler states. African enslaved populations, for example, had to be reproduced and maintained in order to multiply the available workforce, and were therefore racialised as possessing non-dilutable blood. Indigenous populations, on the other hand, were racialised as possessing weak and dilutable blood, allowing the settler state to 'disappear' them in order to take control over always more of their land.

Finally, in chapter 4, we turned to the internal conflicts amongst settler populations and the ways in which settler labour movements positioned themselves towards Indigenous populations and the settler bourgeoisie, as well as settler states. In doing so, a further aspect of settler colonial stability was elucidated: even through internal class struggle, the settler colonial process tends to be reinforced rather than weakened. Indeed, except in rare cases of revolutionary challenge (principally by communists and syndicalists in the early twentieth century), settler labour movements have mobilised and struggled for greater exclusion of Indigenous workers from the labour market and greater control over Indigenous peoples and their land. In this sense, far from forming the basis – as the hopes of some commentators would have it – for class solidarity, settler labour struggles tend to focus on increasing their share of the colonial loot by intensifying Indigenous dispossession, rather than the opposite. Class struggle within the settler population therefore tends to further entrench and solidify, rather than challenge or weaken, the settler state's power.

While the goal of this introduction to settler colonialism has been to familiarise readers with the subject and give explanations for its ability to dominate and stabilise its power – over such a large amount of land, during such a long period of time – one must be careful not to overstate the case. Indigenous and enslaved people have always fought back, and continue to do so. Many settler colonial regimes have been successfully challenged and brought down by Indigenous resistance. Nineteenth- and twentieth-century history is replete with examples, from the Caribbean islands and Algeria, to South Africa, Kenya and Angola, of settler regimes being dismantled by Indigenous populations' struggle. It is to this process of ongoing Indigenous struggle for liberation, in the contemporary settler world, that we now turn.

ONGOING LIBERATION

There is a danger, in the process of recounting and analysing five centuries of conquest, dispossession, exploitation, enslavement and elimination, that one ends up presenting a narrative of settler domination as a situation both inescapable and unchallengeable. In describing how settlers were able to overwhelm Indigenous societies, impose their rule over land and labour, enslave and eliminate millions of people across the globe, one runs the risk of presenting a teleological narrative, one in which the outcome appears to have been determined from the outset, in which Indigenous people never stood a chance, and where settlers appear as all powerful. At the same time, accounting for the structural, cumulative and horrifying levels of violence unleashed in this global and centuries-long process can also give a sense that this history is both finished and irreversible. Indigenous peoples and societies are finished, eliminated, or defeated for good. Settlement becomes a done deal. Such an account leads to the conclusion that the current situation demands, at best, the fair treatment of Indigenous peoples *within* settler states, at worst, a rhetorical mourning of Indigenous disappearance following irreversible genocide. Both approaches preclude entirely the possibility of Indigenous liberation *from* the settler state.

These narratives are dominant in mainstream accounts, and have been for almost as long as settler colonialism itself, as demonstrated brilliantly by Jean O'Brien in her book *Firsting and Lasting: Writing Indians Out of Existence in New England*.[2] Settler colonial studies, as a field, often faces this criticism from Indigenous scholars also, as do anti-racist narratives that fail to account for the specificities of settler colonial relations.[3] These scholars point out, instead, that Indigenous resistance has, and crucially continues to, frustrate settler designs. They further argue that this struggle for liberation and return, as the Palestinian slogan puts it, is ongoing. In that context, failing to incorporate Indigenous resistance, past and present, into the analysis of settler colonialism, risks participating in the naturalisation of settler colonial power and domination, and disappearing Indigenous agency.

When Mahmood Mamdani wrote that '[f]or students of settler colonialism in the modern era, Africa and America represent two polar opposites. Africa is the continent where settler colonialism has been defeated; America is where settler colonialism triumphed',[4] he was, on the one hand, stating a simple truth. The attempts by European states – Portuguese, Spanish, Dutch, Belgian, German, French and British – to settle the African continent, dispossess Indigenous peoples of their lands, displace them into reserves, and force them to labour in mines and on plantations, were defeated by long revolutionary struggles throughout the twentieth century. Settler states were dismantled and settlers were forced to choose between accepting to become citizens of independent states under majority rule, or not. At the same time, settler states have not (yet) been defeated in the Americas. Even in Central and South America, where Indigenous people played a key role in overthrowing Spanish power and, more recently, electing radical progressive governments, social and economic inequalities, Indigenous dispossession, and the struggle for access to land continues.

However, struggles for Indigenous liberation are ongoing and their outcome should neither be assumed, nor should their success be precluded. The central role played by these movements in the last twenty years, throughout the world – for example, in challenging the extraction of natural resources, demanding territorial sovereignty, or challenging exploitation and repression – illustrates Indigenous liberation's importance not only in challenging capital and the state, but also in building a different world in the face of climate catastrophe. Moreover, one might also want to raise questions about whether the struggle against settler colonialism is necessarily over on the African continent. As Andy Clarno has shown in his *Neoliberal Apartheid*, the post-1994 period has seen the continuation of inequality, or even its acceleration, in South Africa, most often (although no longer always) on the same racist lines constructed under settler rule.[5] Without undermining the importance of the political transition out of Apartheid, fought for heroically by the people of South Africa,[6] the striking similarities that Clarno documents between contemporary Palestinian and South African experiences of Apartheid, certainly challenge the idea that the latter can be celebrated as a straightforward example of liberation from settler colonialism. The ongoing struggles in South Africa, emerging from these ongoing and unresolved material inequalities, also highlight the importance of not foreclosing the question of continued struggles for liberation.

The story of settler colonialism and its spread across the globe is not simply one of expansion, encounter and elimination – despite settler fantasies, which imagined that Indigenous peoples would disappear and be replaced. Instead, settler colonial processes are always contested by Indigenous populations, who fight settlers and their states over access to land, resources, and the organisation of power relations. While this might be more directly obvious in certain (post-)settler colonial locales, it is a reality that is often obscured in settler colonial processes following conquest (see below). To paraphrase Cedric J. Robinson's observation about racial regimes: settler colonial regimes are unrelentingly hostile to the exhibition of their discernible origins and mechanisms of assembly.[7]

As we saw in chapter 1, from the moment Columbus initiated the invasion of the Americas, Indigenous people fought back against attempts to dispossess and enslave them. Five centuries later, this struggle for Indigenous liberation continues. This reality of continued Indigenous presence and struggle, in the face of the dispossessing violence of settlers and their states, is where Taiaiake Alfred and Jeff Corntassel root their definition of Indigeneity, as a global, enduring reality:

> Indigenous is an identity constructed, shaped and lived in the politicized context of contemporary colonialism. The communities, clans, nations and tribes we call Indigenous peoples are just that: Indigenous to the lands they inhabit, in contrast to and in contention with the colonial societies and states that have spread out from Europe and other centres of empire. It is this oppositional, place-based existence, along with the consciousness of being in struggle against the dispossessing and demeaning fact of colonization by foreign peoples, that fundamentally distinguishes Indigenous peoples from other peoples of the world. There are, of course, vast differences among the world's Indigenous peoples in their cultures, political-economic situations, and in their relationships with colonizing Settler societies. But the struggle to survive as distinct peoples on foundations constituted in their unique heritages, attachments to their homelands, and natural ways of life is what is shared by all Indigenous peoples, as well as the fact that

their existence is in large part lived as determined acts of survival against colonizing states' efforts to eradicate them culturally, politically and physically.[8]

Nor are Indigenous people marginal either, as the discourse of irrevocable elimination would have it. The authors, for example, point out that '[t]here are approximately 350 million Indigenous peoples situated in some 70 countries around the world.'[9] It goes without saying that the importance of Indigenous peoples should not be reduced to a grisly arithmetic, or a simple headcount – if only for the simple reason that settler regimes' racialisation strategies have made this process, at best, complicated. Yet, restating some simple facts can help undermine ideas of terminal Indigenous defeat and disappearance. Even in the US, where the genocidal process of conquest, reservation, allotment and assimilation has and continues to be imposed with such violence, there are today at least 3 million Indigenous people, from 554 (recognised) Indigenous communities. The reservations have broken up the territories of nations, moved populations out of their homelands altogether, and even denied some nations any territory at all.[10] Yet,

The Diné (Navajo) Nation has the largest contemporary contiguous land base among Native nations: nearly sixteen million acres, or nearly twenty-five thousand square miles, the size of West Virginia. Each of twelve other reservations is larger than Rhode Island, which comprises nearly eight hundred thousand acres, or twelve hundred square miles, and each of nine other reservations is larger than Delaware, which covers nearly a million and a half acres, or two thousand square miles … A number of independent nation-states with seats in the United Nations have less territory and smaller populations than some Indigenous nations of North America.[11]

These material realities further complicate the image of a finished process of Indigenous dispossession, without, nonetheless, underplaying the significance of settler conquest and genocide.

Across the Americas, Indigenous peoples' struggle for land and against the extraction of natural resources confronts states as well as some of the planet's most powerful companies and conglomerates.[12] While waging these struggles against both the state and capital, in places such as Ecuador, Bolivia, and Venezuela, Indigenous struggles have played a key role in the electoral victories of progressive governments. They have also been central in the successful resistance against US-backed coups and destabilisation attempts that these governments have faced. Nor are Indigenous peoples in the Western Hemisphere alone. In Australia, New Zealand, or Palestine – to name but a few – the struggle for liberation also continues in the face of often terrifying violence.

The greatest demonstration of the strength of Indigenous organisation and resistance is that, after 500 years of genocidal violence and displacement, on a planetary scale, Indigenous peoples not only survive but continue to demand their right to land and freedom. This is a struggle for a return to the land from which they have been driven by settler expansion, and the sovereignty that they have been denied in the process. And it is also a struggle over the forms of political, economic and ecological regimes that have been imposed by settler states, which continue to destroy both people and natural environments. In the words of Robert Nichols:

> The stakes of current struggles could not be higher. Although these groups are relatively small minorities in their individual respective contexts, taken collectively, they have a global significance beyond their numbers. Indigenous peoples manage or have tenure rights over approximately thirty-eight million square kilometres, or one-quarter of the Earth's land surface. Found in at least eighty-seven countries on all inhabited continents, Indigenous title lands intersect 'about 40% of all terrestrial protected areas and ecologically intact landscapes (for example, boreal and tropical primary forests, savannas and marshes)'. Given this, defending Indigenous systems of land stewardship will be key to long-term ecological sustainability.[13]

The victory of Indigenous struggles for liberation waged across the settler colonial world is, therefore, intimately imbricated with the global struggle against capitalism, extractive regimes of accumulation, and a way out of the climate catastrophe that was initiated and sustained by the twin process of settlement and capitalist development. This point has been made by the Red Nation, an Indigenous revolutionary collective, which put forward its programme for a 'Red Deal', envisaged as simultaneously an answer to continued settler violence and dispossession, as well as to capitalism and climate catastrophe: 'Thus the Red Deal is "Red" because it prioritizes Indigenous liberation, on the one hand, and a revolutionary left position, on the other. It is simultaneously particular and universal, because Indigenous liberation is for everybody.'[14]

To write off Indigenous struggles for liberation, or ignore their ongoing character, is to preclude a possible and different future for humanity, as well as to participate in settler power's stabilisation by presenting it as unshakable or unchallenged. The struggle, in the words of the old slogan, continues. Rana Barakat goes further still. She points out that while settler regimes fight for domination over Indigenous peoples and their disappearance, this goal has always been, and continues to always be, thwarted by Indigenous resistance. In fact, she sees in this failure a key characteristic of settler colonialism, which 'can strive for triumph through the elimination of the native, but in this sense – it will never triumph.'[15]

In concluding, in a brief overview of two recent iterations of these ongoing struggles, this chapter hopes to point out their long-term roots as well as the light they shine on the wider settler projects that they confront, and the road to liberation that they indicate.

FROM THE RIVER TO THE SEA

Two intertwined processes of intensified settler colonial violence directed at Palestinians, both focused on occupied Jerusalem,[16] led to new mass resistance movements in April and May 2021.[17] Throughout the month of

Ramadan, Israeli military forces multiplied provocations in and around the Al Aqsa Mosque. Palestinian gatherings outside the Old City's Damascus Gate were banned, the mosque compound was stormed several times, and arbitrary limitations on the number of attendees were imposed. The situation was further escalated by a march through Jerusalem, organised by the Israeli anti-miscegenation group Lehava (Preventing Assimilation in the Holy Land), where demonstrators chanted their (usual) genocidal chant of 'Death to the Arabs' and attacked Palestinian passers-by. In the same period, Israeli courts rejected an appeal by Palestinian residents of the Sheikh Jarrah neighbourhood, who were petitioning the court to halt their eviction from their homes. The court rejected their appeal, ordering them to leave, which is to say that their houses were to be handed over to Israeli settlers.

Sheikh Jarrah is one of a number of Palestinian neighbourhoods in East Jerusalem that are targeted for settlement, in an attempt to separate the old city from the surrounding Palestinian population. The immediate issue of the affected families' dispossession is thus connected to a larger Israeli plan to 'judaise' Jerusalem, by fragmenting Palestinian neighbourhoods while encouraging the development of settlements in the city.[18] Today, there are roughly 200,000 settlers in East Jerusalem alone. Moreover, dispossession is part and parcel of Sheikh Jarrah's history as a neighbourhood, not only due to the contemporary settler presence, but also because many of its Palestinian inhabitants are refugees, who fled Israel's ethnic cleansing in 1948.[19] Yara Hawari has argued that this has been crucial in building solidarity with the Save

Sheikh Jarrah campaign, 'because it encapsulates the Palestinian experience of dispossession'.[20]

In response to the planned evictions, demonstrations spread across historic Palestine. In the West Bank as well as within the Green Line, Palestinians mobilised in opposing Israeli colonial violence, in Jerusalem first, and then also in Gaza. Indeed, in the face of growing Israeli military aggression in Jerusalem, directed at both mosque attendants and the Sheikh Jarrah's inhabitants, on 10 May, the Hamas government in Gaza issued an ultimatum: Israel was to pull out its military forces from Al Aqsa and Sheikh Jarrah. If it failed to do so (which it did), it would reply to Israel's military escalation in Jerusalem with rocket fire. Israel, in turn, unleashed yet another indiscriminate military assault on the Strip – as it has done repeatedly since 2008.

The United Nations' Office for the Coordination of Humanitarian Affairs (OCHA) noted that the bombing damaged '[a]n estimated 15,000 housing units … multiple water and sanitation facilities and infrastructure, 58 education facilities, nine hospitals and 19 primary healthcare centres'.[21] Not only were 256 Palestinians in Gaza killed, nearly 2,000 were injured, and 113,000 people had to look for refuge during the Israeli bombardments, of which 8,500 were permanently displaced.[22] Just as in Jerusalem, this was not an isolated incident. Gaza has been under blockade since 2005, causing repeated shortages of food, medicine and building materials, amongst other vital goods. In addition, Gaza has repeatedly been targeted by Israeli military offensives, which have been referred to by Israeli officials as 'mowing the lawn'.[23] The most severe of these attacks, in 2014, killed over 2,200 Palestinians, wounded more than 11,000 and displaced half a million.[24] As in Sheikh Jarrah, the majority of Palestinians in Gaza are refugees from the Nakba, expelled from their lands in what became Israel and forbidden to return ever since. Israel's assaults on Palestinians – in Gaza, Jerusalem, and elsewhere – need to be placed in a much longer history of dispossession and ethnic cleansing.

However, while the world's media focused primarily on the conflict's military aspect – without acknowledging the long-term processes of Israeli settler colonialism mentioned above – much less was said about what was happening in the rest of historic Palestine. Within the Green Line as well as in the West Bank, Palestinians demonstrated against the assault on Gaza and the expulsion of Palestinian families from their homes in Jerusalem. Demonstrators confronted not only heavy repression from the state, but also violence meted out by private Israeli citizens who assaulted Palestinians in the streets and vandalised Palestinian shops and places of worship, as well as houses.[25] The myth of 'mixed' Israeli cities – a euphemism for those cities where Palestinian minorities managed to avoid expulsion during the Nakba, and today live segregated from the Jewish Israeli majority, sometimes even behind physical walls – was laid bare for all to see.[26] Palestinians inside the Green Line organised self-defence committees,[27] while Palestinian refugees in Jordan and Lebanon marched to the state borders, illustrating their continued demand to return. In the West Bank, Palestinians mobilised in large demonstrations that denounced both continued Israeli colonisation and the failures of the Palestinian Authority (PA).

The mobilisations shattered the idea of a fragmented Palestinian people, that is too often reproduced in journalistic, academic, or official state and NGO output.[28] In these accounts, the divisions imposed on the Palestinian people by the Israeli state are reproduced uncritically, with each section of the population treated separately: Palestinian refugees in different countries, Palestinians in the West Bank living under the rule of the PA, Palestinians in (East) Jerusalem in limbo as non-citizen residents of the Israeli state, Palestinians in Gaza under military blockade, and Palestinian citizens of Israel. The latter are then again divided between Druze, Bedouin, Christian, Muslim, etc. Yet, in the spring of 2021, the Palestinian movement burst on the scene across these imposed divisions, demonstrating in practice its continued collective identification with a unified struggle for liberation, as well as its recognition of a shared history of dispossession, and a continued collective experience of Israeli settler colonial rule, albeit in different shapes. In the words of Mouin Rabbani: 'Collectively, the mobilisation sent an unmistakable message that despite all efforts to the contrary, Palestine remains a national as well as an Arab cause.'[29]

The most powerful show of unity came on 18 May, when Palestinians across both sides of the Green Line observed a general strike – referred to as the Dignity Strike – organised in only a couple of days by grassroots activists.[30] Official unions in the West Bank as well as the High Follow-up Committee of Arab Citizens in Israel were forced, by the intense pressure building up from below, to support the call, at least rhetorically. Riya Al-Sanah notes that by the time the call was formulated:

> The whole of historic Palestine was engulfed in struggle. It wasn't that Palestinians in Israel were going out on demonstrations in solidarity with Palestinians being attacked in Gaza, it was asserting that we are part of the same struggle, and we have a fight to fight ... An official strike was called for in Palestine '48 [within the Green Line – that is, the Palestinian lands occupied in 1948], then in Jerusalem and the rest of Palestine. The call for the strike and the eagerness to participate in it crystallised the sense of unity that has re-emerged amongst us as Palestinians during this uprising, but also the desire to disconnect from colonial structures.[31]

The strike was widely respected amongst Palestinians, and massive demonstrations were held in the West Bank's cities.[32] Inside Israel, the construction and transport sectors were hit particularly hard. Although there was some disagreement about the role of Israeli closures in the former industry,[33] it remains the case that a little over a hundred workers out of 65,000 from the West Bank turned up for work on the day, causing an estimated 130 million Shekels (£28 million) of losses.[34] The Israeli Transport Ministry reported that around 10 per cent of drivers did not work on that day, while the Egged bus company had to cancel 'nearly 300 journeys'.[35]

If the strike was primarily political in character, and designed to force the Israeli state to de-escalate in both Gaza and Jerusalem, this economic hit does point to the failure of the Labour Zionist attempts to impose a total policy of Palestinian exclusion from the Israeli labour market. Even if this dependence remains limited to specific sectors, this failure has implications, as the Dignity Strike demonstrates, for the Palestinian Liberation struggle. Sobhi Samour's remark, in the context of the Israeli state's continued demand for Palestinian workers throughout the COVID-19 pandemic, is relevant here also: '[A] materialist appraisal of Israel's demand for Palestinian labour would acknowledge that as long as such demand exists ... Israel's settler-colonial strategy of elimination is kept in check.'[36]

During the strike a statement, known as the *Dignity and Hope Manifesto*, was issued.[37] It understood the significance of what it called the 'Unity Intifada' as a new moment in the Palestinian people's long-term struggle for liberation from Zionist settler colonial rule. It is worth quoting in full:

Here we are, writing a new chapter of courage and pride, in which we tell a story of justice and of the truth that no level of Israeli colonial repression can erase, however cruel and brutal that repression may be.

The story of truth is a simple one in our land: the truth is that Palestinians are one people, one society. Zionist gangs forced out most of our people, it stole our homes and destroyed our villages. Then Zionism decided to shred what remained of Palestine, isolating us and separating us in small strips of our land. They tried to turn us into different societies, each living apart, each in its own separate prison. That is how Zionism has sought to control us, that is how they worked to fragment our political will, and to prevent a united struggle in the face of racist settler colonialism in all of Palestine.

This is how Israel imprisoned us in prisons of isolation; some of us caged in the 'Oslo prison' in the West Bank, some in the 'citizenship prison' in the part of Palestine occupied in 1948, some of us isolated by the monstrous siege and ongoing, devastating assault [in] the 'Gaza prison,' some of us isolated under the systematic Judaization campaigns [in] the 'Jerusalem prison,' and some isolated from Palestine altogether, dispersed across all corners of the globe.

It is now time for this tragedy to end.

In these days, we write a new chapter, a chapter of a united Intifada that seeks our one and only goal: reuniting Palestinian society in all of its different parts; reuniting our political will, and our means of struggle to confront Zionism throughout Palestine.

This long Intifada is, at its heart, an Intifada of consciousness. It is an Intifada to overthrow ... the filth of quietude and defeatism. Because of it, the brave generations to come will have been raised, once again, on the fundamental principle of our unity. It will stand in the face of all the elites working to deepen and entrench the divisions in and between our communities. This Intifada will be a long one in the streets of Palestine and in streets around the world; an intifada that fights the hand of injustice wherever it tries to reach, that fights the batons of cruel regimes wherever they try to strike. This is an Intifada of bared chests and foreheads held high armed with revolutionary goals, deep knowledge and understanding, and the organizational toil and commitment of every individual and collective in the face [of] the bullets of the Israeli occupation wherever they are fired.

Long Live a United Palestine.
Long Live the Intifada of Unity.

While the movement and the strike were undoubtedly a watershed moment, which continues to reverberate at the time of writing in political movements opposing the PA in the West Bank, activists and commentators recognised that it did not come out of nowhere. On the one hand, its roots were located in previous rounds of struggle, including the Palestinian general strikes of 1936 and 1987, the latter of which took place in the context of the First Intifada – the most important and extensive Palestinian uprising since the 1930s.[38] On the other hand, the current wave of struggle was also understood in relation to a series of social movements in the last decade that have shared a number of characteristics, including: their ability to mobilise across the entire Palestinian population, regardless of settler colonial divisions; their grassroots character, and their independence from (or direct opposition to) the framework and institutions developed as part of the Oslo process, such as the so-called 'two state solution', the privileging of nation-building over liberation, and the Palestinian Authority.

Even before the latest uprising started, Amahl Bishara noted that new forms of Palestinian movements were developing,[39] for example, the Great March of Return (GMR) in Gaza, as well as the Tal'at movement. The

GMR was a grassroots movement in Gaza, which called on Palestinians to march to the Strip's edges to protest the ongoing military siege, as well as demand the right to return to their lands. The first march was called to coincide with Land Day – an annual day of Palestinian resistance, which marks the struggle of Palestinians in the Galilee in 1976 against mass landgrabs, when Palestinians marched, struck and resisted the renewed dispossession of their land. Bishara notes that the connection was also made in the name chosen by the organisers of the GMR, which

> … echoes the name of annual marches inside Israel organized by the Association for the Defence of the Rights of the Internally Displaced (ADRID) and its partners. The Gaza March of Return was both a march against siege and for the right of return. In this way, it spoke to the most urgent demand of Palestinians in Gaza as well as one of the most central Palestinian claims.[40]

When Israel repeatedly opened fire on unarmed pro-testors, killing 59 people in a single day, Palestinians mobilised across historic Palestine, including in Haifa and Ramallah. There too, Bishara points out, protestors faced violent repression at the hands of the Israeli and PA police, respectively, which further unified their struggles.

The second example Bishara gives is the feminist Tal'at (Stepping Out) movement, which looked to unify Pal-estinian women and their allies, in the aftermath of the murder of Israa Ghrayeb by her family. The movement mobilised for the transformation of gender relations within Palestine society. At the same time, building connections between women in Gaza, the West Bank and within the Green Line, Tal'at activists raised the connection between gender-based violence, neoliberal reforms and Israeli colonialism. Activists and organisers Hala Marshood and Riya Al-Sanah explain:

Tal'at is part of [a] revolutionary feminist tradition. Our movement is shaped by our lived experience of more than seven decades of Israeli settler-colonial violence. As a people, we are stripped of our most basic rights and needs while crippling our collective development and resistance. This reality compels us to analyse experiences of violence – in their varied forms – as a social and political matter that must be dealt with at their root and collectively, as a society … In its initial call out, Tal'at called to seize the opportunity to build Palestinian, de-fragmented feminist solidarity. In this, Tal'at actively pushes against the tide of geographical, political and social fragmentation engulfing the Palestinian landscape, a process accelerated with the neoliberal-state-building process cemented by the Oslo Accords of 1993.[41]

Hawari mentions still other movements in the lineage of the most recent uprising, such as the movements in 2011, spurred on by the wider Arab Spring, demanding political unity between Palestinian factions, those that challenged the Prawer Plan in 2013, and those that called for an end to the PA-imposed sanctions on Gaza.[42]

Through this – necessarily partial – overview of Palestinian responses to the intensifying Israeli colonial violence and dispossession, in the spring of 2021, what emerges is the importance of understanding the ongoing nature of Indigenous resistance to settler colonialism. Although the settler colonial project in Palestine has not yet been defeated, let alone reversed, telling *only* the story of conquest and dispossession, fails to identify historical continuities and the centrality of previous forms of resistance in making the contemporary iterations of the liberation struggle possible. If Palestinians today are able to develop these unified responses to Israel's assaults, it is because of all the previous rounds of struggle, from which they are able to draw, and which have kept the memory and the possibility of liberation alive. Furthermore, isolating each round of struggle from previous ones, risks reinforcing the idea that they are isolated moments, blips in the larger picture of Israeli domination, rather than the next step in a longer process towards decolonisation, from the river to the sea.

The way these new iterations of the Palestinian liberation struggle are framed, also points to the connections that activists and organisers are making between their specific, settler colonial, context and the wider, global, struggles against exploitation and oppression. By locating their activism within international movements against sexism, oppressive regimes, or capitalism – as Tal'at and the *Dignity and Hope Manifesto* did – they are inscribing their own struggle within ongoing efforts for our world's systematic and radical transformation. In doing so, Palestinian organisers are giving practical echoes to Glen S. Coulthard's words, written in the context of the Indigenous struggles in North America: 'For Indigenous nations to live, capitalism must die. And for capitalism to die, we must actively participate in the construction of Indigenous alternatives to it.'[43]

WATER IS LIFE

In 2016, thousands of Indigenous people set up protest camps in the Standing Rock reservation and on the historic lands of the Oceti Sakowin – often referred to as the Sioux nation by European settlers. They were protesting against the construction of the Dakota access underground oil pipeline, the route of which cuts through ancient burial grounds, crosses unceded Indigenous land, and passes under the Missouri River (twice), endangering underground aquifers and water supplies. In fact, the US Army Corp of Engineers – in charge of the project – had rerouted the pipeline from its original course, in order to avoid crossing the river close to a majority White town (Bismarck), and thus endangering its water supply.[44] However, the US Army Corps' concerns, it seems, did not extend to the Oceti Sakowin. Over 300 different Indigenous nations resisting this process were joined by non-Indigenous activists, international solidarity delegations, and even local farmers similarly concerned about the potential implications for their water supplies. At its height, the camp became the state's tenth largest city, welcoming between 10,000 and 15,000 people.[45]

The movement's key slogan – *Mni Wiconi*/Water is Life – captured the connected struggles on which the #NoDAPL movement was built. Water protectors, as its participants were known, were not only fighting against the pipeline's imposition across Indigenous land. This was also a struggle for the environment, against extractive practices, and for a different relationship with the world around us. By foregrounding Indigenous leadership and concepts, the movement put the immediate conflict squarely within a much longer struggle against ongoing settler colonial dispossession and capitalist destruction of nature. As Nick Estes notes, 'protestors ... weren't simply against a pipeline; they also stood for something greater: the continuation of life on a planet ravaged by capitalism. This reflected the Lakota and Dakota philosophy of Mitakuye Oyasin, meaning "all my relations" or "we are all related."'[46] Theirs was a struggle against settler colonialism, capitalist accumulation, and ecological destruction. The state responded to it by declaring a state of emergency, violently repressing and mass-arresting demonstrators, and imposing the pipeline through sheer force.

There was also a regional context to this process. From the late 2000s onwards, a boom in shale oil and tar sands extraction redrew the energy politics across North America: 'US domestic crude oil production skyrocketed from 2008 to 2016—an 88 percent increase.'[47] On both sides of the border between Canada and the United States, this black gold rush brought the settler states into direct confrontation with Indigenous peoples. Natural resources were either directly located on Indigenous land, or pipelines, railroads, as well as other necessary infrastructure for their extraction and circulation were slated to cut through it.[48] The ecological consequences have been devastating across the board. In Canada, for example:

... tar sands extraction – by companies such as Suncor Energy, ConocoPhillips, ExxonMobil, and Shell Canada – has poisoned water, land, air, plants, animals, and people. Duck and moose – staple foods of many Indigenous communities – have become contaminated with toxins, and harvests of wild berries and plants have been decimated.[49]

If, in certain cases, official leaderships were prepared to collaborate with capital and the state, the defence of land and water became a central mobilising factor for mass Indigenous-led social movements. Before #NoDAPL, other Indigenous campaigns have similarly challenged pipeline construction, the extraction of resources, and the continued dispossession of Indigenous lands. Most notably, in 2012, Indigenous people in Canada mobilised under the banner of 'Idle No More'. Resisting what was called the Jobs and Growth Act (also known as Bill C-45), Indigenous activists highlighted the joint threat of environmental damage – once again, largely to water – as well as the direct assault on Indigenous land rights that the legislation represented. As Coulthard points out, the Bill

... unilaterally undermines Aboriginal and treaty rights by making it easier for First Nations' band councils to lease out reserve lands with minimal community input or support, by gutting environmental protection for lakes and rivers, and by reducing the number of resource development projects that would have required environmental assessment under previous legislation. Bill

C-45 thus represents the latest instalment of Canada's longstanding policy of colonial dispossession.[50]

The Idle No More movement was the result of two inter-related initiatives. On the one hand, the awareness-raising campaign by three Indigenous and one non-Indigenous woman opposing the Bill – Nina Wilson, Sylvia McAdam, Jessica Gordon and Sheelah McLean – led to growing discontent. On the other, in December 2012, 'Chief Theresa Spence of the Attawapiskat Cree Nation began a hunger strike to protest the deplorable living conditions on her reserve in northern Ontario.'[51] These twin developments led to a much wider opposition movement across the country – and beyond. Teach-ins, demonstrations and blockades sprung up across Canada. The Aamjiwnaag First Nation, for example, blocked rail tracks in Ontario for a full two weeks in late December 2012. By mid-January 2013, 'railway barricades [were] erected in Manitoba, Ontario, and British Columbia; [there were] highway and bridge stoppages in British Columbia, Ontario, New Brunswick, and Alberta; as well as … marches, flash-mob round-dances, drumming, and prayer circles.'[52]

Once again, while the movement's immediate focus was opposition to Bill C-45, it raised much wider issues about environmental degradation, capitalist accumulation and settler colonial domination. In Coulthard's words, '[b]uilding on the inspirational work of these women, what originally began as an education campaign against a repugnant piece of federal legislation … transformed into a grassroots struggle to transform the colonial relationship itself.'[53] The wider implications of the movement were visible both in the demands raised and some of its outcomes. For example, Chief Theresa Spence ended her hunger strike following the publication of a 'Declaration of Commitment', which, among other points, called for

> ... a 'national inquiry' into the hundreds of cases of murdered and missing Aboriginal women that have gone unsolved in Canada; improving Aboriginal education and housing; fully implementing the United Nations Declaration on the Rights of Indigenous Peoples; reform of the federal government's comprehensive lands claims policy; the establishment of an implementation framework for First Nations' treaty rights; and, of course, a comprehensive review of Bill C-45, undertaken with meaningful consultation with Aboriginal peoples.[54]

Indigenous people across North America also held protests and rallies – laying the foundation for the spread of resistance across the region. Idle No More, much like #NoDAPL, drew wide solidarity from non-Indigenous people, ecological activists and international groups. In the words of Kim Tallbear, '[t]he view is that Indigenous movements do this not only for Indigenous peoples, but for everyone.'[55] Nor have these struggles – or the pipelines they oppose – ended. Amongst others, the Wet'suwet'en First Nation has mobilised against the imposition of TC Energy's Coastal Gaslink Pipeline on their unceded land,[56] while the Ojibwe campaigned against the construction of Enbridge pipelines cutting through their land and endangering water resources.[57]

As the examples given above demonstrate – and the specific points of the Declaration articulate – women played a key role in the mobilisations. The issue of gendered oppression was central to both movements' demands and practices, and informed their understanding of the multiple structures of oppression they faced, foregrounding once more the gendered character of settler rule and dispossession. The connection between assault on land, environmental destruction, and violence against Indigenous women was repeatedly made by activists. The establishment of the 'man camps' on which extractive industries on Indigenous land depend, for example, systematically lead to sharp increases in sexual assault and violence against Indigenous women.[58] Nor are these camps alone. Border towns, which function as establishments somewhere between settlements and military outposts on the edges of Indigenous reservations, have equally long histories of gendered violence carried out against women as well as Two-Spirit people – largely in complete impunity.[59] It is then perhaps unsurprising that women played such a central role as organisers, initiators and leaders in both movements – much the same was true in the context of the Black Lives Matter movement, as Tallbear points out.[60]

As in the case of Palestine, these struggles are best understood within the longer context of settler colonialism and Indigenous dispossession. This is so not only because of the historic imposition of settler colonial rule, which makes the contemporary imposition of extractive industries possible, but also because the resistance to these projects identified them as the latest iterations of ongoing

Indigenous dispossession, and were able to rely on previous rounds of Indigenous resistance in responding to them. This idea is captured powerfully in Nick Estes' book *Our History is the Future*: if an alternative future is to be built – free from exploitation and oppression, capitalism and settler colonialism, the destruction of the world and its people – it will need to account for, and understand, the past. Its crimes and horrors, of course, but also the alternative ways to live, with and in the world, that it signals.

Estes traces the 200-year-long process of settler colonial violence meted out against the Oceti Sakowin, from the first military encounters with the United States, following the 1803 Louisiana Purchase, to the present: a history of genocide, conquest, dispossession and displacement, but also one of ongoing resistance. While the US state declared the frontier closed after the massacre at Wounded Knee, the struggle against settler colonial violence and domination did not end. In every generation, the struggle renewed itself: resistance against termination, assimilation and allotment. Resistance against forced displacement when the US Army Corps of Engineers flooded much of Oceti Sakowin reservation land in order to build a series of massive dams, designed to power the area's White settler cities. Resistance against the state as well as against Indigenous collaborating elites in the 1973 occupation of Wounded Knee, by the American Indian Movement. Resistance against the erasure of Indigenous sovereignty and the rejection by the US state of nation-to-nation treaty making, which took activists to Geneva and laid the groundwork for the 2007 UN Declaration on the Rights of Indigenous People. Each iteration of the liberation struggle lay the foundations for the next, keeping simultaneously the memory and the possibility of a different world alive. Estes also identified this simultaneous presence of the past and the future in #NoDAPL:

The encampments were about more than stopping a pipeline. Scattered and separated during invasion, the long-awaited reunification of all seven nations of Dakota-, Nakota-, and Lakota-speaking peoples hadn't occurred in more than a hundred years, or at least seven generations … Only in stories had I heard about the Oceti Sakowin uniting, its fire lit, and the seven tipis or lodges – each representing a nation – arranged in the shape [of] a buffalo horn. Historically, this reunification had happened in times of celebration, for annual sun dances, large multi-tribal trading fairs, and buffalo hunts. But the last time was also in a time of war – to resist invasion.[61]

Reflecting on the camps, and drawing direct comparisons with forms of self-government during the First Palestinian Intifada, Estes further points out the systemic implications of this most recent iteration of Indigenous resistance, in the Missouri River basin:

Free food, free education, free health care, free legal aid, a strong sense of community, safety, and security were guaranteed to all. Most reservations in the United States don't have access to these services, nor do most poor people. Yet, in the absence of empire, people came together to help each other, to care for one another. The

#NoDAPL camps were designed according to need, not profit. (There were no prisons or armed bodies of the state.) That's what separated them from the world of cops, settlers, and oil companies that surrounded them. Capitalism is not merely an economic system, but also a social system. And it was here abundantly evident that Indigenous social systems offered a radically different way of relating to other people and the world.

The central role that settler colonial dispossession and accumulation play, in shaping capitalism and expanding its global reach, as we have seen, also underscores these systemic implications of ongoing Indigenous movements for liberation. Across the world, by opposing further resource extraction, dispossession of land, and the violent accumulation of profit at the detriment of people, Indigenous struggles are pointing towards a different – and better – world for all. By maintaining memories of the worlds that were, as well as the worlds that can be, Indigenous resistance concerns us all, if we are to find a way out of the multiple crises – ecological, political, economic – that beset the global present.

To understand settler colonialism, then, as co-constitutive of power structures that continue to dominate us all, is also to engage differently with the ongoing struggles against it. These are not isolated, particularistic, or – worse – xenophobic movements opposed to progress and strangers, as many conservative commentators would have us believe. These are movements that are building, with others, alternatives to colonial, racist, sexist, and capitalist domination. To understand settler colonialism in this way, is then also to join Indigenous blockades and demonstrations in defence of land, water and people. It is opposing settler wars that aim to accumulate land by murdering and displacing Indigenous people. It is supporting and implementing the Palestinian demands for Boycott, Divestment and Sanctions (BDS) against those institutions and businesses that continue to impose – and profit from – Palestinian dispossession.[62] It is also to build practical connections between ongoing Indigenous movements for liberation and other struggles against climate catastrophe, exploitation and oppression everywhere. It is opposing business as usual, refusing existing nation states as our political horizon, and reaffirming that alternative modes of existence, production and relations with the natural word are possible.

Identifying how structures of domination have been built, imposed and reproduced, is necessary in order to dismantle them. But doing so, while crucial, is not enough. Only through sustained struggle, through the building of practical solidarities in action, through principled grassroots organising, can alternatives take shape, grow and emerge as viable challenges to the power of states and capital. No blueprint can be offered, in these pages, or any others. Alternatives must be built through struggle – every time anew.

Notes

INTRODUCTION

1. David Agren and Sam Jones (2021), 'Zapatistas Set Sail for Spain on Mission of Solidarity and Rebellion', *The Guardian*, 4 May, www.theguardian.com/world/2021/may/04/zapatistas-set-sail-for-spain-on-mission-of-solidarity-and-rebellion

2. Quoted in Jérôme Baschet (2021), 'The "Zapatista Invasion" has Begun!', *ROARmag*, 11 May, https://roarmag.org/essays/zapatista-mexico-europe-trip. See the video here: https://vimeo.com/566701998

3. Subcomandante Insurgente Moisés (2020), 'Part Six: A Mountain on the High Seas', *Communique from the Indigenous Revolutionary Clandestine Committee General Command of the Zapatista Army for National Liberation*, 5 October, https://enlacezapatista.ezln.org.mx/2020/10/07/part-six-a-mountain-on-the-high-seas/

4. Ibid.

5. Ibid.

6. On liberal recognition and Indigenous struggles, see Audra Simpson (2014), *Mohawk Interruptus: Political Life Across the Borders of Settler States*, Durham: Duke University Press, and Glen Sean Coulthard (2014), *Red Skin, White Masks: Rejecting the Colonial Politics of Recognition*. Minneapolis: University of Minnesota Press.

7. Manu Vimalassery, Juliana Hu Pegues and Alyosha Goldstein (2016), 'On Colonial Unknowing', *Theory & Event*, 19(4), p. 3.

8. Nor is this a new phenomenon. See Jean M. O'Brien (2010), *Firsting and Lasting: Writing Indians out of Existence in New England*, Minneapolis: Minnesota Press.

9. Patrick Wolfe (1999), *Settler Colonialism and the Transformation of Anthropology: The Politics and Poetics of an Ethnographic Event*, London: Cassell, p. 3.

10. Arrighi Emmanuel (1972), 'White-Settler Colonialism and the Myth of Investment Imperialism', *New Left Review*, 73, 1972, p. 37.

11. On the tendency to erase the continuation of settler colonial rule in the US, see, for example, Jody A. Byrd (2011), *The Transit of Empire: Indigenous Critiques of Colonialism*, Minneapolis: University of Minnesota Press.

12. George Jabbour (1970), *Settler Colonialism in Southern Africa and the Middle East*, Beirut: Palestine Liberation Organisation Research Centre, pp. 7–8.

13. Corey Snelgrove, Rita Kaur Dhamoon and Jeff Corntassel (2014), 'Unsettling Settler Colonialism: The Discourse and Politics of Settlers, and Solidarity with Indigenous Nations', *Decolonization: Indigeneity, Education and Society*, 3(2), p. 27.

14. Rana Barakat (2018), 'Writing/Righting Palestine Studies: Settler Colonialism, Indigenous Sovereignty and Resisting the Ghost(s) of History', *Settler Colonial Studies*, 8(3), pp. 349–63. Older debates can also be traced in Indigenous, settler and European literature. For the sake of clarity and space, the book will focus on the contemporary era.

15. Fayez A. Sayegh (1965), *Zionist Colonialism in Palestine*, Beirut: Research Centre of the Palestinian Liberation Organization. Sayegh's text has more recently been reproduced in part in the 2012 special issue of *Settler Colonial Studies*, 2(1), edited by Omar Jabary Salamanca, Mezna Qato, Kareem Rabie and Sobhi Samour: 'Past is Present: Settler Colonialism in Palestine'.

16. Rosemary Sayigh (2007 [1979]), *The Palestinians: From Peasants to Revolutionaries*, London: Zed Books. In fact, Sayegh also highlights the issue of elimination in *Zionist Colonialism in Palestine*, on pp. 26–7.

17. See also Brenna Bhandar and Rafeef Ziadah (2016), 'Acts and Omissions: Framing Settler Colonialism in Palestine Studies', *Jadaliyya*, 14 January, www.jadaliyya.com/Details/ 32857/Acts-and-Omissions-Framing-Settler-Colonialism-in-Palestine-Studies

18. See for example, Vine Deloria Jr. (1988 [1969]) *Custer Died for Your Sins: An Indian Manifesto*, Norman: University of Oklahoma Press and Howard Adams (1975) *Prison of Grass: Canada from a Native Point of View*, Toronto: New Press, and (retrospectively) Paul Chaat Smith and Robert Warrior (1997), *Like A Hurricane: The Indian Movement from Alcatraz to Wounded Knee*, New York: The New Press. See also J. Kēhaulani Kauanui (2016),'"A Structure, Not an Event": Settler Colonialism and Enduring Indigeneity', *Lateral*, 5(1), pp. 1–8, for a short overview and a discussion of the contribution of Indigenous writers, also in the context of settler colonialism in Hawaii. For a short overview of AIM and the Red Power movement, see chapter 5 in Nick Estes (2019), *Our History Is the Future: Standing Rock versus the Dakota Access Pipeline, and the Long Tradition of Indigenous Resistance*, London: Verso.

19. Paul Chaat Smith and Robert Warrior (1997), *Like A Hurricane: The Indian Movement from Alcatraz to Wounded Knee*, New York: The New Press, pp. 99–100; Roxanne Dubar-Ortiz (2016), 'The Relationship between Marxism and Indigenous Struggles and Implications of the Theoretical Framework for International Indigenous Struggles', *Historical Materialism,* 24(3), pp. 76–91.

20. Omar Jabary Salamanca, Mezna Qato, Kareem Rabie and Sobhi Samour (2013), 'Past is Present: Settler Colonialism in Palestine', *Settler Colonial Studies* 2(1), p. 3.

21. This argument is based on Sai Englert (2020), 'Settlers, Workers, and the Logic of Accumulation by Dispossession', *Antipode*, 52(6), pp. 1647–66.

22. Patrick Wolfe (1999), *Settler Colonialism and the Transformation of Anthropology: The Politics and Poetics of an Ethnographic Event*, London: Cassell, p. 3.

23. Patrick Wolfe (2006), 'Settler Colonialism and the Elimination of the Native', *Journal of Genocide Research*, 8(4), p. 393.

24. Wolfe, *Settler Colonialism and the Transformation of Anthropology*, pp. 1–2.

25. Lorenzo Veracini (2010), *Settler Colonialism: A Theoretical Overview*, New York: Palgrave Macmillan, p. 34.

26. See, for example, Mike Davis (2002), *Late Victorian Holocausts: El Niño Famines and the Making of the Third World.* London: Verso; or John Newsinger (2010), *The Blood Never Dried: A People's History of the British Empire.* London: Bookmarks.

27. Shannon Speed (2017), 'Structures of Settler Capitalism in Abya Yala', *American Quarterly*, 69(4), p. 784.

28. Robin D.G. Kelley (2017), 'The Rest of Us: Rethinking Settler and Native', *American Quarterly*, 69(2), p. 269.

29. Patrick Wolfe (2001), 'Land, Labour, and Difference: Elementary Structures of Race', *American Historical Review*, 106(3), p. 868 n.7.

30. Lorenzo Veracini (2013), 'The Other Shift: Settler Colonialism, Israel and The Occupation', *Journal of Palestine Studies*, 42(2), pp. 26–42.

31. Barakat, *Writing/Righting Palestine Studies*, pp. 350–51.

32. Ibid., p. 351.

33. Jean M. O'Brien (2017), 'Tracing Settler Colonialism's Eliminatory Logic in Traces of History', *American Quarterly*, 69(2), pp. 249–55.

34. Ibid., p. 251; original emphasis.

35. For more on the Japanese settler colonial project, see, for example, Hyung Gu Lynn (2005), 'Malthusian Dreams, Colonial Imaginary: The Oriental Development Company and Japanese Emigration to Korea'; Prasenjit Duara (2005) 'Between Empire and Nation: Settler Colonialism in

Manchukuo'; Alexis Dudden (2005) 'Mission Législatrice: Extraterritoriality and Japan's Legal Mission to Korea in the Early Twentieth Century'; Jun Uchida (2005) 'Brokers of Empire: Japanese and Korean Business Elites in Colonial Korea', and Lori Watt (2005) 'Imperial Remnants: The Repatriates in Postwar Japan'; all in Caroline Elkins and Susan Pedersen (eds), *Settler Colonialism in the Twentieth Century: Project, Practices, Legacies*, New York: Routledge. For recent applications of settler colonialism to India's policies in Kashmir, see Samreen Mushtaq and Mudasir Amin (2021), '"We will memorise our home": Exploring Settler Colonialism as an Interpretive Framework for Kashmir', *Third World Quarterly*, 42(12), pp. 3012–29, and Zainab Ramahi and Azadeh Shahshahani (2020), 'Destroying to Replace: Settler Colonialism from Kashmir to Palestine', *Verso Blog*, 10 August, www.versobooks.com/blogs/4817-destroying-to-replace-settler-colonialism-from-kashmir-to-palestine. For uses of the settler colonial paradigm in China, see, for example, Mette H. Hansen (2005), *Frontier People: Han Settlers in Minority Areas of China*, London: C. Hurst; Jonathan Mirsky (2009), 'Tibet: China's Gaza?', *Asian Affairs*, 40(3), pp. 353–60; Carole McGranahan (2019), 'Chinese Settler Colonialism: Empire and Life in the Tibetan Borderlands', in Stéphane Gros (ed.) *Frontier Tibet: Patterns of Change in the Sino-Tibetan Borderlands*. Amsterdam: Amsterdam University Press, and Jonathan Brooks (2021), 'Settler Colonialism, Primitive Accumulation, and Biopolitics in Xinjiang, China', available at SSRN: https://ssrn.com/abstract=3965577 or http://dx.doi.org/10.2139/ssrn.3965577

36. Gerald Horne (2018), *The Apocalypse of Settler Colonialism: the Roots of Slavery, White Supremacy, and Capitalism in the Seventeenth-Century North America and the Caribbean*, New York: Monthly Review Press; Gerald Horne (2020), *The Dawning of the Apocalypse: the Roots of Slavery, White*

Supremacy, Settler Colonialism and Capitalism in the long Sixteenth Century, New York: Monthly Review Press.

CHAPTER 1 ACCUMULATE, ACCUMULATE!

1. It speaks volumes about the contempt in which indigenous life continues to be held that the invasion of lands inhabited by millions of people can continue to be described in history books and popular culture as a 'discovery'.
2. This long historical process has been captured powerfully by Alex Anievas and Kerem Nişancıoğlu (2015), *How the West Came to Rule: The Geopolitical Origins of Capitalism*, London: Pluto Press.
3. As Jairus Banaji has argued, the existence of forms of capital accumulation pre-date the emergence of capitalism as the dominant global mode of production. See Jairus Banaji (2020), *A Brief History of Commercial Capitalism*, Chicago: Haymarket Books, and Jairus Banaji (2011), *Theory as History: Essays on Modes of Production and Exploitation*, Chicago: Haymarket Books.
4. Karl Marx (1867), *Capital*, Volume 1, Chapter 24, www.marxists.org/archive/marx/works/1867-c1/ch24.htm#23a
5. For a practical application of this approach to capital accumulation, within a settler colonial context, see, for example, Jonathan Nitzan and Shimshon Bichler (2002), *The Global Political Economy of Israel*, London: Pluto Press.
6. Marx (1867), *Capital*, Volume 1, Chapter 31, www.marxists.org/archive/marx/works/1867-c1/ch31.htm
7. Ibid., Chapter 26, www.marxists.org/archive/marx/works/1867-c1/ch26.htm
8. Anievas and Nişancıoğlu (2015), *How the West Came to Rule*, p. 9.
9. See Nancy Marie Brown (2010), *The Abacus and The Cross*. New York: Basic Books, for an overview of these debates.
10. The continued use today of the West Indies to describe the Caribbean region is a remnant of this mistake.

11. David Graeber (2011) offers an important account of the central role of debt in encouraging the rapacious behaviour of the colonisers across the continent in his *Debt – The First 5000 Years,* New York: Melville House.

12. Horne, *The Dawning of the Apocalypse*, p. 16.

13. See Sidney Mintz (1986), *Sweetness and Power: The Place of Sugar in Modern History*, London: Penguin Books, about the role of sugar in reshaping both the colonised and colonising economies; and Eduardo Galeano, *Open Veins of Latin America*, London: Serpent's Tail, about sugar's continued influence on the region's agriculture and international trade in the twentieth century.

14. Eduardo Galeano (2009), *Open Veins of Latin America*, London: Serpent's Tail, p. 15.

15. Ibid., p. 38.

16. Roxanne Dunbar-Ortiz (2014), *An Indigenous Peoples' History of the United States*, Boston: Beacon Press, p. 40.

17. Ibid., p. 40.

18. Horne, *The Dawning of the Apocalypse*.

19. Ibid., p. 19.

20. Ibid., p. 14.

21. Anievas and Nişancıoğlu, *How the West Came to Rule*, p. 137; original emphasis.

22. For an overview of Spanish and Portuguese expansion in the Americas see D.K Fieldhouse (1982 [1966]), *The Colonial Empires: A Comparative Survey from the 18th Century*, New York: Dell, pp. 11–34. Later chapters – especially 2 and 5 – will also discuss the continued resistance of Indigenous people post-military conquest, to this day.

23. See Jeffrey R. Webber (2011), *From Rebellion to Reform in Bolivia: Class Struggle, Indigenous Liberation, and the Politics of Evo Morales*, Chicago: Haymarket, for an excellent account of the interactions between the revolutionary and electoral processes. See also Benjamin Dangl (2019), *The Five Hundred Year Rebellion: Indigenous Movements and the Decolonization of History in Bolivia*, Chico: AK Press,

for a discussion on the connection between contemporary struggles and previous rounds of indigenous resistance.

24. Kevin Ochieng Okoth (2020), 'The Flatness of Blackness: Afro-Pessimism and the Erasure of Anti-Colonial Thought', *Salvage*, 16 January, https://salvage.zone/issue-seven/the-flatness-of-blackness-afro-pessimism-and-the-erasure-of-anti-colonial-thought/

25. Patrick Wolfe (2016), *Traces of History: Elementary Structures of Race*, London: Verso, p. 125.

26. Galeano, *Open Veins*, captures powerfully how colonial regimes moved indigenous and enslaved labour around the settler colonies as they extracted natural resources and cultivated land to exhaustion.

27. Fieldhouse, *The Colonial Empires*, p. 23.

28. John Tutino (2017), *The Mexican Heartland: How Communities Shaped Capitalism, a Nation, and World History, 1500–2000*, Princeton: Princeton University Press, p. 38.

29. Anievas and Nişancıoğlu (2015), *How the West Came to Rule*, p. 131.

30. Ibid.

31. Ibid.

32. Ibid., p. 132.

33. Ibid., p. 133. On the role of witchcraft accusations in repressing women and transforming gender roles, see Silvia Federici (2004), *Caliban and the Witch: Women, the Body and Primitive Accumulation*, New York: Autonomedia.

34. Galeano, *Open Veins*, p. 36.

35. Ibid., pp. 32, 39.

36. Ibid., p. 23.

37. Anievas and Nişancıoğlu, *How the West Came to Rule*, p. 135.

38. Tutino, *The Mexican Heartland*, p. 5.

39. Anievas and Nişancıoğlu, *How the West Came to Rule*, p. 325, n. 137.

40. Horne, *The Dawning of the Apocalypse*, p 29.

41. Anievas and Nişancıoğlu, *How the West Came to Rule*, p. 143.
42. Ibid., p. 143.
43. Ibid., p. 145.
44. Banaji, *A Brief History*, p. 50.
45. For an overview of the history of commercial capitalism and its consequences for production, see Banaji, *A Brief History*. For the connection between this global trade and the rise of capitalism in the Netherlands, see Pepijn Brandon (2016), *War, Capital, and the Dutch State (1588–1795)*, Chicago: Haymarket Books.
46. Anievas and Nişancıoğlu, *How the West Came to Rule*, p. 151.
47. See Mintz, *Sweetness and Power*.
48. Anievas and Nişancıoğlu, *How the West Came to Rule*, p. 159.
49. Ibid., p. 161. In addition, for a classic study of the role of slavery in the emergence of capitalism see Eric Williams (1994[1944]), *Capitalism and Slavery*, Chapel Hill: University of North Carolina Press. See also C.L.R. James (2001 [1938]), *The Black Jacobins: Toussaint L'Ouverture and the San Domingo Revolution*, London: Penguin Books. Not only is this a classic study of slave economies and revolt in the Caribbean, James also makes the argument that the mass and collective nature of enslaved labour on sugar plantations and in their factories was the closest thing to an industrial proletariat, before the industrial revolution in England.
50. Horne, *The Apocalypse of Settler Colonialism*, p. 37.
51. Anievas and Nişancıoğlu, *How the West Came to Rule*, p. 152.
52. See Horne, *The Apocalypse of Settler Colonialism*, for an account of the growing importance of African enslaved labour in the English American colonies throughout the seventeenth century.
53. Wolfe, *Traces of History*, p. 21.

54. See Horne's *The Dawning of the Apocalypse* for a detailed overview of the differences between Spanish and English forms of difference.

55. Donald Denoon (1986), *Settler Capitalism: The Dynamics of Dependent Development in the Southern Hemisphere*, Oxford: Oxford University Press.

56. For detailed overviews of these processes, see Jürgen Osterhammel (2014), *The Transformation of the World: A Global History of the Nineteenth Century*, Princeton: Princeton University Press, and James Belich (2011), *Replenishing the Earth: The Settler Revolution and the Rise of the Angloworld*, Oxford: Oxford University Press.

57. Anievas and Nişancıoğlu, *How the West Came to Rule*, p. 155.

58. Horne's, *The Dawning of the Apocalypse*, p. 12.

59. Mike Davis (2007) has powerfully captured the connection between colonial extraction of resources and mass famine in his, *The Late Victorian Holocaust: El Niño Famines and the Making of the Third World*. London: Verso.

60. See, for example, Horne's *The Apocalypse of Settler Colonialism* for an overview of this double bind for settlers stuck between greed and terror. In particular, pp. 129–41 give a powerful sense of slave rebellions in Jamaica and Barbados in the late seventeenth century.

61. C.L.R. James (2001), *The Black Jacobins: Toussaint L'Ouverture and the San Domingo Revolution*, London: Penguin Books, remains one of the best and most detailed account of the Haitian Revolution. There is also the excellent and more recent biography of Toussaint L'Ouverture: Sudhir Hazareesingh (2020), *Black Spartacus: The Epic Life of Toussaint Louverture*, London: Allen Lane.

62. John Bellamy Foster, Brett Clark and Hannah Holleman (2019), 'Capitalism and Robbery: The Expropriation of Land, Labour, and Corporeal Life', *Monthly Review*, 1 December, https://monthlyreview.org/2019/12/01/capitalism-and-robbery/

63. Lisa Lowe (2015), *The Intimacies of Four Continents*, Durham: Duke University Press, p. 37.

64. Both Iyko Day (2016), *Alien Capital – Asian Racialization and the Logic of Settler Colonial Capitalism*, Durham: Duke University Press, and Manu Karuka (2019), *Empire's Tracks: Indigenous Nations, Chinese Workers, and the Transcontinental Railroad*, Oakland: University of California Press, give detailed accounts of these workers' place in North American settler colonial expansion and racial regimes of control.

65. Denoon, *Settler Capitalism*.

66. Jonathan Hyslop (1999), 'The Imperial Working Class Makes Itself "White": White Labourism in Britain, Australia, and South Africa Before the First World War', University of Witwatersrand, Institute for Advanced Social Research, Seminar Paper 449, pp. 1–19.

67. Eric Hobsbawm (2007), *Age Of Capital 1848–1875*. London: Abacus, p. 150.

68. Belich, *Replenishing the Earth*, p. 108.

69. Karuka, *Empire's Tracks*, p. xiv.

70. Roxanne Dunbar-Ortiz, *An Indigenous Peoples' History*, p. 118.

71. Bellamy Foster, Clark and Holleman, 'Capitalism and Robbery'.

72. Roxanne Dunbar-Ortiz, *An Indigenous Peoples' History*, p. 140.

73. Ibid., p. 141.

74. Ibid.

75. Ibid., p. 142.

76. Deborah Cowan (2020), 'The Jurisdiction of Infrastructure – Circulation and Canadian Settler Colonialism', *The Funambulist*, 17, p. 16.

77. For more on Russian settler colonialism, see Alexander Morrison (2017), 'Russian Settler Colonialism', in Lorenzo Veracini and Ed Cavanagh (eds), *The Routledge Handbook of the History of Settler Colonialism*, Abingdon: Routledge, and

Robert Geraci (2008), 'Genocidal Impulses and Fantasies in Imperial Russia', in A. Dirk Moses (ed.), *Empire, Colony, Genocide: Conquest, Occupation, and Subaltern Resistance in World History*, New York: Berghahn. Interestingly, in his posthumously published *The Russian Revolution: A View from the Third World*, Walter Rodney points out the striking parallels between Russian settler colonialism in Central Asia and other European forms of settler colonialism in the US, Australia and South Africa. See Walter Rodney (2018), *The Russian Revolution: A View from the Third World*, London: Verso, pp. 155–6.

78. Belich, *Replenishing the Earth*, p. 379.

79. Karuka, *Empire's Tracks*, p. 53.

80. See Chapter 1 in Karuka, *Empire's Tracks*.

81. Ibid., pp. 52–7.

82. Ibid., p. 56. This process is also captured powerfully, in romanticised form, in Ousmane Sembene (1986), *Les Bouts de Bois de Dieu*, Paris: Presses Pocket. I am grateful to Cristiana Strava for introducing me to this book.

83. Denoon, *Settler Capitalism*.

84. For more on the Japanese settler colonial project, see the essays by Hyung Gu Lynn, Prasenjit Duara, Alexis Dudden, Lori Watt and Jun Uchida in Caroline Elkins and Susan Pedersen (eds), (2005), *Settler Colonialism in the Twentieth Century: Project, Practices, Legacies*. New York: Routledge.

85. Sir Ronald Storrs, quoted in Nu'man Abd Al Wahid (2012), 'An Account of the *Guardian*'s Racist Endorsement of the Balfour Declaration', *Mondoweiss*, 30 April, https://mondoweiss.net/2012/04/an-account-of-the-guardians-racist-endorsement-of-the-balfour-declaration/

86. On the Nakba see, amongst others, Walid Khalidi (1984), *Before Their Diaspora: A Photographic History of the Palestinians 1876–1948*, Washington, DC: Institute for Palestine Studies; Rashid Khalidi (1997), *Palestinian Identity: The Construction of Modern National Consciousness*, New York: Columbia University Press; Ibrahim Abu

Lughod (1987), *The Transformation of Palestine*, Evanston: Northwestern University Press; Elia Zureik (1979), *The Palestinians in Israel*, Abingdon: Routledge & Kegan Paul Books; Nur Masalha (2011), 'New History, Post-Zionism and Neo-Colonialism: A Critique of the Israeli "New Historians"', *Holy Land Studies*, 10(1), pp. 1–53, and Anaheed Al-Hardan (2016), *Palestinians in Syria: Nakba Memories of Shattered Communities*. New York: Columbia University Press.

87. Jeanne Marie Penvenne (2005), 'Settling against the Tide: The Layered Contradictions of Twentieth-Century Portuguese Settlement in Mozambique', in Caroline Elkins and Susan Pedersen (eds), *Settler Colonialism in the 20th Century: Project, Practices, Legacies*, New York: Routledge, p. 80.

88. See, for example, Gerald Horne (2019), *White Supremacy Confronted: U.S. Imperialism and Anti-Communism vs. the Liberation of Southern Africa from Rhodes to Mandela*, New York: International Publishers Co, amongst many others.

CHAPTER 2 DISPOSSESSING THE NATIVE

1. Roxanne Dunbar-Ortiz (2014), *An Indigenous People's History of the United States*, Boston: Beacon Press, p. 8.

2. Nick Estes (2019), *Our History Is the Future: Standing Rock versus the Dakota Access Pipeline, and the Long Tradition of Indigenous Resistance*, London: Verso, p. 40.

3. Quoted in Anievas and Nişancıoğlu, *How the West Came to Rule*, p. 322.

4. See ibid., pp. 16–31 for an overview of pre-invasion societies across the continent.

5. For a twentieth-century rehearsal of these arguments, with striking echoes of contemporary Zionist narratives in Palestine, see Anne-Marie Kriek (1989), 'South Africa Shouldn't be Singled Out', *The Christian Science Monitor*, 12 October, www.csmonitor.com/1989/1012/ekri.html

6. Lowe, *Intimacies of Four Continents*, pp. 9–11.

7. Dunbar-Ortiz, *An Indigenous People's History of the United States*, p. 60.

8. Ibid., p. 61.

9. Jody A. Byrd (2011), *The Transit of Empire: Indigenous Critiques of Colonialism*, Minneapolis: University of Minnesota Press, p. 198.

10. For a comparative study of the imposition of Indigenous reservations and their consequences, see below and Mahmood Mamdani, *Neither Settler nor Native: The Making and Unmaking of Permanent Minorities*, Cambridge: The Belknap Press of Harvard University Press.

11. Karl Marx (1887), *Capital*, Part VIII, Chapter 26, www.marxists.org/archive/marx/works/1867-c1/ch26.htm

12. Edward Said (2003 [1978]), *Orientalism*, London: Penguin Books, pp. 153–6.

13. For responses to Said's reading of Marx, see, for example, Aijaz Ahmad (1992), 'Marx on India: A Clarification', in his *In Theory: Classes, Nations and Literatures*, London: Verso, and Sadik Jalal al-'Azm (1980), 'Orientalism and Orientalism in Reverse', *Libcom.org*, https://libcom.org/library/orientalism-orientalism-reverse-sadik-jalal-al-%E2%80%99azm

14. For an overview of this argument, see, for example, Franklin Rosemont (1989), 'Karl Marx and the Iroquois', *Libcom.org*, https://libcom.org/library/karl-marx-iroquois-franklin-rosemont, and John Bellamy Foster, Brett Clark and Hannah Holleman (2020), 'Marx and the Indigenous', *Monthly Review*, https://monthlyreview.org/2020/02/01/marx-and-the-Indigenous/

15. Rosa Luxemburg (1951), *The Accumulation of Capital*, www.marxists.org/archive/luxemburg/1913/accumulation-capital/

16. David Harvey (2003), *The New Imperialism*, Oxford: Oxford University Press. For other contributions on this approach, see Silvia Federici (1998), *Caliban and the Witch: Women, the Body, and Primitive Accumulation*, New York: Autono-

media; Massimo De Angelis (2001), 'Marx and Primitive Accumulation: The Continuous Character of Capital's "Enclosures"', *The Commoner*, 2, pp. 1–22, and Michael Perelman (2000), *The Invention of Capitalism: Classical Political Economy and the Secret History of Primitive Accumulation*. Durham: Duke University Press.

17. See, for example, Vine Deloria, Jr. (2003), *God is Red: A Native View of Religion*, Wheat Ridge: Fulcrum Publishing, and Peter Kulchyski (2005), *Like the Sound of a Drum: Aboriginal Cultural Politics in Denendeh and Nunavut*, Winnipeg: University of Manitoba Press.

18. These approaches are echoed also in Brenna Bhandar's critique of abstraction and racial regimes of property, discussed in chapter 3.

19. Glen Sean Coulthard (2014), *Red Skin, White Masks: Rejecting the Colonial Politics of Recognition*, Minneapolis: University of Minnesota Press.

20. For another critique of the supposed developmental nature of settler colonialism, in a different context, see Sara Roy (1987), 'The Gaza Strip: A Case of Economic De-Development', *Journal of Palestine Studies*, 17(1), pp. 56–88.

21. In the Canadian context, see Cole Harris (2004), 'How Did Colonialism Dispossess? Comments from an Edge of Empire', *Annals of the Association of American Geographers*, 94(1), pp. 165–82.

22. Robert Nichols (2020), *Theft is Property! Dispossession and Critical Theory*, Durham: Duke University Press, p. 70.

23. This point is also made by Brenna Bhandar (2018), *Colonial Lives of Property: Law, Land, and Racial Regimes of Ownership*, Durham: Duke University Press. See chapter 3.

24. Nichols, *Theft is Property!*, pp. 46–50. The narrative below follows Nichols.

25. Ibid., p. 47.

26. Ibid, p. 49.

27. See Federici, *Caliban and the Witch*.

28. For an in-depth study of the role of gendered violence in the dispossession of Indigenous peoples in North America, see Andrea Smith (2015), *Conquest: Sexual violence and American Indian Genocide*, Durham: Duke University Press.

29. Aileen Moreton-Robinson (2015), *The White Possessive: Property, Power, and Indigenous Sovereignty*, Minneapolis: University of Minnesota Press.

30. M. Bianet Castellanos (2021), *Indigenous Dispossession: Housing and Maya Indebtedness in Mexico*, Stanford: Stanford University Press, pp. 12–14, 133.

31. Richard Gott (2007), 'The 2006 SLAS Lecture: Latin America as a White Settler Society', *Bulletin of Latin American Research*, 26(2), pp. 269–89.

32. Ibid., p. 14.

33. For a similar discussion of the dispossessing character of neoliberalism for Indigenous peoples in Latin America, see, for example, Macarena Gómez-Barris, *The Extractive Zone: Social Ecologies and Decolonial Perspectives*, Durham: Duke University Press.

34. Bianet Castellanos, *Indigenous Dispossession*, p. 13.

35. Kevin Bruyneel (2007), *The Third Space of Sovereignty: The Postcolonial Politics of US-Indigenous Relations*. Minneapolis: University of Minnesota Press, p. ix.

36. Mahmood Mamdani (2012), *Define and Rule – Native as Political Identity*, Cambridge: Harvard University Press, pp. 2–3.

37. Ibid., p. 6.

38. These ideas are developed by Mamdani in a number of different publications, including Mahmood Mamdani (1996), *Citizen and Subject: Contemporary Africa and the Legacy of Late Colonialism*, Princeton: Princeton University Press; *Define and Rule*, already mentioned, and most recently, Mamdani, *Neither Settler nor Native: The Making and Unmaking of Permanent Minorities*, Cambridge: The Belknap Press of Harvard University Press.

39. Mamdani, *Define and Rule*, p. 7.
40. See James McDougall (2017), *A History of Algeria*, Cambridge: Cambridge University Press, pp. 118–28.
41. Ibid., p. 121.
42. Ibid.
43. Mamdani, *Neither Settler nor Native*, pp. 56–7.
44. Dunbar-Ortiz, *An Indigenous People's History*, p. 11.
45. Estes, *Our History Is the Future*, p. 40.
46. For an account of the brutality of settler violence in the process of secession, see Dunbar-Ortiz, *An Indigenous People's History*, pp. 71–7, and in its aftermath, see pp. 81–92 For a fictionalised account of American secession that foregrounds the question of settlement and Indigenous dispossession, see Wu Ming (2010), *Manituana*, Verso: London.
47. Dunbar-Ortiz, *An Indigenous People's History*, p. 96.
48. Ibid., p. 99.
49. Ibid.
50. Mamdani, *Neither Settler nor Native*, pp. 58–9.
51. Ibid., p. 61.
52. Dunbar-Ortiz, *An Indigenous People's History*, p. 151.
53. Mamdani, *Neither Settler nor Native*, p. 83.
54. Dunbar-Ortiz, *An Indigenous People's History*, p. 159.
55. Ibid., p. 172.
56. For a discussion of the contradictory nature of settler-imposed 'sovereignty' through the IRA and its effects on Indigenous resistance, see, for example, Byrd, *The Transit of Empire*; Coulthard, *Red Skin, White Masks*, and Audra Simpson (2014), *Mohawk Interruptus: Political Life Across the Borders of Settler States*, Durham: Duke University Press. See also chapter 5.
57. Mamdani, *Neither Settler nor Native*, p. 69.
58. Mahmood Mamdani (2015), 'Settler Colonialism: Then and Now', *Critical Inquiry*, 41(3), p. 608.
59. Mamdani, *Neither Settler nor Native*, p. 151.
60. Ibid., p. 152.

61. Ibid., p. 157.

62. Mamdani makes this connection in *Natives and Settlers*. For further details on the process on Israeli settler colonialism in Palestine and the geographic control over the Palestinian population, see, for example, Omar Jabary Salamanca, Mezna Qato, Kareem Rabie and Sobhi Samour (2013), 'Past is Present: Settler Colonialism in Palestine', *Settler Colonial Studies*, 2(1), pp. 1–8; Nadim Rouhana and Areej Sabbagh-Khoury (2015), 'Settler-Colonial Citizenship: Conceptualizing the Relationship between Israel and its Palestinian Citizens', *Settler Colonial Studies*, 5(3), pp. 205–25, and Rashid Khalidi (2020), *The Hundred Years' War on Palestine: A History of Settler Colonialism and Resistance, 1917–2017*, London: Profile Books.

63. For a discussion of the Zionist concerns about replicating the South African model, see Zachary Lockman (2012), 'Land, Labour and the Logic of Zionism: A Critical Engagement with Gershon Shafir', *Settler Colonial Studies*, 2(1), pp. 9–38.

64. Joel Beinin (1990), *Was the Red Flag Flying There? Marxist Politics and the Arab-Israeli Conflict in Egypt and Israel, 1948–1965*, Berkeley: University of California Press, p. 69.

65. For more on this period, see, for example, Leena Dallasheh (2016), 'Persevering Through Colonial Transition: Nazareth's Palestinian Residents After 1948', *Journal of Palestine Studies*, 45(2), pp. 8–23.

66. For a detailed analysis of the PA and its role as a subordinate body, economically and politically to Israel, see Toufic Haddad (2016), *Palestine Ltd: Neoliberalism and Nationalism in the Occupied Territory*, London: I.B. Tauris, and Kareem Rabie (2021), *Palestine Is Throwing a Party and the Whole World Is Invited: Capital and State Building in the West Bank*, Durham: Duke University Press.

67. Leila Farsakh (2005), *Palestinian Labour Migration to Israel: Labour, Land and Occupation*, New York: Routledge, p. 135.

68. For more on the Naqab and the Palestinian Bedouin pop-
    ulation, see Lana Tatour (2019), 'The Culturalisation of
    Indigeneity: The Palestinian Bedouin of the Naqab and
    Indigenous Rights', *International Journal of Human Rights*,
    23(10), pp. 1569–93.

CHAPTER 3 RACISM AS SOCIAL CONTROL

1. Karen E. Fields and Barbara J. Fields (2012), *Racecraft: The
   Soul of Inequality in American Life*, London: Verso, p. 193.
2. Ibid., p. 137.
3. Ibid.
4. Cedric J. Robinson (2007), *Forgeries of Memory and
   Meaning: Blacks and the Regimes of Race in American
   Theatre and Film before WWII*, Chapel Hill: The University
   of North Carolina Press, p. xii.
5. Fields and Fields, *Racecraft*, p. 117.
6. Jody A. Bird (2011), *The Transit of Empire: Indigenous
   Critiques of Colonialism*, Minneapolis: Minnesota University Press, p. xvii.
7. Cedric J. Robinson (1983) in his *Black Marxism: The
   Making of the Black Radical Tradition* (London: Penguin
   Classics, 2021 edn) raised important questions about the
   nature of the relationship between racism and capitalism,
   and the struggle against it. Robinson argued that racism in
   Europe preceded the emergence of capitalism – and that the
   failure of classical Marxism to recognise this fact, led it to
   underestimate the anti-systemic importance of anti-racist
   struggles across the world. This approach has recently been
   rekindled. It is not possible to do it justice in the space
   available here. It is, however, uncontroversial, that until the
   emergence of global European colonial empires, there were
   no global processes of racialisation at play. It is on this process
   that this chapter focuses. See important interventions
   engaging with Robinson's argument, such as Walter Johnson
   and Robin D.G. Kelley (eds) (2017), *Race Capitalism*

Justice, Cambridge: MIT Press; Robin D.G. Kelley (2017), 'What Did Cedric Robinson Mean by Racial Capitalism?', *Boston Review*, 12 January, https://bostonreview.net/race/robin-d-g-kelley-what-did-cedric-robinson-mean-racial-capitalism; Gargi Bhattacharyya (2018), *Rethinking Racial Capitalism: Questions of Reproduction and Survival*, London: Rowman & Littlefield Publishers, and Arun Kundnani (2020) 'What is Racial Capitalism?', *Arun Kundnani on Race, Culture, and Imperialism*, 15 October, www.kundnani.org/what-is-racial-capitalism/

8. For an in-depth study, see Henry Kamen (2014), *The Spanish Inquisition: An Historical Revision*, London: Phoenix Press.
9. Ibid., p. 39.
10. Dunbar-Ortiz, *An Indigenous People's History*, p. 37.
11. The argument here follows Horne, *The Dawning of the Apocalypse*.
12. Ibid., p. 19.
13. Ibid., p. 20.
14. Quoted in George M. Frederickson (1981), *White Supremacy: A Comparative Study in American and South African History*, Oxford: Oxford University Press, p. 8.
15. Ibid.
16. As Patricia Seed has argued, the terms of the debate are important. It was not so much a debate about settler colonialism per se, or even about the rights of the Indigenous peoples being colonised, but about whether it was the Church or the secular powers who could claim control over Indigenous labour and land, and therefore over their lives – and their souls. See Patricia Seed (1993), '"Are These Not Also Men?": The Indians' Humanity and Capacity for Spanish Civilisation', *Journal of Latin American Studies*, 25(3), pp. 629–52. In fact, in Brazil's Amazonian region, Franciscan and Jesuit orders were able to achieve the outlawing of Indigenous slavery by the end of the seventeenth century. The orders then yearly assigned Indigenous labourers, for limited periods of time, to the plantations.

The secular powers solved the problem by extending the use of African slave labour to the region. See Theodore W. Allen (2012), *The Invention of the White Race (Vol. II): The Origin of Racial Oppression in Anglo-America*, London: Verso, p. 34.

17. Ibid., p. 9.

18. For an excellent account of the use of the 'civilising mission' in oppressing Algerian women, see, for example, Neil Macmaster (2009), *Burning the Veil: The Algerian War and the 'Emancipation' of Muslim Women, 1954–62*, Manchester: Manchester University Press. For a discussion of this same argument in the context of the so-called War on Terror, see Lila Abu-Lughod (2002), 'Do Muslim Women Really Need Saving?: Anthropological Reflections on Cultural Relativism and Its Others', *American Anthropologist*, 104(3), pp. 783–90, and Lila Abu-Lughod (2013), *Do Muslim Women Need Saving?*, Cambridge: Harvard University Press.

19. Theodore W. Allen (2012), *The Invention of the White Race (Vol. I): Racial Oppression and Social Control*, London: Verso, p. 31.

20. For an overview of the bloody settler colonial career of these 'Ulster Scots', first in Ireland and then in the 13 colonies, see Dunbar-Ortiz, *An Indigenous Peoples' History*, pp. 51–4.

21. Allen, *The Invention of the White Race (Vol. I)*, p. 31.

22. Ibid.

23. Quoted in Horne, *The Dawning of the Apocalypse*, p. 157.

24. Allen, *The Invention of the White Race (Vol. I)*, pp. 44–5.

25. Quoted in Timothy Mitchell (1991), *Colonising Egypt*, Berkeley: University of California Press, p. 111.

26. See Gayatri Chakravorty Spivak (1993 [1985]), 'Can the Subaltern Speak?', in Patrick Williams and Laura Chrisman (eds), *Colonial Discourse and Post-Colonial Theory: A Reader*, Hemel Hempstead: Harvester, p. 93, for her famous formulation of the gendered justification of empire: 'White men are saving brown women from brown men.'

27. Brenna Bhandar (2018), *Colonial Lives of Property: Law, Land, and Racial Regimes of Ownership*, Durham: Duke University Press, p. 40.
28. Ibid., p. 43.
29. Ibid.
30. Dunbar-Ortiz, *An Indigenous Peoples' History*, p. 37.
31. Patrick Wolfe (2016), *Traces of History: Elementary Structures of Race*, Verso: London, p. 117.
32. Cheryl I. Harris (1993), 'Whiteness as Property', *Harvard Law Review*, 106(8), p. 1714.
33. Aileen Moreton-Robinson (2015), *The White Possessive: Property, Power, and Indigenous Sovereignty*, Minneapolis: University of Minnesota Press.
34. Ibid., p. xxiii.
35. Robin D.G. Kelley (2017), 'The Rest of Us: Rethinking Settler and Native'. *American Quarterly*, 69(2), pp. 267–76.
36. One should, of course, not confuse racial order with reality. It is neither tenable nor the point to imagine either of those three racist categories to be homogenous and neatly separated. What it does indicate is a social order constructed in a context of limited influx of settlers – certainly compared to the Anglo-Saxon settler world – and dependence on Indigenous labour.
37. Jack D. Forbes (1993), *Africans and Native Americans: The Language of Race and the Evolution of Red-Black Peoples*, Urbana: University of Illinois Press, p. 130.
38. Ibid., pp. 181–9 for the Spanish and Portuguese Americas, and especially pp. 190–98 for Anglo North America.
39. Wolfe, *Traces of History*, p. 61.
40. Allen, *The Invention of the White Race (Vol. II)*, p. 262.
41. Ibid.
42. Harris, 'Whiteness as Property', p. 1711.
43. Nell Irvin Painter (2010), *The History of White People*, New York: W.W. Norton and Company, p. 42.
44. Ibid., p. 41.

45. Eric Williams (1994 [1944]), *Capitalism and Slavery*, Chapel Hill: University of North Carolina Press, p. 10.
46. Ibid., p. 14.
47. Fields and Fields, *Racecraft*, p. 126.
48. Williams, *Capitalism and Slavery*, p. 13.
49. Allen, *The Invention of White People (Vol. II)*, pp. 178–9.
50. Ibid., pp. 181–3, 186–7.
51. Ibid., p. 184.
52. Dunbar-Ortiz, *An Indigenous Peoples' History*, p. 61.
53. Ibid., pp. 61–2.
54. Allen, *The Invention of White People (Vol. II)*, p. 213.
55. Ibid., p. 249.
56. Ibid., p. 250.
57. Ibid.
58. Ibid., p. 251.
59. Ibid.
60. Ibid., p. 152.
61. Ibid., p. 253.
62. See, for example, Philip S. Foner's (1982) classic study, *Organized Labour and the Black Worker, 1619–1981*, New York: International Publishers.
63. Fields and Fields, *Racecraft*, pp. 126–7.
64. Williams, *Capitalism and Slavery*, p. 26.
65. Ibid., pp. 32–3.
66. Horne, *The Apocalypse of Settler Colonialism*, p. 130.
67. Ibid., p. 129.
68. Ibid., p. 128.
69. Allen, *The Invention of White People (Vol. II)*, p. 235.
70. Ibid., p. 237.
71. Fredrickson, *White Supremacy*, p. 110.
72. Ibid., pp. 121–9.
73. The 1805 Constitution of Haiti, Articles 12–14: http://faculty.webster.edu/corbetre/haiti/history/earlyhaiti/1805-const.htm, emphasis added. I am very grateful to Ashok Kumar and Robert Knox for helping me find the quote and the right constitution.

74. Here the argument follows Wolfe in *Traces of History*.
75. Wolfe, *Traces of History*, p. 15. It is worth pointing out, as Wolfe does (amongst others), that this same process of universal claims of equality simultaneously increasing regimes of difference was also experienced by Jewish populations in Europe after emancipation. While the French Revolution had promised equal citizenship to Jewish citizens, the late nineteenth century saw the growth of a new form of 'biological' racism directed against them. It was partly their 'invisibility' that scared antisemites and made it necessary for them to identify, exclude and confine them. If the Nazis took this idea to its furthest and most murderous logic, the racial character (and inferiority) of Jews was a much more generally accepted idea in European society. See, for example, Enzo Traverso (2016), *The End of Jewish Modernity*, London: Pluto Press.
76. Bhandar, *Colonial Lives*, p. 43.
77. Quoted in Wolfe, *Traces of History*, p. 49.
78. Ibid., p. 50.
79. Ibid., p. 51.
80. Ibid., p. 56.
81. The classic historical study of this period is W.E.B. DuBois (1999/1935), *Black Reconstruction in America, 1860–1880*, New York: The Free Press, not least because DuBois identifies the central agency of the enslaved themselves in their liberation.
82. Wolfe, *Traces of History*, p. 76.
83. Leon Higginbotham and Barbara Kopytoff (1977), 'Racial Purity', quoted in Wolfe, *Traces of History*, p. 77.
84. Marvin Harris, quoted in Wolfe, *Traces of History*, pp. 113–14.
85. Wolfe, *Traces of History*, p. 137.
86. Noel Ignatiev (2009 [1995]), *How the Irish Became White*, New York: Routledge.
87. Painter, *The History of White People*, p. 142.
88. Ignatiev, *How the Irish Became White*, p. 3.

89. Ibid., p. 212.

90. For a discussion of similar processes in Morocco, as well as their implication for gendered relations and sexuality, see Peter Drucker (2015), '"Disengaging from the Muslim Spirit": The Alliance Israélite Universelle and Moroccan Jews', *Journal of Middle East Women's Studies*, 11(1), pp. 3–23. For a discussion of this process in Tunisia as well as Egypt, and their ongoing contemporary consequences, see Massoud Hayoun (2019), *When We Were Arabs: A Jewish Family's Forgotten History*, New York: The New Press.

91. Despite his recent role in giving intellectual cover to Emmanuel Macron, see Ariella Aïsha Azoulay (2021), 'Algerian Jews Have Not Forgotten France's Colonial Crimes', *Boston Review*, 10 February, https://bostonreview.net/ global-justice/ariella-aisha-azoulay-benjamin-stora-letter

92. Benjamin Stora (2006), *Les Trois Éxils Juifs D'Algérie*, Paris: Éditions Stock.

93. Ibid., pp. 211–13.

94. This reality is powerfully captured in Denis Guénoun (2014), *A Semite: A Memoir of Algeria*, New York: Columbia University Press.

95. Steve Biko (1971), 'The Definition of Black Consciousness', in Aelred Stubbs (ed.) (1987), *Steve Biko (1946–77) – I Write What I Like: A Selection of His Writings*, Oxford: Heinemann Publishers, p. 52. See Annie Olaloku-Teriba (2018), 'Afro-Pessimism and the (Un)Logic of Anti-Blackness', *Historical Materialism*, 26(2), pp. 96–122, for a brilliant discussion on the contemporary relevance of anti-colonial understandings of Blackness.

96. Biko, 'The Definition of Black Consciousness', p. 48.

CHAPTER 4 STRIKING SETTLERS

1. See Eric Hobsbawm's (1996 [1962]), *Age of Revolutions 1789–1848*, New York: Vintage Books and (1995 [1975]), *Age of Capital 1848–1875*, London: Abacus, for a broad

overview of these processes. For a specific overview of settler labour in the Anglo world, see James Belich (2011), *Replenishing the Earth: The Settler Revolution and the Rise of the Angloworld*, Oxford: Oxford University Press.

2. C.L.R. James (2001), *The Black Jacobins: Toussaint L'Ouverture and the San Domingo Revolution*, London: Penguin Books, and John Tutino (2018), *The Mexican Heartland: How Communities Shaped Capitalism, a Nation, and World History, 1500–2000*, Princeton: Princeton University Press.

3. Jonathan Hyslop (1999), 'The Imperial Working Class Makes Itself "White": White Labourism in Britain, Australia, and South Africa Before the First World War', University of Witwatersrand, Institute for Advanced Social Research, Seminar Paper 449, pp. 1–19.

4. It is important to point out that the so-called 'unskilled' nature of Indigenous labour was already the outcome of colonial rule, which consigned these workers to specific jobs.

5. On the failure, for example, of the early Hebrew Labour campaigns. see Steven A. Glazer, (2001), 'Picketing for Hebrew Labor: A Window on Histadrut Tactics and Strategy', *Journal of Palestine Studies*, 30(4), pp. 39–54, and Glazer (2007), 'Language of Propaganda: The Histadrut, Hebrew Labor, and the Palestinian Worker', *Journal of Palestine Studies*, 36(2), pp. 25–38. For a discussion of the place of Palestinians in the Israeli economy, see Salim Tamari (1981), 'Building Other People's Homes: The Palestinian Peasant's Household and Work in Israel', *Journal of Palestine Studies* 11(1), pp. 31–6; Leila Farsakh (2005), *Palestinian Labor Migration to Israel: Labor, Land, and Occupation*, London: Routledge; Nabil Khattab and Sami Miaari (2013), *Palestinians in the Israeli Labour Market: A Multidisciplinary Approach*, New York: Palgrave Macmillan, and Andrew Ross (2019), *Stone Men: The Palestinians who Built Israel*, London: Verso.

6. For a brilliant study of racism in the British labour movement, as well as the ways in which it has been fought, see Satnam Virdee (2014), *Racism, Class, and the Racialised Outsider*, London: Red Globe Press.

7. Patricia Grimshaw (2000), 'Settler Anxieties, Indigenous Peoples, and Women's Suffrage in the Colonies of Australia, New Zealand, and Hawai'i, 1888 to 1902', *Pacific Historical Review*, 69(4), pp. 553–72.

8. The author has developed this argument previously in Sai Englert (2020), 'Settlers, Workers, and the Logic of Accumulation by Dispossession', *Antipode*, 52(6), pp. 1647–66.

9. MEMO (2015), 'China Tells Israel "Don't Send Workers to Settlements"', *Middle East Monitor*, 8 June, www.middleeastmonitor.com/20150608-china-tells-israel-dont-send-workers-to-settlements/, and John Reed (2015), 'Israel Rights Groups Attack Plan to Import 20,000 Chinese Workers', *Financial Times*, 20 September, https://next.ft.com/content/1f0cdc62-5f9a-11e5-9846-de406ccb37f2#axzz4FoXnLfYT

10. Tikva Honig-Parnass (2011), 'The 2011 Uprising in Israel: The Inherent Limitation of a Middle-Class Protest in a Settler-Colonial State', *Israeli Occupation Archive*, 9 January, www.israeli-occupation.org/2012-01-09/tikva-honig-parnass-the-2011-uprising-in-israel/#sthash.SOqZsrK2.dpuf

11. See, for example, Lucien Van Der Walt (2007) 'The First Globalisation and Transnational Labour Activism in Southern Africa: White Labourism, the IWW, and the ICU, 1904–1934', *African Studies*, 66(2–3), pp. 223–51; Georges Spillman (1967), *Du Protectorat à l'Independence, Maroc 1912–1955*, Paris: Plon; Michel de la Varde (1955), *Casablanca: Ville d'Émeutes*, Paris: Editions André Martel; Zachary Lockman (1996), *Comrades and Enemies: Arab and Jewish Workers in Palestine, 1906–1948*, Berkeley: University of California Press, and Musa Budeiri (2010), *Palestine*

Communist Party (1919–1948): Arab and Jew in the Struggle for Internationalism, Chicago: Haymarket.

12. Budeiri, *Palestine Communist Party*.

13. Peter Linebaugh and Marcus Rediker (2002), *The Many-Headed Hydra: Sailors, Slaves, Commoners, and the Hidden History of the Revolutionary Atlantic*, Boston: Beacon Press, p. 34.

14. For an overview of the French left's role and political positions during the Algerian war of independence, see Ian Birchall (ed.) (2012), *European Revolutionaries and Algerian Independence: 1954–1962*, Pontypool: Merlin Press.

15. Theodore Herzl (1896), *The Jewish State*. Jewish Virtual Library, www.jewishvirtuallibrary.org/quot-the-jewish-state-quottheodor-herzl

16. Tom Segev (2000), *One Palestine Complete*, London: Little Brown & Co., p. 47.

17. For more on this history, see, for example, Alain Brossat and Sylvia Klingberg (2017), *Revolutionary Yiddishland: A History of Jewish Radicalism*, London: Verso, and Jack Jacobs (ed.) (2001), *Jewish Politics in Eastern Europe: The Bund at 100*, Basingstoke: Palgrave.

18. Gershon Shafir (1996 [1989]), *Land, Labour, and the Origins of the Israeli-Palestinian Conflict 1882–1914*, Berkeley: University of California Press, pp. 74–5.

19. See ibid.

20. Zachary Lockman describes how Labour Zionist theoreticians argued against replicating the South African model, see his 'Land, Labor and the Logic of Zionism: A Critical Engagement with Gershon Shafir', *Settler Colonial Studies*, 2(1), pp. 9–38.

21. The most important source on this early process is Shafir, *Land, Labour, and the Origins*. Here the text follows his narrative.

22. The JNF, established during the first ZO congress, still exists today and owns roughly 93 per cent of the land within the

Green Line, alongside its successor organisation: the Israel Land Administration (ILA).

23. Lockman, *Comrades and Enemies*, p. 352.

24. Revisionism was a political wing of the Zionist movement, whose most famous leader was Zeev Jabotinsky. The Revisionists believed that the Zionist movement was too conciliatory with the Palestinian population and needed to claim immediate sovereignty over the whole of Palestine and Transjordan.

25. *HaHistadrut HaClalit shel HaOvdim BaEretz Yisrael* – The General Organisation of Workers in the Land of Israel.

26. Zachary Lockman has painstakingly detailed the process through which the Histadrut leadership undermined attempts by some – often communist-influenced – groups of Jewish workers to build alliances with their Palestinian counterparts in his *Comrades and Enemies*. Musa Budeiri's *Palestine Communist Party* traces how even within the PCP, the pull towards Zionism intensified and led to a split of the organisation along national lines.

27. See Zeev Sternhell (1998), *The Founding Myths of Israel: Nationalism, Socialism, and the Making of the Jewish State*, Princeton: Princeton University Press, for a discussion of the Histadrut's role in the development of the future state and its economy, before 1948.

28. Quoted in Lockman, *Comrades and Enemies*, p. 68.

29. For a detailed account of this process see Lockman's *Comrades and Enemies*, his 'Land, Labor and the Logic of Zionism', and Deborah Bernstein (2000), *Constructing Boundaries*, Albany: State University of New York Press.

30. John Newsinger (2010), *The Blood Never Dried: A People's History of the British Empire*, London: Bookmarks, p. 136.

31. Quoted in Lockman, *Comrades and Enemies*, p. 260.

32. Ghassan Kanafani's 1973 volume *The 1936–39 Revolt in Palestine*, Committee for Democratic Palestine, gives a vivid and important account of the revolt and its betrayal.

John Newsinger's *The Blood Never Dried* offers a powerful account of British violence in putting down the revolt.

33. Rashid Khalidi (2020), *The Hundred Years' War on Palestine: A History of Settler Colonialism and Resistance, 1917–2017*, Profile Books: London, pp. 15–16.

34. See Lockman, *Comrades and Enemies*, for a detailed account of this process.

35. John Rose (2004), *The Myths of Zionism*, London: Pluto, p. 130.

36. See Farsakh, *Palestinian Labour Migration*, for the classic study of this process.

37. George M. Fredrickson (1981), *White Supremacy: A Comparative Study in American and South African History*, Oxford: Oxford University Press.

38. Much as in the case of the 'freeing' of enslaved populations discussed in chapter 1, the Indigenous population's electoral enfranchisement should be taken with a pinch of salt. In practice, it was severely curtailed by such qualifications as property requirements, which ruled out the participation of the vast majority.

39. Donald Denoon (1986), *Settler Capitalism – The Dynamics of Dependent Development in the Southern Hemisphere*, Oxford: Clarendon Press.

40. Ibid., p. 65.

41. Ibid., p. 130.

42. Ibid., p. 134.

43. Jonathan Hyslop (1999), 'The Imperial Working Class Makes Itself "White": White Labourism in Britain, Australia, and South Africa Before the First World War', University of Witwatersrand, Institute for Advanced Social Research, Seminar Paper 449, pp. 1–19, and Lucien Van Der Walt (2007) 'The First Globalisation and Transnational Labour Activism in Southern Africa: White Labourism, the IWW, and the ICU, 1904–1934', *African Studies*, 66(2–3), pp. 223–51.

44. Fredrickson, *White Supremacy*, p. 229.

45. Van Der Walt, *The First Globalisation and Transnational Labour Activism in Southern Africa*, p. 227.

46. Fredrickson, *White Supremacy*.

47. Iyko Day (2016), *Alien Capital: Asian Racialization and the Logic of Settler Colonial Capitalism*, Durham: Duke University Press.

48. Van Der Walt, *The First Globalisation and Transnational Labour Activism in Southern Africa*, pp. 229–30.

49. Keith Breckenridge (2007) 'Fighting for a White South Africa: White Working-Class Racism and the 1922 Rand Revolt', *South African Historical Journal*, 57(1), pp. 228–43.

50. Ibid., p. 230.

51. Breckenridge, 'Fighting for a White South Africa', p. 242.

CHAPTER 5 LIBERATION AND RETURN

1. For a discussion of the interrelation between climate change, settler colonialism, and Indigenous struggle, see Glen Sean Coulthard (2014), *Red Skin White Masks: Rejecting the Colonial Politics of Recognition*, Minneapolis: University of Minnesota Press, and Nick Estes (2019), *Our History is the Future: Standing Rock Versus the Dakota Access Pipeline, and the Long Tradition of Indigenous Resistance*, London: Verso.

2. Jean O'Brien (2010), *Firsting and Lasting: Writing Indians Out of Existence in New England*, Minneapolis: University of Minnesota Press.

3. Such critiques have already been mentioned in previous chapters, including Bird, *The Transit of Empire*, and Moreton-Robinson, *The White Possessive*. In addition, they have also been articulated in Brenna Bhandar and Rafeef Ziadah (2016), 'Acts and Omissions: Framing Settler Colonialism in Palestine Studies', *Jadaliyya*, 14 January www.jadaliyya.com/pages/index/23569/acts-and-omissions_framing-settler-colonialism-in-Palestine-studies; J. Kēhaulani Kauanui (2016), '"A Structure, Not an Event": Settler Colonialism

and Enduring Indigeneity', *Lateral: Journal of the Cultural Studies Association*, 5(1), pp. 1–8; Jean M. O'Brien (2017), 'Tracing Settler Colonialism's Eliminatory Logic in Traces of History', *American Quarterly*, 69(2), pp. 249–55, and Rana Barakat (2018), 'Writing/Righting Palestine Studies: Settler Colonialism, Indigenous Sovereignty and Resisting the Ghost(s) of History', *Settler Colonial Studies*, 8(3), pp. 349–63.

4. Mahmood Mamdani (2015), 'Settler Colonialism: Then and Now', *Critical Inquiry*, 41(3), p. 596.

5. Andy Clarno (2017), *Neoliberal Apartheid: Palestine/Israel and South Africa after 1994*. Chicago: University of Chicago Press.

6. Gerald Horne (2019), *White Supremacy Confronted: U.S. Imperialism and Anti-Communism vs. the Liberation of Southern Africa from Rhodes to Mandela*, New York: International Publishers Co., details the international character and the intensity of this struggle, as well as the limits successfully imposed on it by both US and South African ruling classes.

7. Cedric J. Robinson (2007), *Forgeries of Memory and Meaning: Blacks and the Regimes of Race in American Theatre and Film before WWII*, Chapel Hill: University of North Carolina Press.

8. Taiaiake Alfred and Jeff Corntassel (2005), 'Being Indigenous: Resurgences Against Contemporary Colonialism', *Government and Opposition*, 40(4), p. 597.

9. Ibid., p. 599.

10. Roxanne Dunbar-Ortiz (2014), *An Indigenous Peoples' History of the United States*, Boston: Beacon Press, pp. 10–12.

11. Ibid., p. 12.

12. Macarena Gómez-Barris (2017) explores these processes across the Andes in her *The Extractive Zone: Social Ecologies and Decolonial Perspectives*, Durham: Duke University Press.

13. Robert Nichols (2020), *Theft is Property! Dispossession and Critical Theory*, Durham: Duke University Press, p. 151.
14. Red Nation, *The Red Deal: Indigenous Action to Save Our Earth*, http://therednation.org/about-maisha/
15. Barakat, 'Writing/Righting', p. 357.
16. In fact, Jerusalem was unilaterally annexed by Israel in two waves: first, today's West Jerusalem during the Nakba, and then East Jerusalem in 1967.
17. For further reflections on and analysis of the uprising, see Rashid Khalidi (2021), 'Uprisings and Unity: Past and Present; Introduction', *Journal of Palestine Studies*, 50(4), p. 67; Abdel Razeq Farraj (2021), 'Palestine Rises in Rebellion', *Journal of Palestine Studies*, 50(4), pp. 68–72; Safa Joudeh (2021), 'Defying Exception: Gaza after the "Unity Uprising"', *Journal of Palestine Studies*, 50(4), pp. 73–7; Abdel Razzaq Takriti (2021), '"Who Will Hang the Bell?": The Palestinian *Habba* of 2021', *Journal of Palestine Studies*, 50(4), pp. 78–83; Lana Tatour (2021), 'The "Unity Intifada" and '48 Palestinians: Between the Liberal and the Decolonial', *Journal of Palestine Studies*, 50(4), pp. 84–9; Rana Barakat (2021), '"Ramadan Does Not Come for Free": Refusal as New and Ongoing in Palestine', *Journal of Palestine Studies*, 50(4), pp. 90–95; Yousef Munayyer (2021), 'When Palestine Shook', *Journal of Palestine Studies*, 50(4), pp. 96–100, and Nour Joudah, Randa M. Wahbe, Tareq Radi and Dina Omar (2021), 'Palestine as Praxis: Scholarship for Freedom', *Journal of Palestine Studies*, 50(4), pp. 101–5.
18. See, for example, Mohammed El-Kurd (2021), 'If They Steal Sheikh Jarrah', *Mada Masr*, 16 February, www.madamasr.com/en/2021/02/16/opinion/u/if-they-steal-sheikh-jarrah/. The El-Kurd family is one of those targeted for expulsion. See also, for a longer overview of the dispossession of Palestinians in Jerusalem, Norwegian Refugee Council (2017), 'The Absentee Property Law and its Application to East Jerusalem', Legal Memo, 15 February, www.nrc.no/

resources/legal-opinions/the-absentee-property-law-and-its-application-to-east-jerusalem/

19. For an account of contemporary transformations in Sheikh Jarrah from the late 1980s onwards, see Rema Hammami (2012), 'The Exiling of Sheikh Jarrah', *Jerusalem Quarterly*, 51, pp. 49–64.

20. Yara Hawari (2021), 'Defying Fragmentation and the Significance of Unity: A New Palestinian Uprising', *Al-Shabaka*, 29 June, https://al-shabaka.org/commentaries/defying-fragmentation-and-the-significance-of-unity-a-new-palestinian-uprising/

21. OCHA (2021), 'Occupied Palestinian Territory (oPt): Response to the escalation in the oPt', Situation Report No. 1: 21–27 May, p. 1, https://reliefweb.int/sites/reliefweb.int/files/resources/Occupied%20Palestinian%20Territory%20%28oPt%29%20-%20Response%20to%20the%20escalation%20in%20the%20oPt%20-%20Situation%20Report%20No.%201%2C%2021%20-%2027%20May%202021.pdf

22. Ibid.

23. Steve Niva (2012), 'Israel's "Operation Mow the Lawn"', *Middle East Report Online,* 7 December, https://merip.org/2012/12/israels-operation-mow-the-lawn/. See also, for example, Roi Rubinstein (2018), 'Bennett implies IDF should "mow the lawn" in Gaza', *Ynet*, 9 April, www.ynetnews.com/articles/0,7340,L-5341225,00.html

24. OCHA (2015), 'Key Figures on the 2014 Hostilities', www.ochaopt.org/content/key-figures-2014-hostilities

25. Lubna Masarwa and Frank Andrews (2021), 'Lod: Armed Settlers Roam Streets as Mosque Attacked and Night Curfew Ordered', *Middle East Eye*, 12 May, www.middleeasteye.net/news/israel-palestine-armed-settlers-lod-mosque-attacked-night-curfew

26. Nimer Sultany (2021), 'Peaceful Coexistence in Israel Hasn't Been Shattered – It's Always Been a Myth', *The Guardian*, 19 May, www.theguardian.com/commentisfree/2021/may/19/peaceful-coexistence-israel-myth-palestinian-denied-rights

27. Riya Al-Sanah (2021), 'Report on the General Strike in Palestine', *Notes from Below*, 26 May, https://notesfrombelow. org/article/report-general-strike-palestine

28. See Hawari, 'Defying Fragmentation', for a critique of this approach and a discussion of how the 2021 uprising challenged it.

29. Mouin Rabbani (2021), 'A Pivotal Moment for The Palestinian National Struggle', *Jadaliyya*, 13 July, www.jadaliyya. com/Details/43089/A-Pivotal-Moment-for-The-Palestinian-National-Struggle

30. Al-Sanah, 'Report on the General Strike in Palestine'.

31. Ibid.

32. This author is not aware of any Israeli workers who responded to the call, reinforcing the points made in chapter 4.

33. Joseph Daher (2021), 'Palestinian Liberation and the MENA Revolutions', *Tempest*, 5 July, www.tempestmag.org/2021/07/palestinian-liberation-and-the-mena-revolutions/

34. Al-Sanah, 'Report on the General Strike in Palestine'.

35. Lee Yarnon (2021), 'General Strike Highlights Israel's Dependency on Palestinian Workers', *Ha'aretz*, 19 May, www.haaretz.com/israel-news/.premium.MAGAZINE-general-strike-highlights-israel-s-dependency-on-palestinian-workers-1.9824446?fbclid=IwAR0OFbO6xeL48Lfni4zOiLVnI3WcZYPhBX1m5hKBJU6KWdPOhttps://www.haaretz.com/israel-news/.premium.MAGAZINE-general-strike-highlights-israel-s-dependency-on-palestinian-workers-1.9824446?fbclid=IwAR0OFbO6xeL48Lfni4zOiLVnI3WcZYPhBX1m5hKBJU6KWdPOSJidtclYqXgSJidtclYqXg

36. Sobhi Samour (2021), 'Covid-19 and the Necroeconomy of Palestinian Labour in Israel', *Journal of Palestine Studies*, 49(4), pp. 53–64.

37. Anon. (2021), 'The Manifesto of Dignity and Hope', *Mondoweiss*, 18 May, https://mondoweiss.net/2021/05/the-manifesto-of-dignity-and-hope/

38. Al-Sanah, 'Report on the General Strike in Palestine', and Hawari, 'Defying Fragmentation'. For a comment piece placing the strike in a longer historical process of Palestinian labour disputes, see Joel Beinin (2021), 'Palestinian Workers Have a Long History of Resistance', *Jacobin*, 6 June, https://jacobinmag.com/2021/06/palestinian-labor-trade-unions-strike-resistance-worker-solidarity-may-18-labor-history

39. Amahl Bishara (2020), 'Looking Beyond the Struggle for Palestinian Statehood', *Middle East Report*, 294, https://merip.org/2020/06/looking-beyond-the-struggle-for-palestinian-statehood/

40. Ibid.

41. Hala Marshood and Riya Al-Sanah (2020), 'Tal'at: A Feminist Movement that is Redefining Liberation and Reimagining Palestine', *Mondoweiss*, 25 February, https://mondoweiss.net/2020/02/talat-a-feminist-movement-that-is-redefining-liberation-and-reimagining-palestine/?fbclid=IwAR3qJT4HPk83ZheuMqg-j95pZhsKjMRUgQVBUj2TltHok_vxSEfEGs2Es-8

42. Hawari, 'Defying Fragmentation'.

43. Coulthard, *Red Skin White Masks*, p. 173.

44. Estes, *Our History is the Future*, pp. 10–11.

45. Ibid., p. 3.

46. Ibid., p. 15.

47. Ibid., p. 29.

48. For a discussion of some of these processes and their connection to capital accumulation, see Tyler McCreary (2022), 'Crisis in the Tar Sands: Fossil Capitalism and the Future of the Alberta Hydrocarbon Economy', *Historical Materialism*, 30(1), pp. 1–36. For a broader discussion of the US oil Industry, see Adam Hanieh (2021), 'The Commodities Fetish? Financialisation and Finance Capital in the US Oil Industry', *Historical Materialism*, 29(4), pp. 70–113.

49. Estes, *Our History is the Future*, p. 30.

50. Coulthard, *Red Skin White Masks*, p. 128.

51. Ibid.

52. Ibid., p. 164.
53. Ibid., p. 128.
54. Ibid., p. 164.
55. Kim Tallbear (2019), 'Badass Indigenous Women Caretake Relations: #Standingrock, #IdleNoMore, #Black LivesMatter', in Nick Estes and Jaskiran Dhillon (eds), *Standing with Standing Rock: Voices from the NoDAPL Movement*, Minneapolis: University of Minnesota Press, p. 14.
56. For ongoing solidarity between Indigenous peoples in North America, see, for example, Chili Yazzie (2021), 'Letter of Support from Diné Bikeyah to Wet'suwet'en Relatives', *The Red Nation*, 2 December, https://therednation.org/letter-of-support-from-dine-bikeyah-to-wetsuweten-relatives/
57. For more on this campaign, see www.honorearth.org/stop_line_3
58. Zaysha Grinnell, in Jaskiran Dhillon (2019), '"This fight has become my life, and it's not over" An Interview with Zaysha Grinnell', in Estes and Dhillon (eds), *Standing with Standing Rock*, p. 21.
59. Nick Estes, Melanie K. Yazzie, Jennifer Nez Denetdale and David Correia (2021), *Red Nation Rising: From Bordertown Violence to Native Liberation*, Oakland: PM Press, pp. 48–9.
60. Ibid.
61. Estes, *Our History is the Future*, pp. 2–3.
62. For more information, see www.bdsmovement.net

Index

Thanks to our Patreon subscribers:

Andrew Perry
Ciaran Kane

Who have shown generosity and
comradeship in support of our publishing.

Check out the other perks you get by subscribing
to our Patreon – visit patreon.com/plutopress.
Subscriptions start from £3 a month.

The Pluto Press Newsletter

Hello friend of Pluto!

Want to stay on top of the best radical books
we publish?

Then sign up to be the first to hear about our
new books, as well as special events,
podcasts and videos.

You'll also get 50% off your first order with us
when you sign up.

Come and join us!

Go to bit.ly/PlutoNewsletter